Deadly Therapy

Deadly Therapy

Lessons in Liveliness from Theater and Performance Theory

Michael Karson

JASON ARONSON

Lanham • Boulder • New York • Toronto • Plymouth, UK

Published in the United States of America
by Jason Aronson
An imprint of Rowman & Littlefield Publishers, Inc.

A wholly owned subsidiary of
The Rowman & Littlefield Publishing Group, Inc.
4501 Forbes Boulevard, Suite 200, Lanham, Maryland 20706
www.rowmanlittlefield.com

Estover Road
Plymouth PL6 7PY
United Kingdom

British Library Cataloguing in Publication Information Available

Library of Congress Cataloging-in-Publication Data

Karson, Michael.
  Deadly therapy : lessons in liveliness from theater and performance theory / Michael
Karson.
     p. ; cm.
  ISBN-13: 978-0-7657-0445-0 (cloth : alk. paper)
  ISBN-10: 0-7657-0445-5 (cloth : alk. paper)
  1. Psychotherapy. 2. Drama—Therapeutic use. 3. Drama. I. Title.
  [DNLM: 1. Psychotherapy—methods. 2. Drama. 3. Professional Role. 4.
Psychological Theory. WM 420 K182d 2008]

  RC480.5.K3594 2008
  616.89'1653—dc22   2008001174

Printed in the United States of America

♾™ The paper used in this publication meets the minimum requirements of American
National Standard for Information Sciences—Permanence of Paper for Printed Library
Materials, ANSI/NISO Z39.48-1992.

For Ethan and Max, and for their liveliness

Fear them not therefore: for there is nothing covered, that shall not be revealed; and hid, that shall not be known. What I tell you in darkness, that speak ye in light.

—Matthew 10:26–27

The Emperor of the South Sea was Fast; the Emperor of the North Sea was Furious; the Emperor of the center was Oneness. Fast and Furious met from time to time in the land of Oneness, who treated them very generously. Fast and Furious were discussing how to repay Oneness's bounty.

"All people have seven holes through which they look, listen, eat, breathe; he alone doesn't have any. Let's try boring them."

Every day they bored one hole, and on the seventh day Oneness died.

—Chuang-Tzu

Consider the work of God: who can make straight what he has made crooked?

—Ecclesiastes 7:13

Were Pavlov's dog improvising, he would still salivate when the bell rang, but he would feel sure it was all his own doing: "I'm dribbling," he would say, proud of his daring.

—Peter Brook

Contents

Preface ix

Acknowledgments xv

1 Lessons from Deadly Theater 1

2 Lessons from Performance Theory 29

3 What Am I Doing to Irma? 59

4 Status Games 69

5 Gender Is Something We Do, Not Something We Are 87

6 Deadly Multiculturalism 105

7 Therapeutic Privilege 117

8 Is Science Just Another Party Line? 137

9 Critical Thinking About Critical Thinking 159
with Janna Goodwin, Ph.D.

10 Applying Theory to the Therapy (and Not Just to the Patient's Life) 177

11 Deadly Supervision 193

12 Fourteen Things We Can Do to Make Our Therapies Livelier 203

References 217

Index 225

About the Author 231

Preface

Human systems benefit from—and are plagued by—rules that tell people what to do. The benefits are legion. Rule-governed behavior—action based on directions and suggestions—uses other people's discoveries, communicated by language and drawings. Thus, clinicians need not invent exposure therapy when they first treat minor compulsions; they can read about and employ what has been learned by those who came before them. Rules prevent us from responding precipitously to unusual events because they summarize lessons across a wide range of circumstances. In other words, rules help us stick with the best strategy. For example, a clinician may choose to explore the meaning of a request to change some aspect of the therapy because a rule requires exploration of all requests, even when the change would be simple and convenient. Finally, rules can prevent mistakes associated with trial-and-error learning, which is especially important when the costs of mistakes are dear. "Don't touch the stove" can prevent a burn, and "look both ways before crossing" can prevent death. In therapy, "don't touch the patient" and "constantly monitor suicidality in seriously depressed patients" are analogies.

Rules often define categories rather than continua and either-or situations rather than probabilities. These provide the great advantage of simplifying complex situations, which is an advantage because people generally find ambiguity upsetting, especially when intense emotions are involved. Categories in turn define expectations based on the categories, and these too have distinct advantages. Expectations of how things should go and how people should behave reduce anxiety associated with chance and enhance the sense of social efficacy that depends on knowing what will work and what will not.

Some of the disadvantages of rules are well known to clinicians. Most notably, rules can never be as closely tailored to a specific situation as trial-and-error learning. Even a detailed specification of when and how to apply a rule can't compete with a prepared individual with a flexible repertoire who can gauge the particular situation. Also, rules famously have unintended consequences. If blindly followed, even the most careful delineation of when it's a good idea to touch a patient will miss a reassuring handshake or physical assistance. This is the reason that good psychotherapy training teaches students *how* to think about clinical material, not *what* to think about clinical material: *what* to think is too tied to specific cases to transfer usefully to new cases. Finally, rules are hard to change because they are impervious to new information. Whether cast as the organizing principles of self-psychology or the schemas of cognitive therapy, the patient's rules have a way of incorporating rather then yielding to the therapist's efforts to change them. For example, a therapist challenges, whether directly or indirectly, a patient's rule that it is best to avoid help because helpers wind up trying to control you, and the patient assumes the therapist is acting out of a desire for control rather than in an effort to help.

Many of the disadvantages of categories are also known to clinicians. Diagnosis—and any other labeling—is useful only if the things being grouped together are uniform and only if the grouping tells us what to do. Otherwise, diagnosis dismisses individual differences. The ways in which people idiosyncratically label themselves, others, and situations can tell us a lot about them, and the way a profession uses labels can likewise reveal a great deal. The major disadvantage of expectations emphasized in clinical work is *confirmation bias*. We tend to see what we expect to see, ignoring or minimizing contradictions and focusing on confirmatory evidence. This describes the process by which old, outdated maps or schemas persist—evidence of their being outdated is ignored. For example, a man accused of sexually abusing his son brings a toy to a visit, and the gift is seen as an effort to seduce to the boy, but if he doesn't bring a gift, he's punishing the boy for affirming the abuse—whatever he does confirms the belief that he sexually abused his son.

Other disadvantages of rules, categories, and expectations are well known to theater artists and performance theorists but get little notice in psychotherapy training. This book is about these disadvantages and what to do about them.

When following a rule, a person's success means the rule is useful under those conditions. But regardless of a rule's utility, people who promulgate the rule will frequently reward obedience to it. They often do so because experience has taught them that the rule is useful and they want to pass that knowledge on to others, as when a supervisor praises a trainee for discussing difficult emotions even if it didn't work with that particular patient. Equally often, though, promulgators reward obedience because they get something out of obedience per se. Their prestige as rule makers may be at stake, for example, or the rule may be part of a system that legitimizes their authority. Since rules are promulgated by humans, it isn't surprising that human motivations affect their promulgation. Rules and systems of rules come to define political hegemonies—empowered subsystems populated by those who benefit from adherence to the rules. Hegemonies may benefit because their legitimacy is at stake in the validity of the rules or because the application of the rules keeps the hegemony in power.

The most important rules are those that define what kind of situation we are in because the applicability of all other rules is affected. In therapy, we make rules for the benefit of our patients, and these rules apply both to the patients' lives and to the therapy itself. Thus, we have enormous power over patients to define what kind of situation the therapy is, partly because we have more power than patients to begin with and partly because patients are often consulting us in the first place because their ability to define situations has become problematically idiosyncratic. I address these problems in chapter 3, where I review what happens when the hegemony of doctors gangs up on patients; in chapters 4 and 7, where I explore the power differential in therapy; and in chapter 10.

Rules constantly need to be questioned, or they won't be tailored to new situations or responsive to new information. Unfortunately, since those with power probably like the rules, those most likely to question them aren't likely to have much power in the system being questioned. The stability of any system of rules largely depends on the way it handles being challenged—systems without some method for managing questions would not be very stable. Some systems of rules dismiss questioners by demonizing them, some by labeling them as unpatriotic, and some by pathologizing them. In therapy, we are particularly apt to pathologize patients who question what we do. This issue is taken up in chapters 4 and 7. In chapter 6, I critique rule-based approaches to multiculturalism and cultural competence that depend on categorizing people. In chapter 11, I apply many of these ideas about therapy to supervision.

Science is seen as a subculture (Longino, 1990; Skinner, 1957) that facilitates the questioning of rules with evidence and critical thinking. But science is as susceptible to human motivations as any other practice. The availability of science and critical thinking as a check on rule-making hegemonies and on rule making in therapy is explored in chapters 8 and 9.

Rules in social situations function as behavioral and presentational expectations based on the category the person is in—Goffman (1963) calls these expectations *identity norms*. Categories and expectations kill behavioral flexibility. Goffman teaches us how pervasively humans are aware of identity norms and how acutely aware we are of falling short of them. Especially common are identity norms regarding status and gender. I investigate how these expectations play out in therapy in chapters 4 and 5. General problems associated with identity norms, especially the problems associated with living up to them and disguising the failure to do so, are discussed in chapter 2.

Theater practice has a long history of questioning political hegemonies. This statement is especially true if *political hegemony* also means the small acquisitions of power made in families or even within individuals by the self-serving functions of rule making and if *theater practice* includes the small enactments that metaphorically reveal and express the marginalized questioning of those hegemonies. Theater practice is also a place to learn how to manage backstage–front-stage problems, which are ubiquitous in a world that expects certain behaviors and presentations. Additionally, theater practice teaches us how to communicate important human narratives effectively, which is one of the main functions of psychotherapy. Performance theory can be summarized as a dramaturgical view of life. The dramaturgical view of therapy is the focus of chapter 1.

If I say we *perform* the part of ourselves, I do not mean that the performance is insincere or artificial. What I like about the word *perform*, besides the analogy to learning a role in the theater, is that it also conveys that other roles are possible. If the Self is a performance, the implication to me is that change is possible, either in the grand sense of learning a new Self or in the smaller sense of learning to play different roles for different occasions. The distinction between the person and the role being played also invites a friendly discussion of what the person is doing as opposed to a more personalized and therefore defensive discussion of the person. "You're domineering" can hardly be expected to create a genuine discourse as compared with "When you issue orders, it makes me want to do the opposite."

Identity is performance, and some people are so attached to their identities that they cannot try anything fundamentally new. Some other people so detest the roles they have been cast in that they cannot relax and enjoy their situations. The goal is to accept that one has an identity but, rather than drown in this acceptance, to use it as a jumping-off point for becoming—acting like—someone else.

The human tendency to ignore or suppress information that contradicts the party line produces much unhappiness and psychopathology. Psychotherapy, like science, universities, and America under the Bill of Rights, is supposed to be an exception. Science is supposed to account for contradictions, universities are supposed to foster the free exchange of ideas, America is supposed to protect the communication of upsetting information, and psychotherapy is supposed to welcome the marginalized. But psychotherapy, like science, universities, and America, is practiced by humans. This book examines the party lines that emerge in psychotherapy and suggests methods, derived from performance theory, for checking ourselves.

Acknowledgments

In 1997, after practicing psychotherapy for over 20 years, I fell in love with Janna Goodwin, a theater artist (playwright, actor, composer, director). Such is the nature of theater artists and of therapists that we spend a great deal of time talking, talking about talking, and, when things get out of hand, talking about talking about talking. The ubiquity and complexity of our conversation only got worse when she became a communications professor.

As with other friends, I asked her for some key books I could read the better to know her by. She gave me Keith Johnstone's *Impro* and Peter Brook's *The Empty Space*. In these works about stagecraft, I found a world similar to my own. Johnstone's investigation of improvisation and status transactions and Brook's investigation of deadliness made me rethink what I was doing as a therapist.

Then Janna started reading Goffman, and I did too, both of us reveling in his dramaturgical vision of reality. One consequence of all this reading was Janna's 2001 paper on deadliness in the classroom, which got me thinking about deadliness in therapy. This book might have been titled, *What if Johnstone, Brook, and Goffman Had Been Clinical Supervisors?*

I am grateful to the University of Denver and its Graduate School of Professional Psychology, where I have found a stimulating collegial environment. Substantive conversations that have influenced this book include those with Peter Buirski, Shelly Smith-Acuña, Fernand Lubuguin, John McNeill, and Jonathan Shedler, but all my colleagues at DU have helped me think about therapy and training. I'd also like to thank the students at DU for engaging me in dialogue about these ideas. Bonnie Clark and Kathy Corbett also may find their voices threaded through these pages.

Janna helped me organize the chapters and cowrote one of them. Max, Ethan, and Tara are always on my mind as cheery reasons to write and teach, but this time Max also copyedited the manuscript, improving virtually every paragraph. Tom Farrington read a draft and gave me useful feedback, as did Karen Farrington.

This book would never have been written if not for the none-too-gentle encouragement I received from Jason Aronson.

Chapter One

Lessons from Deadly Theater

The basis of the craft of the shoemaker is to make shoes that don't hurt; the basis of the theatre craft consists in producing, with the audience, from very concrete elements, a relationship that works.

—Brook (1993, pp. 75–76)

THEATER AND THE PARTY LINE

For a little more than a hundred years, therapists have tried to help people narrate important human conflicts, understand liberating and uplifting ideas, and engage in meaningful and illuminating interactions. For thousands of years, theater professionals have been working the same agenda. Maybe therapists have something to learn from them.

The parallels between theater and therapy extend beyond narration, education, and engagement. When it is done right, theater is also a place where the invisible, liminal, and marginalized can emerge (Shechner, 1988). In every system, be that system a person, a couple, a therapy, a family, a business, or a country, there is an executive—a hegemony of powerful interests. The executive uses words to create what Goffman (1959) calls a *party line*, a shared understanding of how people should behave that leaves itself well off. There are also less powerful interests, parts of the system that are *out of line*. In an unhealthy system, the hegemony alternately ignores and condemns that which is out of line. As Gandhi put it, "First they laugh at you, then they ignore you, then they fight you." He added, "Then you win," meaning that a system at war within itself will eventually collapse.

All hegemonies exercise the privileges of dismissing or condemning those out of line or, when the hegemony is within the individual, those aspects of

1

the self that are out of line. Different hegemonies do this in different ways, such as demonizing, belittling, dehumanizing, disparaging, or—clinicians' specialty—diagnosing. The system between the party line and those out of line can become in systemic terms a *runaway*, a mutual interaction where each side's response incites an enhanced complementary or symmetrical response from the other side. The more a subsystem is dismissed, the more insistently it announces itself; the more insistently it announces itself, the easier it is to dismiss as hysterical ranting. The more it is demonized, the angrier it becomes; the angrier it becomes, the easier it is to demonize it. In a healthy system, this runaway is constrained, governed by mutual concern, empathy between subsystems, legislative limits, a feedback loop from the marginalized to the privileged, shared values for a higher-order principle than acquiring power, recognition of the self-interest served by democracy, or tempered revolution.

Theater has always served the function of announcing the marginalized, whether by articulating the conflicts involved in human drama or by displaying political themes covertly. Governments have always been suspicious of theaters, partly because political hegemonies do not like large gatherings and partly because hegemonies are much more sensitive to criticism than they pretend to be. The Nazis shut down Renoir's film *Rules of the Game*, which was ostensibly a screwball comedy about a social gathering at a hunting lodge that made fun of the French. The Elizabethan government routinely censored and even executed playwrights for writing plays "perceived to have 'application to the times'" (Wood, 2003, p. 155). Similar concern about retribution may have contributed to Jesus's preference for the plausible deniability of parables when preaching revolution (Asimov, 1969). Thus, the history of theater teaches us that those out of line need a method of expression that will escape recrimination from those in line, and the techniques of theater teach us how this can be achieved.

To apply these ideas to therapy, we must realize that in clinical work there are typically several hegemonies in operation. One operates within the therapy system, where the therapist typically embodies the executive function and the patient is typically the person who is out of line. Other hegemonies operate intrapsychically, or between the patient and his family or society. The patient's symptoms are a form of theater in which aspects of the self that are out of line are expressed in metaphor to avoid reproach from the patient's internal party line or from his family. Similarly, the therapist develops a performed self at work and considers other aspects of herself to be out of line, usually under the rubrics of unprofessional conduct or countertransference. The pervasiveness of psychological hegemonies in therapy makes it a good place to learn how to use power wisely, how to pursue feedback, how to provide feedback, and how to manage marginalization gracefully but expressively—which are often the very things that patients need to learn to cope effectively with finding themselves out of line either socially or intrapsychically.

DEADLY THEATER

Most of this book explores the parallels between therapy, psychopathology, and society, emphasizing the establishment of party lines to protect powerful interests and the creation of strategies to cope with being out of line. These ideas stem from performance theory and performance art. In this chapter, I focus on more direct parallels between theater and therapy and the lessons we can learn from theater. The title of this book derives from Peter Brook's (1968) analysis of theater practice in *The Empty Space*, where he differentiates deadly theater from good theater, while my thesis in some ways follows Goodwin's (2001) application of Brook's ideas to the classroom.

Brook identifies *deadly theater* as a major artistic problem, describes it, and suggests what to do about it. By deadly, he means many things, which can apply to whole companies, to whole productions, or to mere moments in otherwise lively offerings. Basically, deadly theater is theater that does not engage, enlighten, uplift, challenge, or change the audience. Sources of deadliness include production motivations, audience motivations, artistic constraints, and poor stagecraft. Each of these sources has analogues in therapy practice, which I will expand on later. For now, I want to focus on the overall meaning of deadliness in therapy.

If lively theater engages, uplifts, reveals, edifies, and changes the audience, then lively therapy has these effects on the patient. In both theater and therapy, the basic process of deadliness is failure to engage, and the basic outcome is failure to change. This is important in a psychotherapy context because of the parallels between deadliness and psychopathology. One source of deadliness is the stultifying effect of society's party line on the patient; another is the effect of the patient's interior party line on himself. In psychological theory, psychopathology is generally considered a form of deadliness if deadliness means nonresponsivity to the immediate environment.

PSYCHOPATHOLOGY AND DEADLINESS

There are many definitions of psychopathology, depending on the theoretical frame of reference and the general therapeutic goals. I think a useful definition that crosses most theoretical lines would include *disadvantageous*

behavior based on prior experience (one would also want to include something about conflict and emotions transcribed for the particular theory). The
deadly aspect embedded in this phrase is the sense that pathological behavior
is not responsive to the immediate environment. "That was then, this is now"
(J. Shedler, 2005, personal communication) is the central idea of the major
approaches to therapy. Prior experience interferes because it creates psychoanalysis's unconscious conflict, behaviorism's response generalization, poor
cognitive maps, systems theory's fixed role definitions, or cognitive therapy's
irrational beliefs about the world. Problematic prior experience leaves the
person responding to outmoded expectations about or trivial features of the
current environment rather than to what is really going on. Patients are like
the apocryphal 19th-century mule that would not move. When a woman
smacked it on the head with a piece of timber, her husband complained about
her cruelty to the animal. "Cruelty?" she responded. "That wasn't cruelty.
That was just getting his attention." If we want to help them, we have to shake
them out of their complacency, resistance, secondary gains, and dedication to
the past. In other words, engagement in the immediate present is a treatment
for psychopathology. (Patients are actually more like the husband in the story
than the mule since we usually engage them with metaphor; one suspects that
the woman was performing for her husband's benefit.)

Because psychopathology insulates people from immediate environments,
it also turns them into automatons. Without responsivity options, pathological behavior just goes through the motions. Kubie (1958) declares this feature
to be key in determining whether an act is pathological. "The measure of
health is flexibility, the freedom to learn through experience, the freedom to
change with changing internal and external circumstances, to be influenced
by reasonable argument . . . the freedom to respond appropriately to the stimulus of reward or punishment, and especially the freedom to cease when
sated" (p. 20). Thus, "any moment of behavior is neurotic if the processes that
set it in motion predetermine its automatic repetition" (p. 21). I quote Kubie,
a psychoanalyst, not just because his view leads naturally to a lively therapy
but also because he touches on behavioral and cognitive-behavioral concerns
in describing pathology. The overarching point is that psychopathology is itself a form of deadliness, and a lively therapy is needed to change it.

THEATER HISTORY

The origins of theater are beyond our ken. Even Aristotle's 350 B.C.E. account
of Greek tragedy was retrospective by 400 years when it was written. Still,
some awfully smart people (Aristotle and Nietzsche [1966b] in particular)

have thought about where theater came from, and the following account, which relies on them (plus Geisinger [1971] and Brockett [1982]), is as sensible as any.

Theater probably developed from the interweaving of three threads: ritual, celebration, and storytelling. *Ritual*, whether considered in a context of devotion, culture, or superstition, provided a model for theater as a form that consisted of a set piece with multiple actors and that started and ended with clear demarcations. As in celebration, there is no clear boundary line between performer and audience in rituals (at least not until anthropologists started studying them).

Celebration means the human practice of dancing and singing with no purpose other than to dance and sing. Was theater born in a barrel? Agriculture is sufficiently older than fermentation to dispel any illusions that the primary purpose of civilization is to make wine, but alcohol has played a part in celebration festivities since well before the existence of anything that looked like theater. The word *tragedy* comes from the Greek for "goat song," and Nietzsche is sure that this is because of its origins in Dionysian revelry. With agriculture came a food surplus, and with a food surplus came free time, and with free time came boredom. Anything that alleviates boredom has great value, and before television, that meant revelry, storytelling, music, and so on. (One of the reasons jesters were given so much leeway at court was because royalty were so bored [Asimov, 1970].) Getting drunk and dancing wildly is fun for many people, but watching them carry on is fun for even more. In my version of theater history, Dionysian rites of orgiastic celebration, intrinsically fun for the revelers, began to draw a crowd of onlookers. Nothing dampens an orgy (I am told) like being observed; in fact, the whole point of orgiastic revelry is to have a few hours without the otherwise omnipresent monitoring by self and others. Revelers reacted to being watched by trying to involve the onlookers, much as a preacher attends to the congregation's visiting nonmember, or as a family, self-conscious with the inclusion of a member's new fiancé, repeatedly addresses him with concerns about his assessment of them while reaching out to include him in their rituals (I am told).

As the need to deal with onlookers developed, so did the spaces in which the reveler–onlooker interaction occurred. The open-air Greek theaters included a *skene* (or booth) where a spokesman for revelers could stand to address the onlookers, a backstage where the revelers could prepare (because people who are watched need a backstage, just as nude models for an art class need a screen to disrobe behind), an *orchestra* (or dancing place) where the group would revel, and a *theatron* (or seeing place) where the onlookers could sit. An early technique for involving onlookers was to help them understand what was going on, again as a churchgoer might speak in an explanatory aside to a visiting friend about the rituals taking place there. For this purpose, a chorus emerged whose role was to comment on the action and to engage the audience, while the revelers maintained the illusion of revelry. I call this an illusion because once steps are taken to account for monitors, true revelry is lost. Consider the difference between dancing on a crowded versus empty dance floor, where your self-consciousness about how you look depends on how well you can be seen.

Meanwhile, the third strand of theatricality was introduced into the theater, the art of *storytelling*. Goffman (1974) points out that while speech is useful for conveying information about the world, a great deal of what we actually say is storytelling for the purpose of entertaining others and establishing a definition of who we are. Geoffrey Miller (2000), in his book *The Mating Mind*, suggests that our big brains evolved not to manipulate the geographical environment but to win mates in courtship as interesting conversation became the way to a partner's heart. Whether or not one goes as far as Miller, there is no doubt that a good story has long been a valuable social commodity. A conductor I know told me that music undoubtedly developed around a campfire where harmonies and chords were discovered by experiments in singing. Around that same campfire, storytellers may have discovered that they could make their stories more interesting by playing the parts—speaking the voices of the characters and not just narrating.

Eventually, in the theater, someone had the idea (legend says it was a fellow named Thespis) to assign an actor to play a specific character throughout the revelry. Initially, this meant going beyond the incorporation of the god into the body through dancing and singing (and drinking) by having someone impersonate the god in conversation. This thespian did so by standing on the scene and answering questions posed by the chorus. (Greek for "answerer" gives us *hypocrite*, by which performers are disparaged for merely playing a part.) Eventually, the revelers and the chorus disappeared, and all that remained were the audience and the thespians, who have been trying ever since to figure out how to engage the audience.

DEADLY THERAPIST MOTIVES

Now let's look at useful versus problematic motivations on the parts of therapists, patients, artists, and audiences that affect the liveliness of the enterprise.

Wanting a Reputation for Competence

Both therapists and artists normally want a reputation for competence, and the natural motive to acquire such a reputation can conflict with artistic and therapeutic concerns. Because of the private nature of therapy and rehearsal and because of the ephemeral nature of live performance, a reputation for competence does not come easily. It can be very difficult to determine how good an actor, director, or therapist is at her job. Even to have an informed opinion, you have to be there. Recordings do not help, as they distort as much as they reveal. Even worse, the extra layer of what Goffman (1974) calls lamination deadens the theater or therapy recording, as anyone knows who has seen a filmed stage play. (Successful plays must be rewritten and reconsidered directorially to become successful films.) Thus, a recording not only distorts competence but actively misrepresents it as well since a recording that looks competent may play too much to the camera to have been a successful performance for the live audience. And, apart from the way therapy looks in a recording, the very act of recording a psychotherapy session introduces such a powerful change in conditions that the result is not a good indicator of how therapy goes when there is no recorder.

The fact that it is hard to assess competence of live work is both a frustration and a boon for theater and therapy professionals. On the frustration side, I met a woman who wrote and directed a play that won an international prize and was celebrated with a 2-week run in Edinburgh. In all, 300 people saw it. Renown for competence in the theater is so hard to get that, despite the prize, the potential audience was dubious enough to avoid the commitment of time and money needed to see the piece. Wise producers stress other aspects of a show to draw an audience. The Duke in *Huckleberry Finn* (Twain, 1946, p. 379), trying to entice a small-town crowd to a performance of Shakespeare, paints at the bottom of the sign, "LADIES AND CHILDREN NOT ADMITTED." "'There,' says he, 'if that don't fetch them, I don't know Arkansaw!'" Once producers realize that artistic proficiency is not all that important in attracting a crowd (with some notable exceptions), they lose interest in art. This makes a theater career frustrating because it is hard to parlay excellence into success.

The analogous problem for therapists is that our success does not have nearly as much to do with proficiency as marketing strategies based on other factors. Niche therapy—for lesbian professionals, anorexics, and children of bitter divorces—is easier to market than plain competence. Once a niche has been established, marketing forces compel therapists to keep other therapists, regardless of competence, out of the niche. Credential tests are created, and competitors practicing without the credential are disparaged. Sometimes, the credential needed for working with a particular niche is the race, sex, or ethnicity of the therapist. The ultimate test is a statutory one, which will protect a niche from outsiders—statutory tests having a way of including everyone on the statute-writing committee, their close friends, and as few others as possible. In therapy as in theater, the road to worldly success is not paved with competence. (Not sour grapes, by the way. I was in a lucky situation and had about as many patients as I wanted; my niche was working evenings.)

There is also an upside to difficulties in getting recognition for competence. It can actually put the dedicated theater or therapy professional in a position to concentrate on competence, unencumbered by fantasies of recognition. Knowing that a play will not be picked up by Broadway producers, much less Hollywood studios, the company can concentrate on engaging the audience in the art of theatercraft. Similarly, the therapist can be liberated from concerns of fame and glory and focus on the patient. In this respect, as a therapist I want to be an artist—someone whose work of course responds to market forces, politics, and personal needs but whose primary motive is to keep making it better. Artists (and therapists) may disagree as to what constitutes "better," but two people arguing about improvement on this dimension are at least arguing about the right thing.

Whenever someone gets a good reputation as a therapist, I am suspicious. How can anyone who was not involved have a basis for an opinion, and how can anyone who was involved have any objectivity? Often, we infer the quality of the therapies a person conducts from her behavior in other settings. When that behavior is markedly disordered or unintelligent, then it is probably correct to infer that the therapies she conducts are no good. Otherwise, the person's performance in the role of therapist is no more implied by her public conduct than is her performance in the role of romantic partner or mother. Therapists should of course be careful to present themselves socially, like the proverbial banker, in a manner that will get them the professional reputations they want; for therapists, that usually means temperate, considerate, insightful, and accepting, but it can also mean iconoclastic and disruptive for certain therapeutic approaches. But such a social presentation merely means that the therapist is reasonably concerned about her reputation or that she is so overly identified with the role of therapist that she does not know how to have a good time. It does not mean that she behaves that way in sessions.

Theater is vastly more public than therapy. Critics and other professionals see the work and report on it. Thus, even though I have never seen Edwin Booth or Sarah Bernhardt act, I can accept the proposition that they were very skilled. But even with these exalted figures, you never know if the reputation was truly deserved. They may have tailored their performances to applause rather than to artistic engagement. Thus, the pursuit of a reputation for competence, which we all would enjoy, conflicts with liveliness when there is a conflict between engaging versus pleasing the audience or changing versus pleasing the patient. Goffman (1959) discusses this conflict between showing and acquiring competence, as do biologists and economists. A business diverts funds from research and development for marketing and advertising, and genes divert energy from becoming poisonous to predators to appearing poisonous to predators. Therapists need some sort of reputation to stay in business, but some of their energies spent on reputation would be better spent on mastery. I see this when clinicians spend time at conferences, which are essentially about glad-handing, that could be spent reading.

Wanting to Further Our View of Health

Analogous to the production that puts its artistic agenda ahead of engaging a specific audience, therapists often put their culture-bound and theory-bound health agenda ahead of engaging a specific patient. A health agenda is not always deadly, just as artistic concerns in a production are not deadly as long as they inform rather than replace audience engagement. When theater pushes the artistic envelope with nonnarrative drama and random music, it leaves the audience behind and deadliness follows.

Even nonartistic motives need not be deadly. Brook recognizes, accepts, and even celebrates a host of such motivations, including making a living, showing off, being good at something, and spending time with outlandish people. If theater is to avoid deadliness, nonartistic motivations must be subordinated to the artistic enterprise by a pervasive and passionate interest in engaging, honoring, and edifying the audience. A cornerstone of this attitude is Brook's insistence that, despite the fact that there are some bad audiences, the audience must never be blamed. Blame undermines the artistic endeavor of reaching them. I hear in Brook's words the crux of intersubjectivity (Buirski & Haglund, 2001; Stolorow, Brandchaft, & Atwood, 1987): the centrality of engaging the patient, the futility of blame, and the cocreation of an edifying experience.

Therapists have many reasons for doing therapy, including the furtherance of health, but these must be subordinate to the therapeutic goals—those the patient and therapist agree to achieve. In the theater, goals vary according to the audience involved and according to the company's artistic agenda, which also dictates which piece is presented. In therapy, goals vary according to the particular patient (analogous to the audience) and according to the therapist's concerns about what constitutes health (analogous to the artistic agenda). The analogue of the piece that the company presents is the type of therapy selected by the therapist and the content of sessions selected by the patient. Some therapists deny that they have health concerns and claim only to work toward the stated goals of the patient. They may even claim that their therapies are value free, as if such a thing were possible among humans.

I asked a putatively value-free therapist how his work would differ between a 90-pound and a 390-pound woman with the stated therapy goal of losing weight. He claimed that in either case he would explore what she thought she would get out of weight reduction. However, he finally admitted that he would eventually stop subjecting the fat patient's reasons to scrutiny, while he would never stop examining the thin patient's reasons. Other therapists I have met clearly have value-laden agendas in treatment and do not admit to them—not because they claim the patient controls the therapy contract but because they are unaware of their own agendas. A particularly alarming case was the male therapist who agreed to help a 16-year-old girl justify a medical need for breast augmentation. Rather than question her dissatisfaction with her breasts, he agreed to her stated goal of documenting her dysphoria so her insurance would pay for the surgery. Tellingly, her unhappiness centered on the fact that her breasts were different sizes, and at no time in the treatment was reduction of the larger breast considered. Failure to articulate his preference for large breasts led him to enact that preference without due consideration.

The therapist's health agenda is culture bound. In my view, culturally competent psychotherapy does not mean wholesale deference to the client's culture. It means awareness of my own cultural preferences and values, so I can decide which to impose and which to defer. If I am not aware of them, I will surely impose them all. Unawareness also runs the risk of perpetrating such serious breaches of etiquette that I lose the client, even when the etiquette in question is of no real importance to me. For example, I like to start every therapy with a handshake, which to me signals more than an American greeting. It also signals the start of an agreement that whoever we may be in the waiting room will not dictate who we are in the office: the handshake says, "The game is on." But if I know the client is an orthodox Jewess, then why blow the therapy by cavalierly disregarding her culture? A slight bow will do.

Beyond etiquette, examination of my own values and preferences makes me culturally competent because it reminds me that my values and preferences are not universal, leaving me prepared to find out about my client's. This is even more important with clients who seem to be from my own culture because with clients who are obviously different from me, I know not to assume that they see the world as I do. My definition of health—the way my core values translate into goals for myself and others—affects the priority of my motivations for doing therapy and affects what I am up to when I am, like an artist, trying to do it well. For me personally, these goals include, as in Freud's terse summary, love and work and, I would add, social justice, or what Adler (1937) called "the useful side of life." Others may have different values or different ways of organizing them. My patients' love, work, and sense of social justice are my artistic concerns as a therapist. They need not dominate every move I make or every therapy I do, but they are my yardsticks for evaluating how I am doing independent of praise, gratitude, and money. However, when they are more important to me than engaging the patient, the effect is deadly.

Wanting Money

Brook notes the deadliness associated with money limitations in the theater. He cites the lack of needed rehearsal time when money is scarce, which leads to formulaic solutions to dramaturgical problems. He also emphasizes how the high price of theater tickets makes it difficult for the company to experiment with their production, for fear of not giving value, and for the audience to experiment by going to alternative spaces, for fear of not getting value. In sum, "theatre cannot remain dynamic and adventurous if it depends uniquely on the box office" (Brook, 1993, p. 69), but sponsors create other problems since they are typically corporations that want productions they feel comfortable using to entertain clients.

Let's face it: we do therapy for a living and the money is important. I do not think that it is generally realistic to expect to make as much doing therapy as we might make in business, law, or engineering, not to mention other areas of psychology or medicine. On the other hand, a busy practitioner can see 15 people a week for $100 to $150 an hour and gross $70,000 a year for what amounts to half-time work (with paperwork, phone calls, and so on). If that is not attractive, you may be in the wrong line of work.

There are direct parallels between the economic deadliness Brook mentions and what we face as therapists. When therapists charge hefty fees, it makes them tentative for fear of losing the source of income. It also makes patients suspicious of the type of intimate consulting situation that I find ideal: a small office with no receptionist, secretary, answering service, or transcriptionist, with an adjoining waiting area that never has other patients in it. This arrangement seems sensible to a patient paying a moderate fee, but when a lot of money is at stake, the patient expects some bustle. Also, a large fee can make the patient, well, impatient, leading to mutual declarations of progress by the therapist to justify the fee and by the patient to end it.

The money, it is sometimes important to make clear to patients, is for our time, not for the treatment. Ideas, relationship management, humor, respect, and warmth—these are all gratis. Financial motives become problematic only when the therapist feels she needs more money than she has. This can make her yield to the temptation of gratifying the needs of her patients rather than helping them change their behaviors. And it can make her picky and small about late payments and missed sessions. (I am not recommending a policy for missed sessions. Later in this chapter, I will recommend not having a policy.

Here, I am focusing on the way a subjective need for money can make therapists focus on payments maladroitly and bureaucratically.)

I avoided this problem by never trying to make a living doing therapy. I
have always had other irons in the fire, whether a full-time job in a clinic or
private industrial and forensic work. I also charge less than others with my
credentials to avoid a financial sting when the patient gets better and leaves.
Nonetheless, when I saw my first private patient, although I was working full
time in a psychotherapy service, I felt I needed the money. I had rented an office with a friend rather than starting off renting by the hour from someone
with an established practice, and I didn't want to run in the red (although this,
like much subjective need for money, was mostly about pride). I also had an
infant at home, and we were feeling the pinch. (In middle age, I have come
to define wealth as a condition where, when bills come in, you just pay them.)
For my first referral, the referring source called me to let me know he had sent
me a patient. This is standard practice, creating a mutual fiction that some superficial information needs to be exchanged to facilitate the referral when really the referring professional wants credit for the referral even if the patient
never follows through or in case she doesn't mention the source to the new
therapist. It is considered overkill to give a patient three names and call all of
them and tell them you have made a referral to them. (I give only one name
and tell the patient to come back for another if it doesn't work out. I find that
giving multiple names leads the patient to evaluate not the level of trust and
mutuality offered by the three therapists but rather the level of superficial
gratification.)

After Doug called me and told me about the referral, I was excited and re-
lieved. I might be in the black even in my first month of practice. Unfortunately, the patient didn't call and continued not to call as I became increasingly desperate. Doug had told me her name, a practice frowned on in big
cities but necessary in a small town where there's always a pretty good
chance of knowing someone unexpectedly. I can't recall what I was thinking
as I looked her up in the phone book, but as I dialed the number (yes, it was
that long ago: I dialed), I concocted a scheme to tell her that Doug had told
me that I was to call her, and, oh, did I get that part wrong? When I heard the
first burr of the ring, I was overcome by whatever grace may be, and I hung
up before she answered. She called me a few days later, and my private practice was under way.

Therapists must manage various financial quandaries from time to time.
What would you do if a patient lost her job and couldn't afford to pay for sessions? Lower the fee and inadvertently communicate that you see her as
pitiable? Defer payment and cultivate an out-of-therapy dependence? See her
every other week and communicate that it is the overall being-in-therapy that

matters and not the work you do together? Interpret her predicament as somehow motivated or her request as entitled, thereby making her feel blamed?

And what do you do if a patient misses a payment? Should you collect fees every session or every month? Do you accept insurance? Who fills out the insurance forms? What do you do if you start at a reasonable fee but see the patient for years? Do you raise the fee eventually? What if she inherits a fortune? What if her check bounces? What if she misses a session? What if she called first and told you she had a lunch date? What if her mother died and she attended the funeral?

Keeping in mind my definition of deadliness as anything other than furthering mutual engagement in the service of achieving therapeutic goals, my answer to all such quandaries is that it depends on the details of the specific situation. It is foolish to negotiate tricky terrain with a map, whether it be a map of practice policies or a map of psychological theory; tricky terrain requires attention to the terrain, not to the map. A therapist's concern about money can distract him from the patient in front of him and lead to his pulling out a reified, deadly policy.

Wanting Gratitude

One of the main sources of deadliness in therapy is the therapist's motivation to be perceived positively. This often manifests itself in a desire to be perceived as helpful when the situation calls for playing some other role. Behaviorally, insistence on being seen positively interferes with the benign effects of exposure to threatening people. Many patients have had bad experiences with authority figures and have aversive expectations of them now. They require overt signs of niceness or they become fearful. When we withhold niceness, it exposes the patient to the authority figure to extinguish these fears, as we do not dismiss the fears but neither do we confirm them (I hope) by being mean. The patient initially construes our withholding as mean, but it isn't really mean because it isn't a precursor to insult or injury. Dispelling the patient's construction with niceness to gain approval keeps this exposure therapy from occurring and leaves the patient still fearful of authority figures who won't go out of their ways to assure him or her of their kindness. This was a main theme of my book on child abuse (Karson, 2001): "While the ends may not justify the means, neither do the means justify the ends. Bad outcomes should not be applauded merely because they were produced by gentle, optimistic, and humane methods" (p. 234).

The therapist's desire for gratitude can also be expressed as a need for admiration. Actors present themselves to audiences and understandably feel exposed and vulnerable afterward, seeking an almost Kohutian reassurance from others that their exhibition was appreciated. It took *two* Oscars for Sally Field to conclude that the community really liked her. If that vulnerability seeps into the performance itself, deadliness follows because the performance turns from engaging the audience around the themes of the play to engaging them around meeting the performer's needs. Therapists also expose themselves and want patients to make them feel appreciated—a reversal of the usual self-psychology stance, often not discussed, that can make the therapy about mutual reassurance instead of the therapy goals.

Wanting Renown

Another slant on the therapist's deadly motivation to look good is the desire for renown. Brook (1993) again: "One often sees actors, sometimes very great actors—and opera singers above all—conscious of their reputation, totally involved with themselves and only pretending to play with their partner" (p. 38). I attended a fairly intimate play reading, at the Northampton Film Festival in Massachusetts, with Judd Hirsch in it. The play was being workshopped that afternoon, and I got to go to the first read-through just before the audience came in. Hirsch was very much the famous actor, breezing into the theater, treating all around him as entourage, and, after the public workshop, attending the cocktail party but appearing bored and too important to be spoken with. Onstage, however, he was utterly attentive to the two other actors, submerging the celebrity in the role and seeking only the truth of the script. For the duration of the reading, he was the father in the play, not the Hollywood star. His performance onstage was an example of someone who could play for fame choosing not to. His performance offstage was probably an adaptation to avoid fawning or envious people, as intersubjective in its way as his performance onstage.

We play for fame within sessions when we shine with brilliance and cast the patient into shadow. We play for renown when we seek the patient's approval and applause and when we privilege our own assessment of an intervention over the patient's reaction to it, as if the applause we are seeking is from ourselves. Buirski (2006) cautions, "Of course, the test of whether an articulation is attuned is not to be found in the intention of the transmitter, but in the subjective experience of the receiver feeling understood."

We play for fame outside of sessions when we say things in sessions that we know we'll repeat to colleagues or friends. At the time I decided to take the magazines out of my waiting area, reported later in this chapter, I was not thinking about the useful anecdote I would someday commit to paper or the story I would and did tell my colleagues. At the time, I was thinking about what I was doing to the patient and how I could fix the paradoxical communication, not my reputation.

To keep the desire for renown from infiltrating the performance, one must construct a confidential space in which fame is not a factor. In theater, a distinction between rehearsal and performance can accomplish this. In therapy, it is more challenging because the rehearsal space in which alternatives are tried and the performance space in which they are shown are identical. Theater rehearsals, according to Brook, must be private, but of course performances are not. About rehearsals, Brook (1993) writes, "When you have this security, then day after day you can experiment, make mistakes, be foolish, certain in the knowledge that no one outside the four walls will ever know, and from that point you begin to find the strength that helps you to open up, both to yourself and to the others" (p. 120).

In current clinical practice, confidentiality is largely protected in the service of the patient's legal rights. Malpractice, tort, and contract law, in conjunction with ethical obligations, prohibit our breaching confidences. Informed consent from patients legally and ethically frees us to talk to whomever we want. But, as Brook's words remind us, the true purpose of confidentiality is not to protect the patient's right to privacy—it is to create a lively play space. The patient's freedom to reveal and to experiment is likely to be impaired by a lack of privacy, and so is the therapist's. The potential for an external audience is bound to get the therapist playing to that audience instead of responding to the patient. Lively, engaging therapy must be confidential therapy.

Buddha gives us a lesson on the relationship between confidentiality and renown. In the version of the enlightenment I first heard, in an art history class, Siddhartha was very close to enlightenment and resolved to sit under the Bodhi tree until he achieved it. Mara, a god assigned to keep him from getting there, sent the most beautiful women imaginable to distract him, but Siddhartha ignored them. Mara then sent his warriors to frighten Siddhartha into leaving, but he ignored them as well. Finally, playing his ace, Mara congratulated Siddhartha on his imminent triumph and suggested that he let people know about this world-historical moment, to celebrate it and to glorify himself. Siddhartha touched the ground as if to say, "The earth is my witness." I am no Buddha, but when I feel like breaching a confidence, I touch the ground.

(I feel a scholarly obligation to note that most writers say that Mara's final challenge was to ask the Buddha-to-be what entitled him to achieve enlightenment, and the response meant that the earth had witnessed his many incarnations of sacrifice and wisdom. I don't like this version because it seems to me not very Buddhistic of him to say he deserves it.)

DEADLY PATIENT MOTIVES

Just Being There

Brook outlines several audience motivations that contribute to deadliness, and these have counterparts in patients. Frequently, spectators seek *culture* per se rather than the kinds of experiences that are called cultured. It's fine for people to go to the opera or to a Brecht play for culture if once there the opera or play moves, challenges, and edifies them—but deadly spectators attend primarily for the purpose of having attended. Brook (1993) says that culture for these people must be "reassuringly boring" (p. 68). On the same theme, Lorenz Hart, the songwriter, says the lady is a tramp who "likes the opera and never comes late," meaning that the status of being upper class is inconsistent with truly appreciating art. Arnheim (1966, p. 13) tells the story of an art collector who complained to him about her "Philistine" husband; the husband did not like Picassos in the dining room because he could not eat in their presence. The Philistine, not the deadly art collector, was responding to the art. Such theatergoers account for sentiments like Brook's (1968): "One look at the average audience gives us the irresistible urge to assault it" (p. 55).

Once in the audience, the culture-seeking spectator can be engaged unless she is dead set against it. One of my favorite moments in any theater was at a production of *Midsummer Night's Dream*, presented in the round, where you could watch the actors and audience members at the same time. I was way in the back, in the graduate student seats, while closer to the stage I could see some more dignified patrons decked out in expensive jewels, furs, and dinner jackets. The play within the play, Shakespeare's broadest and lowest comedic scene, was performed so well that the audience was literally doubled over with laughter, gasping for air. The sight of elegant ladies and gentlemen managing snot and tears, glimpsed through my own, was one of engagement.

Wealthy culture seekers spend much of their public lives fending off ordinariness, and if they want to rise above a bunch of actors, they can easily do so. Besides coming late and leaving early, they can use their opera glasses to spy on other audience members, whisper to their neighbors, and even bring a radio to listen to the sporting events they are missing. Perhaps their greatest defense is simply to think to themselves how cultured they are when performers do manage to connect with them. Of course, defensiveness is facilitated by performers who sense the audience's purpose and leave them alone by turning the piece into a distant and deadly showcase, much like the mutual unspoken agreement to create a deadly classroom that emerges between teachers who hide behind PowerPoint presentations and students who hide behind laptops. Professors who sense that students are there because the course is required or because it is a prerequisite for something else lose interest in engagement, teach avoidantly, and drive away the engageable students, thus fulfilling the expectation that the students are not there for the content.

Do patients come for therapy just to be in therapy rather than for help? Of course they do. In fact, they all do, at least to the extent that seeking therapy helps define the situation as the kind of situation that needs therapy; any definition, even a needful, pathological one, can be palliative compared to feeling lost. This behavior takes several different forms. The primary case is the patient who comes for therapy to communicate to his social network that he is doing something about the problem. Because psychopathology is nonresponsive and maladroit, it is annoying to other people. The pressure to behave differently can be countered by the patient's claim that he is trying his best. Psychotherapy is especially useful for this since our society often gives a free pass—or at least leeway—to annoying people who can frame their annoying behavior as pathological. Thus, calling a therapist communicates to the patient's associates not only that he is doing something about it but also that it is not really his fault because the annoying conduct is a product of sickness (or family history or inner angst). And even a patient with no associates to impress may undertake therapy to make *herself* think that she is doing something about it, at least to ward of the internal accusations of laziness and self-pity.

Attending therapy can also enhance your status, especially if it is framed as self-exploration and not as needing help. In a dispute over who had messed up the meeting time for a social occasion, one psychoanalyst had the temerity to tell her friend that the unconscious motivation to mess up the dinner must have been the friend's since the analyst's own training analysis precluded her from having such difficulties. Any former patient can make such claims of freedom from neurosis, not just psychoanalysts. A patient can also use reports of therapy to trump his wife's reproaches. "My therapist says you are insecure" has surely been said more than once. The patient does not anticipate this specific parry when seeking treatment, but he may sense that he needs someone on his side.

Couples often seek therapy as a step in the ritual of breaking up or reconciling. Divorce seems impulsive in some circles if not preceded by marital therapy. Just kissing and making up can seem to minimize one or both partners' hurt feelings, and attending couple's therapy can demonstrate that the hurt feelings needed attention.

All too often the therapist does not address, much less use, the patient's extratherapeutic reasons for seeking treatment. Perhaps she is afraid of losing him or insulting him if she openly scrutinizes his statement that he wants help. My own position is that a good time to start involving the patient in the psychotherapy process is when the therapy starts. Like a theater company that wants to shock its culture-seeking audience out of its complacency, I like to ask patients some time in the first session where they were when they first got the idea to call a therapist, who else knows they called and what they think about it, what was going through their minds in the waiting room before I got them, what went through their minds when I asked them that, and what is going through their minds right this second. "Never leap over the garden wall" is a tried-and-true axiom of ego psychology, meaning that the therapist should work on understanding the meaning and function of defenses rather than bypassing them. If the reason for coming to therapy is itself defensive, then it too should be understood rather than bypassed. Moving directly to what defensive behavior avoids is only likely to exacerbate defensiveness, while chipping away at defensive behaviors is more likely to produce gradual, ameliorative exposure.

Understanding Rather Than Changing

Brook reports another deadly audience behavior that is much like the defense of intellectualization. The *Diagnostic and Statistical Manual of Mental Disorders* (*DSM-IV*; American Psychiatric Association, 1994) defines intellectualization as dealing "with emotional conflict or internal or external stressors by the excessive use of abstract thinking or the making of generalizations to control or minimize disturbing feelings" (p. 756). Brook gives the example of an English professor who, during the performance of a classic play, thinks about whether the text has been accurately presented or the operagoer who monitors the performance for false notes. I would also include the spectator whose interest in the meaning of the play insulates her from being engaged by it.

The inverse of the intellectualizer, or what Bullough (1912–1913) called the overdistancer, is what he called the underdistancer. The former understands the art but does not apply it to himself, as if viewing it through the wrong end of a telescope. The latter responds emotionally to the themes but is too close to them to learn anything from them. Parallels to obsessive-compulsive isolation of affect and hysterical emotionality are obvious. One man closely follows each image in Lear's parting scene with Cordelia but does not reflect at all on his relationships with his own father and his own children. Another man sobs through the scene, goes home, and embraces his children, perhaps even demanding a statement of mutual affection (ironically, since Lear starts all the trouble by doing just that), and then forgets the whole thing.

Patients also come in too-distant and too-close varieties (I am not for the moment considering personality but motivation for treatment). The most obvious example of the too-distant patient is the one who comes for therapy as a requirement for training, whether for a psychoanalytic institute or for graduate school. Her whole approach to the therapy is, at best, one of curiosity and, at worst, one of completing an assignment. Too distant also is the patient who comes at the behest of others or who comes to learn about psychotherapy. Even if she does recount some personal narratives, her therapist is hard pressed to engage her around them. Instead, the dyad is apt to drift off into an interpretation of symbols, patterns, and thoughts, like two literature critics deconstructing a text. Even more likely is for the pair to avoid any meaningful personal narratives at all, turning the experience into something more reminiscent of a seminar than an engaged interaction. I have already (Karson, 2006) drawn the analogy to foster children having to pretend that they are engaged with their foster parents and how difficult it is for even concerned foster parents to tell the difference. A kiss goodnight looks a lot like a kiss goodnight, whether it is offered in gratitude or duty. Patients pretending to be engaged by therapy, who are really there to comply with someone else's agenda or as a field study, can complete a wholly as-if treatment without the therapist ever knowing. This is one reason that therapists need a way to assess progress independent of the patient's conscious representations about how things are going.

Faced with such a patient, therapists have a limited array of options to engage them. The easiest is to ask the patient to set aside his motivation and find something real to work on "since we're going to be here anyway." This sometimes works, just at it sometimes works in the theater when the actors speak directly to the pedant to distract him from his removed stance. (Apparently, direct address of the audience has been a sporadic dramatic technique for over 2500 years because it is so effective at engaging overdistancers.) The whole therapy can be organized around the patient's relationship to authority and whether obedience to the requirement of attendance can coexist with liveliness.

Minuchin says that therapy must include the person who wants change, the person who can change, and the person who has to change. I interpret this wisdom to mean that individual therapy works best when all three are the same person—but often they are not. When the overdistancing patient is there to comply with the wishes of friends or family, systemically minded therapists invite these people into the treatment. With patients complying with educational requirements and court orders, inclusion of the referral source is not practical. If a theater company is to perform for an audience known to be fulfilling a course requirement, it can take certain steps toward engaging them. For example, the actors might begin the show "out of character" and let the audience in on the director's placement of them in the scene, even staging some disputes between actors and director. This is Milton Erickson's strategy (Haley, 1973) when he starts sessions with reluctant adolescents by telling them that *his* boss told *him* he had to meet with this patient.

I tried this technique once with a sullen 12-year-old girl who refused to walk with me from the waiting room at the Department of Social Services to the office where I was supposed to evaluate her. As I stood in the hallway, looking perplexed, the area director asked me why the long face. I told her my problem, and, when she asked if she could help, I took her at her word. I suggested she tell the kid a made-up story that my work there was being evaluated, that I had trouble getting kids to meet with me, and that if the girl refused to meet with me, I could lose my job and my kids would suffer. The area director said exactly this to the girl, who responded, "Fuck 'im." Then she looked the area director in the eye and said, "And fuck you, too." I am tempted to write that not every patient is engageable, but the truth is that I am no Erickson.

Therapists have some major advantages over actors in their efforts to engage others. We do not have to anticipate what kind of audience it is because we can get a feel for them as we begin and change our strategy accordingly. Also, we have more than a single evening to work with, so we can take our time to make genuine contact. These are only advantages if we remain aware of the desirability of genuine contact and if we use the time we have; otherwise, these are disadvantages since the luxury of repeated contact and prior assessment can lead us to delay engagement efforts indefinitely. The greatest lesson we can learn from Brook is to recognize deadliness when it occurs and to motivate ourselves and each other to change it. Thus, as long as we remember that the deadliness we experience with the overdistancing patient is not productive work (though it might be intellectually interesting), we can use the time to build a trusting relationship and gently bring the patient's narrative material to life in the room. All too often, though, a slower pace becomes an excuse for dragging things out, and I have great sympathy for those who shrug and dismiss patients who don't want to work.

Making the Therapy Only About the Therapist

Underdistancing patients are also common. These are the people who come to therapy not to change but to get their needs met. They are like theatergoers who ogle the good-looking actors, enjoy the air conditioning, cry during the sad parts, exult when the main characters exact their revenge on the bad guys, and leave the theater feeling refreshed but not otherwise changed by the experience. As patients, they seek help with loneliness, insignificance, or inadequacy, among other things, but instead of working to change themselves, they cure their loneliness through social connection with the therapist, their insignificance through attention and affirmation from the therapist, their inadequacy by besting the therapist, and so on.

Occasionally, the underdistancing audience member disrupts the theater performance, as in the story of the spectator who shouted a warning to Caesar that Brutus was plotting to kill him. (Caesar responded to the shouter's warning as he did to the soothsayer's, such is fate.) Otherwise, these audience members are the bread and butter of commercial theater. They come for various pleasures and various pleasures are provided. Costumes get tighter or disappear altogether, the seats get softer, the plays get simpler, swordfights get more exciting, and everyone goes away happy, just as they do at a fast-food joint—content but malnourished. These types are also the bread and butter of consulting rooms, paying us for validation rather than therapeutic change.

The conscientious therapist wants to convert the steady patient into a working patient even if it means the patient gets better and leaves. A flurry of activity is not the answer, as research repeatedly shows that many therapies take a year or two, whether they are conceptualized in terms of a long-term relationship, as in psychoanalytic therapies, or in terms of brief treatment and lengthy follow-up, as in some cognitive-behavioral therapies. Instead, the therapist needs to parlay the patient's interest in extratherapeutic gratifications into a working relationship. You can look at Kohut's (1971, 1977) contribution as a coherent rationale for why therapy takes so long so that therapists gently trying to convert misalliances into working alliances need not get discouraged about the pace. This conversion is largely achieved by teaching the patient the advantages of, in Goffman's (1974) terminology, an extra layer of lamination or, in Bateson's (1972c) language, metacommunication (i.e., communication about how we communicate). I will revisit this issue in other chapters—for now I want to emphasize the way talking about the patient's storytelling and not just about the stories can change an underdistancer into someone who can appreciate and learn from narrative.

Deadly Stagecraft and the Empty Office

Brook (1968) titled his book about deadly and lively theater *The Empty Space*. His idea was that filling up the stage with scenery, props, costumes, theories of acting, and theories of directing is deadly because objects and methods constrict the freedom of actors to experiment with each other and the play itself. Liveliness is achieved in the theater by abandoning preconceived notions about how to do a play and instead trying things out and seeing what works. In this context, we may infer that what Brook means by liveliness is esponsivity to the immediate environment, which is certainly a characteristic of living organisms. Good actors can create an amazing array of landscapes and situations with a few words and gestures as long as there is nothing in view to refute the impression they are creating. Actors in neutral garb—currently, this means black pants and black T-shirts—can play ancient Romans, but actors in togas can *only* play ancient Romans (and frat boys). In Brook's view, sets, costumes, and actors must function in the service of the play's message and not the other way around. When a method or prop preexists the acting, the actors must accommodate it, limiting their flexibility. His preference is to create dramaturgical illusions with flexible elements, like gestures and words, so they can change as needed. Brook (1968) asks theater artists to start with "the premise that a stage is a stage—not a convenient place for the unfolding of a staged novel or a staged poem or a staged lecture or a staged story—then the word that is spoken on this stage exists . . . only in relation to the tension it creates on that stage within the given stage circumstances" (p. 37).

How shall I appoint my office to maximally enliven the therapy I do there? It isn't practical to redo the consulting room for each patient. As with a set design that will have to serve for an evening of one-act plays, minimalism will serve better than scenery. That means choosing furniture, props, and costumes that are neutral, that is, highly expected. A literally empty office plus two chairs and a wall clock would be so shocking as to require accommodation by the patient as much as an office cluttered with memorabilia and family photos. Thus, the office shouldn't force the patient's narrative to accommodate it.

Local norms will be important. An office in a small town in the South will support bare floors that in a major city might make the room seem unfinished. Likewise, a business suit might be invisible in one location and blatant in another. Whatever these normative expectations may be, though, we should not yield to them to the point of making the office something other than a place in its own right. Thus, spare and somewhat humble furnishings will communicate an expectation of intimacy that expensive art and grand wainscoting will not. Patients are often surprised by the absence of a receptionist, although this unfortunately seems to be a thing of the past, as not only patients but also therapists seem increasingly to accept the physician's office as a model for our own.

Further prescription on how to construct an empty office would be paradoxical. Prescription means rules, and rules, no matter how well they codify liveliness, are deadly. The real issue is the effect on patients. The real issue is to change the things we can and to apologize for or at least accept with equanimity the patient's feelings about the things we cannot change. In this respect, our office's imperfections make us like parents who can't afford to take their kids to Disney World. It is better to tell the children "I wish I could afford it" than "You are a greedy and unappreciative child" or "Disney World represents capitalist excess and alienation of the soul." All too often, though, patients' direct and indirect complaints about our offices are interpreted as reflections on them, not as reflections on the office.

For a long time, I did therapy in a shared office that had its own little waiting room, a consulting room with an entrance from the waiting room and a separate exit, and a bathroom accessible from either space. One day a patient was talking about his efforts to sort out the paradoxical communications he received from his mother, which amounted to "You should always think about how you don't have to think about me." Out of the blue, he mentioned an article he had seen in a magazine in my waiting room. I commented on the paradox of my communicating that we start precisely on time each week while also providing magazines, which communicated an expectation that he would arrive early and wait for me. For the next several years, when I arrived at the office I would pack up all the magazines in the waiting room and put them in a desk drawer and then put them back when I left. When my office mate left the state and I kept the place for myself, I finally just threw the magazines away.

THE EMPTY THERAPIST

Besides an empty office, I can also offer an empty vessel. This is what Bion (1967) meant by advocating an absence of memory, desire, or understanding. I strive to be open to playing whatever role the patient needs to cast me in to put up his production, but like many younger brothers, I resisted patients' efforts to cast me in the role of the person in charge. Becoming a father got me used to playing the role of authority figure, and my flexibility with patients improved accordingly. Now I can play authority, associate, or subordinate, as need be. Some particularly unappealing roles—abuser and abandoner— are still trouble for me, and I have a deadly tendency to remind the patient that I am really a good guy underneath, like a movie star playing a creep who insists on outlandish makeup to show us that he is not the character he is playing.

WHY CAN'T THE PATIENTS LEARN THEIR LINES?

We have therapy technologies that would work every time if only the patient would play the role assigned to him. Why can't he learn his lines? He

.s supposed to complain about depression, not about the way his colleagues respond to his depression. When I cognitive-behaviorally explain to him that he is depressing himself, he is not supposed to tell me that I am minimizing his feelings about being gossiped about at work. When I explain to him, still cognitive-behaviorally, why it is irrational for him to upset himself about gossip, he is not supposed to comment on the fact that I report on his diagnosis to his insurance company. If only these knuckleheads would say their lines correctly, the way Beck and Horney and Kohut wrote them, the therapy would go smoothly, and they would get better.

Many problems in technique faced by therapists can be framed as clients not behaving correctly (the operation is successful but the patient dies). The therapist's frustration is like the actor's frustration when the audience refuses to laugh at the laugh lines. Surely there are actors who say, "The material is funny; the audience is humorless." This is what Brook means by the deadliness of blaming the audience because an actor who thinks that way will not discover how to make the material funny for that particular audience. Similarly, therapists who are convinced that their theoretical orientation and technique are correct ignore signs of failure until they can't be ignored, and then they say, "I guess he didn't really want to change." Or worse, they will enhance the diagnosis (I call this throwing the book—the *DSM*—at the patient): "I may have missed some borderline traits," they say, after the patient gets angry or quits.

IMPROVISATION IN THERAPY

Every lively theater action is improvisational. No matter how sacred the text and no matter how rigid the staging, every lively moment on the stage involves a tailoring of the text and staging to the cues from the specific audience (and other actors) in the specific moment. One audience may communicate, via silent and rapt attention, that it is following nearly every phrase in a Shakespearean tragedy. Lively actors respond by taking their time with every speech. Another more likely audience communicates its inability to follow the text, and lively actors respond by showing the audience what it needs to see to follow the plot while deemphasizing the words. If the audience gets Mercutio's jokes, the other actors can play friends who will not admit that their buddy is funny; if the audience does not get Mercutio's jokes, then at least some of the other actors must laugh to show the audience how clever he is. Lively improvisation, as a method of engaging the audience and tailoring the production to them, is an aspect of what intersubjectivists call attunement (Buirski, 2005; Buirski & Haglund, 2001).

Similarly, therapists must improvise, no matter how tried and true the think their text is. Even when discussing the limits of confidentiality or the expectations of getting paid, the therapist must be alert to signals from the patient that a tailoring is needed. The tailoring itself is simple and almost always involves some form of the question, "What is going through your mind right now?" or "How is that striking you?" The subtlest form of this question is a posture of silent curiosity. The hard part is remembering to question the text's effects in a context where the therapist thinks the text is sacred.

Since this book is about performance, I want to show the man behind the curtain as much as is feasible. All such efforts are of dubious sincerity (Goffman, 1974) since every public posture, even the posture of full disclosure, has a backstage. Like a movie about a movie, in Goffman's metaphor, you can never see the camera showing the camera. And even if you do see the second camera, you can't see the third camera showing it. Still, I want to sound authoritative about improvisation in therapy, which might mean citing and discussing Meares (2001), Ringstrom (2001a, 2001b), Knoblauch (2001), and other writers who have taken up this topic. On the other hand, this is a book about deadliness, and I find such diversions deadly. Therefore, I am writing this aside both to cite and not to cite. I will comment that Ringstrom (2001a, 2001b) has a nice discussion of what is lively and deadly in the theater and in therapy, and Meares (2001) is spot on when it comes to trying to figure out what has worked and what has not worked in therapy. Interestingly, Ringstrom cites Langs's "voluminous work" as an example of deadly prescriptions as to how to behave as a therapist. I always felt that there were two completely distinct Robert Langses. One was utterly committed to listening to metaphorical speech by patients as guideposts to conducting psychotherapy; the other abstracted from these metaphors rigid rules to live by. The former was lively in tailoring every therapy move to the patient; the other was deadly in legislating therapy practice. Langs (1976, 1978) stands for me as an example of what happens when lively, successful ideas turn into a "school" or a "system," whether on stage or in therapy. As Brook (1993) puts it, "A form, once created, is already moribund" (p. 56).

Good actors not only improvise at every moment in their efforts to engage the audience, they also improvise at every moment in their efforts to engage each other. Any successful improv company can tell us the importance of "accepting offers," or a "yes, and" mentality (Johnstone, 1981; Ringstrom, 2001b). However, psychotherapy is not like the improvisation of an improvised show; it is like the improvisation of a play with a text. Psychotherapy is going somewhere, not just anywhere, with the somewhere fined by the therapist's value goals, the patient's value goals, and the therapy contract. Brook's (1993) comment is relevant: "If you really want to know what boredom is, watch an improvisation where two or three actors get going and 'do their thing' without being stopped" (p. 79). Lively psychotherapy involves the kind of ubiquitous improvisation of accomplished actors who respond to what is happening in the moment on the stage to create a lively encounter with which to engage the audience. No matter how fixed the text and staging, good actors respond to each other as if it were happening for the first time. I asked an accomplished performer what the term for this was when actors learn to respond to each other. "It's called *acting*," she replied.

To respond in a lively manner while onstage requires focused attention on the immediate environment. Actors trying to remember their next line or merely waiting for their turn to speak are bound to act badly. Therapists who are waiting for their chance to speak are bad therapists. No matter how fixed the text, whether a written play or a prepared interpretation or a theoretical formulation, the actor and the therapist can make it lively by attending carefully to what is happening in the moment. This means listening. It seems to me that good actors can often find a lively and true response to what is happening onstage not by digging deep for a Stanislavskian sense memory but by listening to and believing what the other person onstage is saying and doing. Good therapists take the patient's presentation as is, not as a variation on or defective version of an expectation based on theory.

Lively actors must fully understand the character of the role they are playing and the meaning of the scene and the production that the character is in. This knowledge enables them to respond to the audience and to the other actors in character. This is especially useful when other actors forget their lines, and even text must be improvised, but it is also necessary for engaging the audience and making lively decisions onstage without driving the production off course. Similarly, therapists need to engage patients both as audience members for the production of therapy and as fellow actors for the coproduction of what happens inside the therapy. To do this effectively, without "breaking frame" (Goffman, 1974), they must fully understand the role of therapist and the production they are in. The role varies according to the contracted goals, the personality of the therapist, the therapist's assessment of what the patient needs, and the therapist's value goals. It is just as important for the therapist to have a comparative understanding of her role preferences as it is for her to understand her cultural preferences. That translates into a reasonable familiarity with all the major schools of therapy and with an array of cultural values.

DEADLY MONOLINGUALISM

Therapists have a way of declaring that the school that brought them some successes, as judged by patients' gratitude and supervisors' approval, is the one true school. We sometimes treat all the other schools of therapy as false versions of the one true school. We may characterize our superficial exposure to another school as a thorough understanding of it, like the tourist who spends 3 weeks in Namibia and claims an understanding of its culture. (One famous anthropologist, asked how long it takes to understand a foreign culture, said, "Thirty years." I think that it takes a lot less than 30 years to pick up systems theory or behaviorism because these are really more like foreign languages than foreign cultures, but a prerequisite to picking up other languages is humility about not knowing them yet and respect for its speakers.) We can't fully understand our role as therapist and therefore can't fulfill that role in a lively manner unless we understand it comparatively, just as we can't understand the patient's character without learning first about all kinds of people.

We also need a comparative understanding of our values and of their applicability to the patient. To me, this means that the therapist needs to be conversant with literature, philosophy, and history. One of the most shocking experiences I have had in the past few years was having to argue this point among psychologists on my forensic listserv. Some psychologists adopted an unabashed position that literature, philosophy, and history were irrelevant to the practice of forensic psychology. Here, I hope I have laid out at least one reason why that is not true: lively and useful improvisation depends on knowledge of the role and the production.

Chapter Two

Lessons from Performance Theory

Shared staging problems; concern for the way things appear; warranted and unwarranted feelings of shame; ambivalence about oneself and one's audience; these are some of the dramaturgic elements of the human situation.

—Goffman (1959, p. 237)

There is a Smile of Love
And there is a Smile of Deceit
And there is a Smile of Smiles
In which these two Smiles meet

—William Blake, *The Smile*

Performance theory combines two overlapping intellectual traditions. One is largely an attempt to explain the philosophical underpinnings, social effects, and artistic history of performance art. The other is an attempt to explain human behavior as an ongoing series of performances. In this chapter, we review selected highlights of artistic performance theory to set the stage for many of the remaining chapters in this book. Then we examine social performance theory for its implications for conducting psychotherapy.

PERFORMANCE ART

Performance art is a development in the visual arts that began roughly in the 1960s—instead of creating art in a studio and displaying the created object in a gallery, the artist herself appeared in the gallery doing something that was

29

itself the art. These performances were distinguishable from theater only in that most theater at the time was more formalized, scripted, time consuming, and deadly. As performance artists got more skilled at communicating with audiences, their productions began to look more like a reinvigorated theater so that the distinction is currently difficult to sustain.

Performance art is suspicious of common knowledge and conventional wisdom, seeing both as platform planks in the party line of hegemonies whose function is to maintain themselves. Like postmodernism and deconstructionism, performance art is essentially revolutionary, seeking to give voice to the marginalized, the silenced, and the underprivileged—certain individuals, certain classes of individuals, and certain aspects of individuals. Performance art celebrates and attempts to empower the bodily in terms of the conceptual, the feminine in terms of the masculine, the marginalized in terms of the privileged, and the individual in terms of the society.

In a narrower sense, performance art attempts to restore the role of the artist as social critic, revolutionary, and revealer of the invisible. Because of the forces and motivations the artist must negotiate, discussed in chapter 1, all too often the artist stops doing art that critiques the prevailing ideologies and concentrates on art that is applauded, bought, and condoned. Co-opted by the system she is supposed to question, she becomes a painter, actor, writer, or sculptor rather than an artist. Every major development in every field of art can be viewed as an overthrow of what is working economically and politically in search of what makes, in Brook's (1968) words, the invisible visible.

Carlson (1996) summarizes these themes in his definition of theater:

> a specific event with its liminoid nature foregrounded, almost invariably clearly separated from the rest of life, presented by performers and attended by audiences both of whom regard the experience as made up of material to be interpreted, to be reflected upon, to be engaged in—emotionally, mentally, and perhaps even physically. This particular sense of occasion and focus as well as the overreaching social envelope combine with the physicality of theatrical performance to make it one of the most powerful and efficacious procedures that human society has developed for the endlessly fascinating process of cultural and personal self-reflexion and experimentation. (pp. 198–199)

The performance artist is a model for the therapist. She creates opportunities for self-reflection by occasioning meaningful narratives and interpreting them in a way that challenges the party line.

The performance artist is also a model for the patient, who is often coping with what Goffman (1959) calls being "out of line." Otto Rank (1936, 1989) wrote that the artist and the neurotic have much in common, as both are in conflict with their conventional contexts. The neurotic protests unconsciously and self-defeatingly, but neither neurotic nor artist toes the party line. Both re-fuse to be co-opted; both either cannot or will not accept the mainstream def-inition of the situation. Peter Brook (1968) writes, "It is not the fault of the holy that it has become a middle-class weapon to keep children good" (p. 46). In other words, whatever questions the party line is typically either marginal-ized or co-opted by the authorized version of what is going on. In psy-chotherapy, the patient's lack of power often recapitulates her predicament. The aspects of the patient that have been marginalized and ignored need a voice, but psychotherapy is often no more responsive to those aspects of her functioning than are her family or her own dominant traits. I address these problems in chapters 4 and 7.

Performance art, as noted, celebrates the bodily and the feminine. It is far from clear why masculinity is so characteristic of people in power. Is it be-cause men have more political power than women, so their traits are glori-fied? Or is there something about what is labeled masculinity that makes it appealing and problematic beyond its association with men? I tend to think the latter if what is meant by masculinity is certainty, abstraction, and ration-ality and if what is meant by femininity is contextualization, physicality, par-ticularity, and emotionality. In fact, masculinity may mean nothing more than the way the powerful behave, and the label has become conflated with the so-cial power of men. To distinguish gender from people's sex, as explained in chapter 9, I prefer to use the terms "yin" and "yang" for "femininity" and "masculinity." Later in this book, we visit the issues of gender in psychother-apy, including the question of the effects on yin when doctors team up with each other rather than with their patients, the deadly appeal of deductive cer-tainty, the role relationship between doctor and patient, and the potential for using a tool like critical thinking, steeped in yang, for empowering yin.

PERFORMANCE THEORY

Social performance theory is an intellectual tradition, exemplified in the work of Erving Goffman (1959, 1963, 1967, 1974) and Kenneth Burke (1945, 1966), that equates life and the theater. Performance theory can be seated in evolutionary biology in the latter's emphasis on the importance of reputation in all species capable of fostering reputation since a good reputation is essen-tial to taking advantage of reciprocal altruism (Trivers, 1985), competing ef-fectively in dominance hierarchies, and advertising in mate selection (Zahavi & Zahavi, 1997; see also chapter 4).

Goffman (1959) writes, "All the world is not, of course, a stage, but the crucial ways in which it isn't are not easy to specify" (p. 72). His analysis of human behavior emphasizes the performative aspect of it—the extent to which people act as if they are being watched. His views are thus consistent with systems theory, a major feature of which is the idea that a crucial causative factor for any behavior can be found in its effect on the relevant social system.

SYSTEMS THEORY

Systems theory and its offspring, game theory, derive from mathematical analyses of engineered systems. Systems theory explains and uses related interconnections rather than units. Game theory looks more specifically at how strategies are interconnected—how one person's goals interconnect with another's and how each must take into account the *moves* of the other. Both theories have been thoroughly applied to evolutionary, biological, economic, political, and psychological problems, largely through the work of Gregory Bateson. Bateson's father was a famous biologist who coined the term *genetics*. Bateson's wife was anthropologist Margaret Mead. Bateson was also an anthropologist, and he spent a lot of time studying human behavior in mental hospitals. Thus, he was particularly well placed to bring the new ideas into the human arena.

Systems theory says that human beings manage the interconnectedness of things by defining situations in a way that dictates what role they are playing so they will know what to do. In order to achieve this, the evolution of the mammal brain had to reach a point where distinctions could be made between situations and definitions of situations, or between what Bertrand Russell called levels of logical typing. This evolutionary development, as Bateson explains in his seminal article "A Theory of Play and Fantasy" (1972d) allows us not only to define situations but to understand other people's definitions of situations as well. It allows for abstraction, the creation and management of paradox, play, fantasy, and metacommunication.

Each definition of a situation also articulates the roles to be played in it. This observation has generated almost the whole of Goffman's work, as he explores the performance of a role, the definition or framing of a situation, the way a situation is like a theater, and what happens to people who fall short of playing the role they are attempting.

The key elements of performance theory, described here, are performance, game theory, signals, logical types, metacommunication, frames, roles, backstages, channels, and teams. As we consider them, we'll see what they tell us about psychotherapy and psychopathology. Then we'll investigate the most alarming aspect of performance theory, namely, its seeming disparagement of authenticity: if everything is a performance, does that mean that all behavior is insincere?

PERFORMANCE DEFINED

Early definitions of performance emphasized the presence and the observations of others. Dell Hymes (1973, quoted in Goffman, 1974) moved away from defining performance by structural factors and toward defining it according to its function: "And there is a sense in which *performance* is an attribute of any behavior, if the doer accepts or has imputed to him responsibility for being evaluated in regard to it" (p. 124, fn. 1). A functional definition helps explain why a therapist, alone in her office and about to open the waiting room door, will check her fly and will do so surreptitiously. In behavioristic terms, we learn only imperfectly to distinguish being alone from being watched because so often in childhood we discover that we have been unexpectedly watched. Thus, we are often performing even when we are alone, and the performance is often for ourselves, sort of like cheating at solitaire.

SIGNS, SIGNALS, AND GAME THEORY

The ability to define a situation for the sake of clarifying roles and expectations required the biological development of an ability to distinguish definitions from situations. Bateson (1972d) observed the play of monkeys and analyzed how they manage to communicate to each other whether a bite is to be taken as aggression or play. In other words, can other species recognize the difference between *signs* and *signals*, between evidence and communication? In his paper, Bateson begins with the biologist's assumption that animals evolved to read and emit signs in order to facilitate cooperation and reproduction and to avoid territorial disputes, among other reasons. Game theory — the analysis of strategic behavior that accounts for the strategies of others — is useful in understanding evolved signing and responding. To illustrate game theory, let's look at cuckoos' tendency to lay eggs in other birds' nests. Genes in other birds that did not enable those birds to distinguish their own offspring from interlopers gradually died out because they led those birds to waste resources on cuckoo chicks. Genes that enabled parent birds to distinguish and feed their own offspring thrived, and therefore cuckoo infants that looked different from natural offspring died out. Cuckoo genes that led cuckoos to lay their interloping eggs in nests of species that looked like them as infants thrived. Cuckoo genes that produced cuckoo chicks that looked like the chicks that belonged there also thrived. Thus, game theory frames the evolution of interspecies conduct in a way that makes sense of it, but no particular animal's behavior needs to be accounted for. Eventually, host birds got better and better at distinguishing interlopers from natural offspring, while interloper chicks looked more and more like host chicks.

The great communicative leap occurred when the possibility of signaling a sign came under operant control—when signaling became something the animal could do in response to cues from the immediate environment rather than something the animal exhibited regardless of the advantages and disadvantages of showing a sign at that moment. This leap meant that animals had to learn how to detect the difference between faked and authentic signs. There is plenty of faking in biology: a firefly attracts mates by blinking in a certain way, but when she is hungry, she blinks in a pattern that attracts males from another species and she eats them. Her blinking patterns are fixed by her genes (even though these are turned on and off by internal and external cues). The genes are blind, and all the tinkering with strategy must be accomplished across generations (Dawkins, 1986). In general, the more responsive an animal is to its immediate environment, the more adaptively it can act but the greater the expense it will incur in the investment in a bigger brain to manage environmental stimuli and to retain learning. Learning also has a disadvantage in that it requires an infancy, which in turn requires a greater investment from parents to raise the infant until it has learned enough to fend for itself. With bigger brains, animals also evolved with the ability to emit signals when it was immediately advantageous to do so, not just with the clunky on-off switches used by genes.

Game theory then had something to say about immediate interactions. Baby cuckoos could conceivably have evolved to emit a range of behaviors in the nest until they struck on one that got them fed. That did not happen, but its analogue has happened in other species. The shorthand version of this conduct is that animals can represent and misrepresent signs rather than merely emitting them. The Darwinian/Skinnerian account is easier to follow by using the words *represent* and *misrepresent*, as if the animal is doing something on purpose.

Bateson (1972d) emphasized the evolution of the ability to emit signals rather than signs, to emit communications about the animal's state rather than evidence of the animal's state. Under many conditions, an animal realizes an advantage from communicating a signal even when the underlying state isn't there. In humans, signals are usually carried by language, or, more precisely, language is the information on a channel for exchanging signals. Few vocalizations in humans after infancy are pure signs: even yelps of joy and moans of despair are in most cases partly performative, and anyone who has wept alone at night with a broken heart knows that, though spontaneous, the weeping is also a performance for the absent lover. George Eliot (1995) described the transition from sign to signal: "On this Jacob, feeling the danger wellnigh over, howled at ease, beginning to imitate his own performance and improve upon it—a sort of transition from impulse into art often observable" (p. 478).

LOGICAL TYPES

With the evolution of signaling came logical types and metacommunication—the potential to distinguish the definition of a situation from the situation itself. The concept of logical types clarifies the fact that the word *book* is not itself a book, that the word *noun* is not itself a noun—or is it? Bertrand Russell (Whitehead & Russell, 1910) pointed out the inherent paradoxes in language that stem from the fact that bits of language can be a member and a class at the same time. *Noun* refers to nouns but is also one of the things it refers to. The class of all phrases is itself a phrase and therefore a member of itself. Some classes are members of themselves, and some are not. Russell examined the class of all classes that are *not* members of themselves. If that class is a member of itself, then, by its own definition, it is not. But if it is not a member of itself, then it must belong to the alternative class of all classes that *are* members of themselves, in which case it *is* a member of itself. Logical typing, or levels of abstraction, must produce such paradoxes. This is similar to Gödel's (1962) proof that any system of logic complicated enough to produce simple arithmetic will produce statements that cannot be proved or disproved. The similarity lies in the limits of language as an explanatory system. Thus, problems occur when information of one logical type is treated as if it were information of another logical type—when words are treated as things, classes as members, maps as territories.

METACOMMUNICATION

Metacommunication has two meanings, both of which involve a logical type a step or two above straight information exchange. The broad meaning is talking about talking, language about language, talking about what is going on rather than just participating in what is going on. The more particular meaning refers to the aspects of every communication that direct the receiver how to take the message. A message always has some content, but it also always implies a definition of the situation—a definition of the role relationships involved. Since the latter function may be considered a label that is about the message, it is *meta to* the message, meaning that the expressed definition of the situation operates at a different level of logical typing. In Bateson's view, much of what passes for psychopathology can be usefully construed as logical typing errors. For example, depression often depends on the confusion of statements that define situations, such as "there's nothing I can do about it" or "life is bare," with the situations themselves. Clarifying that these are just *about* situations opens the way to construing them differently and to behaving differently within them.

Paradoxes, or binds, form a class of important logical typing errors. Binds occur when a message is inherently paradoxical, that is, when the definition of the situation is unsustainable or when the definition of the situation directly contradicts the content of the message. For example, *Do these pants make me look heavy?* simultaneously puts the listener in the roles of supportive spouse and aesthetic judge, which, in many marriages, are mutually contradictory. The question creates a bind because the usual spousal frame cannot support

Figure 2.1.   "Would You Still Love Me If I Were Somebody Else?"

an aesthetic judgment about the speaker. Various solutions to this bind have been suggested, including the mandatory *no* and the diplomatic *you look great in everything* (both of which hostilely set up the pants wearer not to look his best, but it is a form of hostility that does not violate the marital frame). A potentially more productive solution is to engage in metacommunication about how to manage such situations. This conversation may not come on a mutually satisfying solution, but just having the conversation helps both parties recognize that there is an intrinsic bind. This recognition opens the door to such statements as *I love your butt, so wear something that makes it look nice* or *You said you'd stop putting me in this situation* or *Are you asking me as your spouse or as a judge of clothing?* Metacommunication even opens the door that leads back to the mandatory *no*, once it has been established via this conversation that the only role relationship being defined by the question is that of supportive spouse.

Metacommunication is a solution to many paradoxes and binds. Therapists know this. A patient asked me if I wanted to see her next week. I replied, "If I say yes, it seems to imply that I need to see you or that I especially look forward to seeing you. If I say anything other than yes, it seems to imply that I don't care if I see you. I don't like either message." Raising the conversation to a higher logical type changed the definition of the situation from patient with either a careless or an overinvolved therapist to patient with a therapist who talks about what is going on. Many binds are not obvious, and some training in recognizing them is needed before metacommunication can be invoked. When I was in graduate school, I asked my mother how long she nursed me. "It depends," she said. "Depends on what?" I asked. "Well," she said, "if you're studying overprotective mothers, 4 months, but if you're studying abandoning mothers, 14 months." Mom knows a bind when she's in one.

Bateson, Jackson, Haley, and Weakland (1972) also articulated the *double bind* as a source of psychopathology. This is a bind that involves dependency on a powerful speaker and a rule that metacommunication is not allowed. A double bind, then, is a bind from which the listener cannot escape and about which the listener cannot speak. Since that means that no definition of the situation can be sustained, including a definition meta to the situation, it also means that no consistent role or identity or self can be sustained. Bateson et al. give the example, "Go to bed, you're very tired and I want you to get your sleep." The message is caring but the meta-message is, "I'm sick of you. Go away" (p. 214). The child is not allowed to comment on the paradox because to do so would violate the parent's line as perfectly caring.

Another crucial logical typing error involves the mistake of a class for a member, or what the behaviorists are lately calling *fusion* (because the words and what they represent are fused together as if they are the same). The classic case is name-calling, where the sticks-and-stones lesson is forgotten and the word is taken as harmful. *I am anxious* can become much more than a description of a person, much more than a signal; it can be mistaken for a state of mind. *I deserve better* can be taken so literally that the person stops making efforts to improve her life and spends her days licking her wounds and licking the rim of her margarita glass. Here, too, metacommunication is the answer. Circular questions (Selvini Palazzoli, Boscolo, Cecchin, & Prata, 1980) that contextualize the use and function of such statements turn them back into behaviors or communications and stop them from being pronouncements writ on stone tablets. The therapist might ask when the sense of deserving better occurs to her or might even say, "I noticed that you went into your *I deserve better* routine just as we were talking about looking for work," which takes advantage of the therapist's presence when the behavior occurs in the office. Even this minimal bit of contextualizing communicates that the statement is a thing she does, not a thing she is.

FRAMES

Framing defines situations metaphorically by circumscribing or punctuating them—dictating which events constitute the situation and which do not—and technically by identifying the relevant discriminative stimuli. Goffman (1974) begins *Frame Analysis* by quoting William James's famous question, "Under what circumstances do we believe that things are real?" (p. 2). Goffman's answer is that we are all pretty good at changing frames, but we view some frames as primary, and when an event is in a primary frame, we consider it to be real. That is, a frame is a definition of a situation (with implied rules, roles, and contingencies), and a primary frame is one that does not seem to be defining a situation but seems instead just to be what the situation actually is. A familiar example is the clinical phenomenon that can be explained chemically, evolutionarily, cognitively, psychoanalytically, behavioristically, or systemically—an angry gesture, say. A frame that locates the gesture's potential survival value in prehistory can coexist peaceably with a systemic frame that examines its effect on the person's spouse. The evolutionary psychologist may be likely to view the systemic frame as a transcription of what is really going on, while the systemic clinician is more likely to invert what is real and what is transcribed. When Emily Dickinson writes, "I like a look of agony because I know it's true," she is telling us something about her primary, depressive frame (depressive because of the kinds of looks she thinks she knows are real). When I label it depressive, I am telling you something about my primary frame. As Alexander Pope (1970) said, "All seems infected that th'infected spy/As all looks yellow to the jaundic'd eye" (p. 161).

Frames can operate within frames, which is just another way of approaching the problem of logical types. Consider an actor playing an actor on stage: in *A Midsummer Night's Dream*, actor Jack Smith, say, plays Bottom playing Pyramus. The play within a play ends, and the actor sheds the mask of Pyramus and now just plays Bottom. We do not consider Bottom to be Smith's real self because the role of Bottom is strongly framed by the theater and stage. Smith continues to play Bottom until the lights come up, the actors take bows, the audience applauds, and the theatrical frame ends. We go backstage and tell Smith how much we enjoyed the play and his performance in particular. He asks us where we're going for drinks and says he'll join us. We leave. Have we just seen the real Jack Smith, or have we just seen a performance of the role of actor-who-does-not-need-praise-and-maintains-his-social-self-even-right-after-a-performance? Has he seen our real selves or just the role of friend-going-backstage? How we frame the interchange will tell us the answer. If our primary frame is one of politeness and social grace, then we will consider ourselves to have seen his true face. If our primary frame is one of intimacy, we will say no, that was not his true face. If our primary frame is behaviorism, we will never say we saw a true face, but we will say that he was responding to the situation as he has learned to do, possibly because he finds excessive praise aversive and has learned to move potentially praising interactions back onto a social track to avoid them. The point is that our assessment of when we have glimpsed the real self depends entirely on which frames we view as primary.

But which frames really are primary? The pragmatist would ask instead which frames serve a given purpose. Because reality can be construed in an infinite variety of ways, there are an infinite number of useless and unrealistic frames as well as an infinite number of useful and realistic ones. A dog barks, and I cross the street to avoid it. An evolutionary frame puts a fight–flight construction on the event, a performance frame notes how I managed to look like I had to cross the street for some other reason, a behavioral frame highlights the negative reinforcement of increasing the distance between me and the dog, a systemic frame emphasizes how I have reinforced the dog's barking, a cognitive frame examines my beliefs about barking dogs, a psychoanalytic frame might question my relationship to my own animality, and a biochemical frame underlines the release of adrenaline. Notice how some frames are more pragmatic for the therapist than other frames since some of them put the therapist in a position to intervene.

Most people hold some frames as really real, as not transcribable, as depicting what is really going on. Some therapists focus on the affect, some the social network, some the organizing principle, and so on. When these are not used as heuristic devices for solving a clinical problem but instead are seen as the ultimate explanation, certain advantages and disadvantages follow. The main advantage of fully believing in a primary frame is that the therapist may inspire the patient to believe that the therapy will work. When the cognitive therapist teaches the patient that thoughts cause behavior, she imbues disputation of irrational beliefs with a seriousness and consequentiality that would be sorely lacking if she said, "Of course thoughts don't cause behavior. I mean, I believe I'm brilliant but that belief doesn't improve the quality of my utterances. But if you'll pretend that thoughts cause behavior, then I can change your behavior by disputing your thoughts." The primary disadvantage of sincere belief in your preferred language or frame is that its use becomes inflexible when it is wrong for the occasion—for the specific patient or the specific problem.

Theory Fusion

Mischief ensues when the therapist believes that her definition of the situation is *the* definition of the situation. While this inspires confidence in the patient, it also inspires devotion to the therapist's primary frames. Put differently, many psychological problems that lead people to treatment can be conceptualized as the use of old maps for negotiating new territories. The therapist who is fused with her frame teaches the patient to use *her* maps to negotiate new territories and instead should be teaching the patient to examine and respond to map/territory discrepancies. Patients are often looking at the manual rather than looking at the problem, and giving them another manual can help only so much. This goes double for trainees, who are often even more anxious than patients during therapy sessions to find a right way to do things. Supervisors who believe their frame is *the* frame teach trainees to manage anxiety through obedience rather than through listening.

> An atheist dies and goes to Heaven. St. Peter shows him around: lovely parks, sloping meadows, babbling brooks, even a beach—but they're all nearly deserted. Scattered around are enormous halls of worship—temples, cathedrals, ashrams—from which prayer and music emanate. The atheist says, "Okay, so I admit I was wrong about Heaven, but I still don't see myself spending all that much time in worship. Why don't people spend more time outdoors?" St. Peter replies, "Going outdoors reminds them that their religion is not the only one up here."

A major source of deadliness in therapy is the therapist's tendency to put the theory ahead of the facts, to use the treatment to show the patient how he fits into the therapist's theory. This is deadly partly because it reduces the patient's narrative to an example of something rather than treating it as important in its own right. It is also deadly because it squeezes what is unique out of the therapy. The analogy in theater is the actor who is constantly thinking about her next line rather than attending to what is going on around her. Good actors recognize that lively interaction requires them to learn their lines so thoroughly that they can make other things up as they go along. They are then free to respond to each other physically and emotionally, and the words they say become responsive to the immediate situation rather than taking them out of the immediate situation.

Therapists who wait patiently for their turn to speak, concentrating on what they are going to say next, create deadly interactions. Even if the therapist knows what she is going to say next, she must listen to the patient carefully and speak when her line will be responsive. Therapists who are committed to their theoretical frames find themselves often in the position of putting text ahead of interaction. A good way to learn not to be fused with a theory, as suggested throughout this project, is to learn more than one theoretical orientation thoroughly. This enables the therapist to maintain the inspirational advantage of having really good maps for negotiating new territories while also reminding her that her maps are only maps. The same process occurs when a person learns a second language: knowing how to say the same things in another language helps keep the individual from fusing words and what they represent.

Fusion with a favorite theory also makes mischief because it keeps the therapist from wondering if *her* map might be in error. Even though every major theory is robust enough to account for any clinical phenomenon, fusion with it strengthens the therapist's tendency to believe she is right when she defines the immediate situation in its terminology. Thus, the therapist defines the situation in a way that makes her look good, often at the patient's expense, emphasizing, for example, the patient's narcissism rather than her own narcissism. If the distribution of blame is blanketed by a flurry of knowledge rather than a flurry of opinion, it will be harder to deconstruct. Freud did this when he chided a patient for objecting to his use of a spittoon during sessions: Freud's psychoanalytic explanation of the patient's sensitivity made it harder for the patient to fight back. When our definition of what's going on conflicts with the patient's, we must avoid the temptation to couch our own definition in terminology that reminds us that we are the better-educated, healthier, and more mature member of the dyad. Putting our definition in the language of our theoretical orientation lends it undeserved authority, as a religious person can bolster her preferred definition of a situation by citing scripture.

ROLES

A definition of a situation articulates roles that tell the individual what to do and what others ought to do. Goffman (1974) points out how hard it is for a person to play a role sincerely—how vulnerable to being discredited a performance is—when it is framed as real. He identifies casting problems. An individual can have personal characteristics or a social history that prevents him from playing a role, like the aging actor who still wants to play the leading man opposite an ingénue, or how Woody Allen's offscreen exploits interfere with his ability to become embedded in any role. Casting problems in therapy include age, sex, religion, ethnicity, and even costume—one sophisticated 14-year-old girl told me, "I could never be in therapy with someone wearing those shoes."

A role makes certain claims on a performer, even when she is out of character. The classic example was the banker who had to be a model of discretion and moderation, even when not banking. Today, the better example is the politician or preacher who is expected to be in character at all times, scrutinized by a press that feeds on discrediting the performance of rectitude. When therapists think twice about marching for gay pride, posting a photo on Match.com when seeking a mate, or writing a political letter to the editor of the local paper, they are managing the claims the role has on them. Since the role varies so much with each patient, many therapists have found it advisable to maintain anonymity in all aspects of their lives. Others with more specialized practices can safely express certain aspects of themselves without fear of losing patients, but casting problems will follow nonetheless. Images of the therapist donating time and services to a good cause will confuse a religious patient who needs gentle and gradual exposure to a therapist seen as heartless.

In discussing the claim a role can have on a person, Goffman mentions the porn actress whose character has sex onscreen. Society does not allow her to disassociate herself from onscreen sex, so she is a porn actress, not a legitimate one. A vast array of film actresses, of course, disassociate themselves from onscreen sex when the sex is foreplay but not when genital penetration is shown. Michael Caine said in an interview that he avoids onscreen sex scenes because his wife, who will accept him as a murdering villain or a contemptible cad, accuses him of actual foreplay in the sex scenes. Social conventions dictate which actions the therapist can disassociate herself from and which she cannot. Pregnant therapists find themselves smack dab in the center of this issue—the role of therapist often excludes reproductive interests, but the claim is too great to defer to. Metacommunication about the problem is usually more productive than self-righteous proclamations about the right to live as you choose. A good policy, as in all such matters, is not to have a policy but instead to see what works and what does not. Most therapists find that sexual and aggressive departures are disruptive, while other revelations from behind the curtain, including emotional displays besides sex and aggression and bodily expressions like sneezing, are either tactfully disattended by patients or incorporated into the role definition. Again, metacommunication helps.

Some roles give the performer leeway to depart from the role while in character. The higher the prestige associated with the role, the more leeway given, so that the president may swear or joke and remain in character but the doorman may not. The relationship between performer and audience affects leeway, such that familiarity and friendliness breed tactful disattention by the audience to discrediting conduct by the performer. Performers who claim their version of a role is special must stay tightly in character so that a lecturer presented as brilliant must not make a single factual error. The pervasiveness of the role's claim on the performer also depends on how the performer herself responds to departures—musicians must learn not only to play the right notes but also to wear a crooked smile after playing a wrong note to communicate that the musical frame is not the primary one, at least not during mistakes.

In therapy, patients are also constrained by their roles. We may run into depressed patients at a restaurant and catch them acting energetic and cheerful, but in therapy, they need to keep up the mopey appearance of unrelenting depression. The degree of leeway afforded patients depends on the way their role has been defined. A view of patients as really disturbed makes more claims—and makes change more difficult—than a view of them as acting disturbed.

THE BACKSTAGE PROBLEM

When people perform roles according to their definitions of situations, there is always a backstage where thoughts and feelings are examined privately and that must not be revealed for fear of discrediting the performance. Goffman affirms the presence of a real self underlying performance in his discussion of the backstage problem, but he also describes how evanescent and situational this real self is. In the same breath as affirming the self as a construct, Goffman (1974) says, "There is a relation between person and role. But the relationship answers to the interactive system—to the frame—in which the role is performed and the self of the performer is glimpsed. Self, then, is not an entity half-concealed behind events, but a changeable formula for managing oneself during them" (p. 573). The paradox is that the self can only be glimpsed unintentionally and cannot be revealed on purpose without creating a further, unrevealed backstage. One consequence of this paradox is that the real self is often the self that is hidden, and since we tend to hide what we are not proud of, most people come to think of themselves as less desirable than they are. The real self is conflated with an embarrassing self. At the end of the day, we all need a place—for some, it's therapy—to which we can retire, loosen our belts, and kick off our shoes. Persons lacking such a retreat get worn down by social obligations.

WHAT CHANNEL ARE WE LISTENING TO?

Goffman (1974) describes different communicative channels to clarify how people maintain their backstage areas and tactfully respect each other's. Besides the content channel, he describes other channels as directional, disattended, concealed, and overlaid.

Goffman uses the term *directional channel* for the metacommunicative labels that Bateson (1972c) and Watzlawick, Bavelas, and Jackson (1967) describe. According to these systems theorists, every communication contains content information (or, as they call it, a report function) and relationship-defining information (or, as they call it, a command function). Often, content is in the text and direction is in the way it is said, but both are intermingled in all modes of communication. Thus, when a therapist asks a patient her sexual orientation, the content of the communication is a request for personal information, but the directional channel carries a message that the relationship will be interrogatory, more like a job interview or even a police investigation than an expressive psychotherapy. The conflict between content and position can create paradoxes that, like other paradoxes, are best resolved by metacommunication (moving up to the next logical type). The power differential in the relationship makes it difficult for patients to bring up touchy subjects about the therapy, so the therapist typically has to initiate metacommunication.

A good example of the importance of the directional channel might be the peace offer sent by British General Howe to the Americans shortly after the rebels declared independence. The envelope was addressed to "George Washington, Esq." (instead of General George Washington), and both Washington's adjutant and later Washington himself clearly understood that the address automatically invalidated their efforts to define the war as a conflict between two separate countries (McCullough, 2005). The incident was managed by refusing delivery of the envelope, even after ceremoniously admitting the British emissary into Washington's presence. Washington conducted himself with the dignity appropriate to the commander in chief of a sovereign nation rather than the impromptu posturing of a rebel gang leader, prompting John Adams to call him one of the great actors of the age.

The *disattend channel* carries communications that discredit the performance or the performer's definition of the situation; that is, it carries glimpses of an invalidating backstage. Humans are socialized to ignore such inadvertent communications—hence the name, disattend channel. Goffman says that the crucial counterpart for a sincere performance of a social role is tact, by which he means the mutual agreement to ignore discrediting information. Examples include anything from sneezes and stifled yawns to statements that are obviously incorrect. Generally, audiences are more tactful in the face of a performer's power and prestige but are less tactful if the performer claims that the role she is playing is complete, sincere, or special.

The *concealment channel* is that which carries information between teammates designed to be hidden from an audience. Its use also strengthens the team by highlighting the boundary between team and audience. In Goffman's (1959) lexicon, a team is "any set of individuals who co-operate in staging a single routine" (p. 79). Goffman points out that a team, which he considers to be the basic unit of performers, can be composed of various aspects of a single person. This agrees with a systemic view of the psyche (Karson, 2001), which sees the individual as an organization of figures, archetypes, response repertoires, or self-object internalizations. This approach places self-talk in the concealment channel when its purpose is to tweak the performance and it's intended to be hidden from the audience. Self-talk can also *be* a performance when its purpose is to convince a part of the self about your intentions or nature. Performing for yourself drives the concealment channel into a mode that the individual is not conscious of. Cognitive and psychoanalytic therapists induce the patient to articulate the unconscious concealment channel: cognitive therapists teach the patient to hear and present it, while psychoanalytic therapists try to make the concealment unnecessary by acting nonpunitively. Self-talk can also occur in the disattend channel when we respond to embarrassing thoughts and fantasies by acting as if they did not happen.

The *overlay channel* is like the scrawl at the bottom of a news broadcast. It is not meant to be disattended or concealed, but it is meant to be secondary, like a witty comment called out during a case conference. Which channel is defined as content and which as overlay can vary, and lengthy or complex communication does not work well in the overlay channel. Lengthy, complex communication can't even occupy the content channel satisfactorily if there is an active overlay. Patients will find it difficult to tell emotional and intimate stories if asides, mm-hmms, and stage business are actively overlaying the stories. On the other hand, a private overlay need not disrupt a story. The thoughts that go through our heads while we are doing therapy are typically in the overlay channel, and good therapists learn to follow the patient's narrative and their own overlay at the same time.

WE'RE ALL TEAM PLAYERS

Although the contents of a concealment channel always remain hidden from the audience, Goffman notes a difference between showing and hiding the very existence of the concealment channel. Two people at a meeting can subtly exchange a look or openly pass a note back and forth. The content of the exchange is hidden in either case, but the note announces the presence of a concealed exchange. This example helps us think constructively about the difference between a therapy whose contents are confidential and one whose very existence is hidden from others. When the concealment channel itself is concealed, it is easier to discredit the therapist–patient team's performance by its discovery; when the channel is not concealed, the performance of teamwork is harder to discredit, but defining others as not on the team risks antagonism toward the therapy.

Goffman (1974) defines the *audience* not as whom a speech is made *to* but as whom a speech is made *for*. Just as a team can be constituted within a single individual, Goffman (1959) recognizes that a person can be her own audience. She can execute a routine or make a silent or oral speech for her own benefit, as when a religious southerner follows hostile thoughts about another person with the reflexive thought, "Bless his heart." When the performance is for yourself, the team's concealment channel is what in psychoanalysis is called the unconscious.

THE IMPORTANCE OF BEING EARNEST

If life is a series of performances, is there no sincerity—no real self? Goffman's answer is a complicated yes and no. He points out the paradox in letting others see your backstage—a backstage pass turns the backstage into a front stage, and the invitation then has a backstage to which it is impossible to welcome admittance (because the welcoming would create another level of backstage).

Although the word *performance* tends to signal insincerity, it can also stand for the profound importance to us of other people and their reactions to us.

One of Goffman's main points is that we tend to assume that we are specially sensitive to what others think of us because we do not have access to its importance in others. We believe that a cowboy is genuinely indifferent to the appraisal of others because he acts the part so naturally. "To be 'natural,' then, is not merely to seem at ease, but to be acting in such a way as to convince others that the apparent frame is in fact the actual one" (Goffman, 1974, p. 487). Sometimes, we learn a part so thoroughly that we convince even ourselves that there is no backstage. This is where Freud came into the picture, insisting that neurotic behaviors had backstages even if the patient had convinced herself they did not. The dramaturgical approach to human affairs does not smirk at human sincerity; instead, it emphasizes how social an animal we really are.

Goffman says there is a real self, but it cannot be revealed—it can only be stumbled on. This is familiar territory for any therapist who wonders, no matter how intimate the disclosure, why at this moment the patient is telling this particular story or demonstrating this particular emotion. As therapists, we prefer signs that seem unintentional to signals. For example, in treating an arrogant patient for the lack of satisfaction he experiences in close relationships, we spot signs of arrogance in the sessions and track these for change. When the patient reports that his wife now truly loves him and he is still dismissive of our ideas, we suspect that he has bullied her into acting more lovingly. These *clinically relevant behaviors* have recently been discovered by behaviorists, who have an annoying way of acting as if they were the first to see them, like Columbus discovering America. In fact, when you think about it, these behaviors are precisely what Freud meant by transference: in-therapy conduct that provides an unintentional window into the presenting problem.

Other unintentional revelations of a real self are provided by projective testing (Goffman, 1959) and by free association (asking the patient to say whatever comes to mind or to tell you what is really going through her mind at a particular moment). The primary purpose of asking patients to free-associate is to gain access to their backstages—their real selves—in a way that is difficult for them to manipulate. Psychoanalytic therapy thus functions as intimacy exposure. Aversive experiences in intimate relationships are often what bring patients into therapy because these experiences make the person angry or avoidant in intimate circumstances. Psychoanalytic therapy exposes the patient to an intimate relationship that does *not* replicate harm, and the exposure extinguishes his aversive reactions to intimacy. Exposure is more effective when it is highlighted, which is one way of looking at what interpretation does. A great deal of what is called technique operates in the service of creating intimacy by revealing the patient's backstage, protecting that backstage from intrusive or hurtful interaction, and highlighting the exposure process via interpretation. That is not the whole story, but it helps explain how just having the relationship promotes health.

Goffman's affirmation of the psychological person behind the roles she plays is a highly constricted one: usually you just find more roles. The real self is expressed infrequently and in small doses. When other people are present, there is almost always a role to play. When they are not present, we often act as if they are, like the man who returns a few paces to his car to check that the door is locked but pretends he left something in the backseat so that nonexistent observers won't think he's a compulsive double-checker. When others are not present, we prepare for their presence, rehearsing stories and writing scenes for later. Just as a novelist or playwright almost constantly imagines his characters interacting, in preparation for the production of plot points and dialogue, we almost constantly imagine ourselves interacting with others, also in preparation for the production to come. When we aren't rehearsing alone, we often perform for ourselves, usually the role of good person, and we disattend to stray, discrediting thoughts much as audience members try to pay no attention when an actor stumbles on a line. These considerations shrink the opportunity to locate an underlying real self to those instances when we *accidentally* reveal the face behind the mask, to extremely intimate encounters, and to those moments alone when we are not rehearsing or revamping social interactions.

THE SEARCH FOR AUTHENTICITY IN
A WORLD THAT'S A STAGE

Assuming that Goffman is right and we are almost always playing roles in performances designed to promote and respond to the cultural and personal way we have framed a situation and assuming that conscious efforts to reveal the true self are paradoxically impossible, then does that mean that psychotherapy is just a lesson in duplicity? Or is there a place for authenticity in a world that's a stage?

Does the cultural and personal arbitrariness of framing mean that nothing is genuine? Is the onstage liveliness that we are trying to apply to therapy false to its core? Nietzsche (1996) (and others) would say that the way to develop authenticity is to fake it until it feels real. In my opinion, there are several situations in which true authenticity can occur, but they boil down to metacommunication, the backstage pass, teamwork, and what Dewey (1934) calls the consummate experience and what others call aesthetic engrossment.

Authenticity and Metacommunication

Metacommunication is authentic when it is framed as such and does not pretend to be something else. Discussing the frame creates authenticity because even though the real self is not revealed, neither is its presence pretended. When the therapist takes steps to define the therapy situation as a helping relationship, he is implicitly acknowledging that he has unhelpful impulses that do not fit this frame. A patient struggling with sexual guilt wants to know how the therapist manages his own sexuality. Metacommunication in the form of a question or an observation about the patient's interest hides the therapist's sex life, but it doesn't pretend not to. Even the statement "I am not going to discuss my sex life" hides nothing compared with the therapist who pretends not to have a sex life. The therapist who says, "I like sex," can only pretend to reveal the true self, and what is left backstage is treated as if it does not exist. The therapist who acknowledges or discusses his sex life may be defining the situation as one in which he has no backstage or as one that rejects the traditional therapy frame because it is authoritarian or class based. Thus, discussion of the frame—the definition of the relationship—promotes authenticity not because it reveals much but because it does not pretend to reveal. It is genuinely authentic but not revealing to say, "What would it be like if I discussed my sex life?" The treatment advantages of metacommunication, in the areas of teaching circumspection and resolving conflicts, are compounded by metacommunication's liveliness: both parties can engage in it energetically without fear of accidentally straying backstage.

Authenticity and the Backstage Pass

All of us are born into a situation where our primary caregivers have a backstage pass, so to speak, although some caregivers use their pass too rarely, and others do not observe the various expiration dates on these passes. The right to continuously monitor the child's backstage expires early on, and the pass becomes a visa rather than a green card. In quick succession come expirations to dominion over the child's body, the right to define the child's physical state, and the right to define the child's emotional state. Eventually, in adolescence, the child revokes the pass entirely and allows the parent backstage only on a case-by-case basis. At this time, the child claims the right to define situations as much as or almost as much as the parent, and the parent who tactlessly denies the child this mutual right soon learns that another backstage gets constructed behind the backstage to which the parent demands access.

It is very difficult for a parent not to mismanage backstage access. A character played by James Garner in an otherwise forgettable movie summed it up when his late adolescent son complained about not being taken seriously. Garner's character replies by telling the son that when he, the father, used to change the son's diaper, he would get him all cleaned up and washed, and then he would lean over and kiss the son's soft little butt. "Once you've done that," says the father, "it's hard to take someone seriously." Thus, it is the very object constancy and role relatedness that make for good parenting in childhood that also make for trouble in adolescence: the parent learns to relate to an infant and forever after is a step or two behind the child's developmental need for tact. The challenge is even greater for a mother, who once related to the child as literally part of herself.

The inevitability of mismanaging backstage access in childhood makes its delicate management in therapy an important feature of the relationship since it gives the therapist a chance to remediate the harm done. As with other restorative aspects of the therapy relationship, its benefits can be accrued either via sensitive handling in the first place or via sensitive management of mistakes. The effective therapist can use her backstage access carefully, or she can stumble around and then carefully manage the effects of her ineptitude by metacommunicating about them. The patient learns either that granting access need not disrupt relationships or that disruptions caused by access need not be permanently damaging to relationships. The patient learns that her defensive maneuvers are outmoded and not needed.

In therapy, the paradox of not being able to show oneself authentically (because such efforts always create a further backstage) deadens interactions because it makes them interchanges of masks rather than of selves. This is overcome by licensing the therapist to peek backstage at her discretion. The therapist does this by commenting, in effect, "What you're really saying is . . . ," which in normal society would be tactless. The patient's real self is revealed not through performance but through eavesdropping, and since the therapist controls the revelation, the paradox is avoided.

Authenticity and Teamwork

When the patient and therapist are on a team, they are likely to experience some forms of authenticity, but these will depend on confidentiality. Again, by confidentiality I do not mean an agreement to discuss the patient only with persons the patient has given informed consent to talk to; I do not mean an agreement with exceptions like colleagues, dinner companions, and life partners; I mean actual privacy. Breaches of privacy need not disrupt the teamwork of therapist and patient, but they do broaden the audience from therapist and patient to include others. The effect is analogous to sitting in a theater and realizing that the actors are performing for the newspaper critic or the dignitary sitting in a box rather than performing for us. The audience for the therapist's performance ought to be the patient, and the audience for the patient's performance ought to be the therapist, but the audience for the *therapy* should be the patient, the person who purchased a ticket and whose engagement is vital to success. We all know the misery of listening to monologists who only *act* as if we're their audience but whose speech is actually for themselves or some generic version of a listener. Patients often speak not for the therapist but for the record, and therapists who examine this form of barriered communication promote liveliness and authenticity. Therapists frequently say things that are not designed for the particular moment but are instead generic statements, such as the obligation to report child abuse or the idea that perfectionism is stultifying. When the therapist is truly able to say such things *for* the patient, they need not be deadly. But all too often, the therapist is also speaking to get things on the record or to impress a supervisor or colleague or himself, and then the patient too knows what it's like to realize she isn't the actual audience.

Aesthetic Engrossment

Another kind of authenticity available in therapy is what Dewey (1934) calls the consummate moment, or what has also been called aesthetic engrossment or enthrallment. Whether creating or appreciating, we seem capable of forgetting that we are performing when what confronts us is sufficiently captivating. We can be ourselves, then, when we are not trying to be, when we are not even thinking about ourselves, when we are absorbed in something else. That may have been the whole point of Dionysian celebration, and it still seems to be a benefit of drugs, sex, rock and roll, and wild carnival rides. Engrossing moments come cheaply with tried-and-true dramatic formulas: tearjerkers, shockers, low comedy, revenge plots, and suspense are all examples. So are games and puzzles. These moments are more dear when they not only enthrall but also edify or enlighten. Theater professionals have been trying for millennia to engross their audiences, and performance theorists have some ideas about how this is accomplished.

Engrossment may be healthy for people regardless of content. Winnicott (1965) explained how a child's engrossment in play while in the presence of someone else leads to the ability to be comfortably alone as an adult. Unfortunately, engrossment can activate strong feelings of insignificance in other people, as it signifies that the other person is secondary to your experience. In many families, it is impossible to read a book or to become absorbed in a television program or a daydream without stimulating intrusive remarks. Good therapists learn to interrupt long speeches whose function is to avoid engrossment and to avoid interrupting long stories that engross the patient—therapy becomes a place where expectations of intrusion when engrossed can extinguish. Trauma and insecurity, like stigma, increase situation consciousness and interfere with engrossment—as anyone knows who has tried to follow a complicated story or read a book while upset. Engrossment requires an absence of situation consciousness. Engrossment can be a sign that posttraumatic situation consciousness has been reduced, while inducing engrossment even though the person isn't fully able to enjoy it yet can extinguish the effects of trauma and insecurity via exposure to the experience of not being situation conscious. The person learns that nontraumatized, secure ways of behaving need not be disrupted.

There are three major factors in facilitating a consummate moment: the degree of lamination between audience and event, the treatment of the frame as primary, and the management of the role conflicts between frames.

Lamination and engrossment. In most situations, there is an ideal degree of lamination between audience and event. By lamination, Goffman means logical type, or level of metacommunication, or number of internal brackets that frame a narrative. An example might be *Butch Cassidy and the Sundance Kid* (Foreman & Hill, 1969). Screenings for test audiences found the movie falling flat, and George Roy Hill realized that the problem was an opening title: "Not that it matters, but most of what follows is true." This bracket pushed the involvement with the film's characters one level too far away, from a rendering-on-film of possibly fictitious events to a *nonserious*-rendering-on-film of possibly fictitious events. When the title was changed to "Most of what follows is true," audiences laughed at the bracket itself but did not watch the film through an extra lamination of the film not mattering.

Too few laminations fail to create an aesthetic distance. Appreciation and not action is the desired audience response (Fry, 1920; Goffman, 1974). Underlaminating an event puts the spectator in a position to do something about it and keeps the aesthetic attitude from framing the event. Underlaminations are famous in art when audiences take unnecessary action, like the Renaissance Italians who tried to brush the painted fly off Giotto's canvas or Welles's radio production of *War of the Worlds* that some listeners supposedly took seriously. Underlamination is sometimes a function of the audience member rather than of the production. Bullough (1912–1913) described underdistancers as those who improperly frame artistic activity as too real, like the many fans who supposedly mistake actors for the roles they play in soap operas. Bullough's overdistancers are those who add extra laminations to art and make the art seem so artificial or intellectual as not to be engrossing.

In therapy, the underdistancer is the patient who thinks the therapy is all too real, like the patient who learns in therapy not that she is lovable but only that her therapist loves her. There are also patients who think we are really trying to humiliate them by forcing them to admit they are not perfect. One way to describe a personality disorder in performance terms is a tendency to convert metacommunication into content by underlaminating so that efforts by the therapist to discuss the frame are seen merely as efforts to operate within the patient's frame. For example, the therapist attempts to discuss how the patient is sexualizing the relationship, and the patient just gets turned on. At the other end of the lamination continuum is the patient who treats the therapy as a purely intellectual exercise or who constantly brings up the payments and professionalism in the relationship. "You only accept me because I'm paying you" overly laminates the relationship and prevents engrossment.

Engrossing presentation of frames as primary. Aesthetic engrossment requires taking the brackets around the event as if they are primary. Coleridge's (1985) "willing suspension of disbelief" means an acceptance of the frame of the presentation as real. Literally, the boundaries of the stage are treated as the boundaries of the world, and what is offstage is treated as nonexistent. Games and puzzles are engrossing because the tight rules create a frame that can be accepted as primary—that's why it matters if rent is collected on a Monopoly square and why it matters who wins. In painting, the literal frame is treated as the boundary of the world. An anthropologist found that women newly exposed to photography could not at first recognize pictures of their own children, but with a little training they could (Herskovits, 1959). The training they received was not in facial recognition but in how to accept the boundaries of a piece of paper as a frame for the experience of looking. If they had been placed in a room with a window 5 by 8 inches and then if the photograph had been held up to the window, they would probably have recognized their children the first time because they already presumably knew how to use a window frame.

Performers have two main responsibilities in helping audience members accept the presented frame. First, they must not discredit the frame themselves. The audience is perfectly willing to overlook muffed lines or minor stumbles, but if the actor then comments on it, the disattend channel cannot be sustained, the discrediting material becomes content, the frame is seen to be arbitrary, and the engrossment is destroyed. In therapy, the psychoanalytic therapist must not suddenly interpret the patient's productive attitude of trust as a *transference*, and the cognitive therapist must not reveal that the causality of thoughts is only a metaphor and that the environment actually causes *both* thoughts *and* behavior. Neither therapist can be caught with an erection.

Second, performers must not burden the artistic frame with more than it can hold. A stage can hold a skirmish and a swordfight, but a full-scale battle needs film to contain it. A play longer than about 90 minutes needs an intermission.

A painting that is more than several yards long cannot operate as a typical painting; it must become a mural, and its subject must change accordingly. Many therapy frames are unable to contain what is presented in them. Hugging patients is an understandable impulse, but it usually wrecks the therapy frame and replaces it with a social frame that cannot sustain the other intimacies of productive psychotherapy. Suicidal patients often present content—threats of self-destruction—that the therapy cannot contain, leading to phone calls, extra sessions, and medication regimens that replace the therapy frame with a case management frame. Some psychotic thinking, violent fantasies, or bad choices make therapists think it is their job to set the patient straight, and regardless of the usefulness of abandoning the therapeutic frame in such moments, its abandonment means that the patient will no longer be able to accept it as real once it is reestablished. The patient thereafter will hunger for moments when the therapy manifests the frame now considered to be real, namely, when the therapist drops her neutrality and acceptance and tells the patient what to do. This has the same effect as an actor commenting on her performance during the play: it is amusing for Juliet to turn to the audience and say, "Remember! She's only 14!" But after that, the audience will not become engrossed again in her Juliet, waiting instead for the actor-to-audience bracketing that she has presented as even more primary than Shakespeare's. (An entirely different play can be written, of course, in which such breaches are presented as primary, and then engrossment is still possible between breaches because the breacher, rather than the playwright, becomes the storyteller. The movies *Alfie* [Gilbert, 1966] and *Ferris Bueller's Day Off* [Hughes, 1986] did this well, with Michael Caine and Mathew Broderick commenting to the camera between otherwise engrossing scenes.)

Unengrossing role conflicts. An important source of content that cannot be bracketed by the therapy frame is content associated with the patient role. This needs explaining. Both parties in a therapy always play at least two roles. The therapist plays a person trying to make a living by helping people, and then within the therapy she plays whatever roles the patient's psychology and her approach dictate. Psychoanalytic therapists tend to play roles dictated by the patient's psychology (e.g., rejecting father, demanding mother), while cognitive therapists are more likely to stay in the teacherly role demanded by the technique. Patients play the role of a person seeking help by paying a therapist, and then within the therapy they tend to reproduce the roles associated with their problematic definitions of situations (e.g., adored or neglected child). Indeed, a great underlying advantage in psychotherapy is that its intrinsic power differential, fiduciary aspects, caregiving, and limit setting are like a parenting relationship, and many psychological problems have their roots and their current expressions in just these sorts of relationships.

Content exceeds framing when the therapist undertakes to assist the patient not only with the problems in living that have brought her to therapy but also with the life problems that make it difficult for her to be a patient at all. If the therapist starts the therapy in the patient's home or discusses bus schedules with her to find a way for her to get to the sessions while the children are in day care, the therapist is conflating the roles framed by society and the roles framed by therapy. These interventions are sometimes necessary to help at all, but they will also ensure that the case management frame will always be primary, and attempts by these patients in the future to locate themselves in the primary frame by demanding extratherapeutic assistance should not be surprising.

PSYCHOTHERAPY AND FRAMES

Following Bateson (1972d), Goffman sees psychopathology as an abnormal application of frames, that is, as a tendency to frame situations incorrectly or idiosyncratically. An incorrect frame is one that defines roles that are bound to be discredited. As in every major approach to therapy, patients are seen as applying old maps to new territories. Care must be taken not to pathologize all framing discrepancies, only those that are in error. This echoes Rank's (1936, 1989) view of the artist and the neurotic as alike since both question the legitimacy of their society's primary frames. Therapy presents an opportunity for the therapist to observe framing problems and to correct them, so the therapy should be structured so as to occasion the patient's framing errors.

Therapist anonymity and silence facilitate the patient's demonstration of her framing problems because reduced amounts of information free the individual to fill in the blanks with idiosyncratic expectations. "You have the right to remain silent," I tell trainees. The patient reports an angry fantasy about his sister's baby. I can reassure him, I can pathologize him, or I can silently await information about how he is framing this disclosure. Reassurance teaches him he's okay, pathologizing teaches him to constrain his self-expression, and silence followed by interpretation teaches him to change the way he relates to himself. Projective testing capitalizes on the same effect, as ambiguous stimuli invite idiosyncratic frames. Confidentiality occasions framing errors because secrets are usually broadcast as gossip or to build teams, and a conscientious therapist will confuse the patient about whether the therapy is private or public, a confusion that will be imbued with idiosyncratic expectations. This source of information about framing errors is especially pertinent to our own psychotherapies, where we may wonder just how curious our therapist is about *us* versus how curious she is about the gossip we report about other professionals we discuss with her. She can re-assure us about her disinterest—or she can silently wait for us to demon-strate our framing errors. Intimacy also produces framing errors, presumably because society is unable to easily observe such situations and teach indi-viduals how to frame them.

Games produce framing errors when it is unclear what is in the game and what is not. In my friendly poker game, it is against the rules to gain an ad-vantage by irritating other players, but in Las Vegas such behavior is within the rules. When a Las Vegas player acts annoyingly, other players may have difficulty framing the situation, as it is unclear whether the annoyance is or is not part of the game. Bateson says that therapy is a special kind of game that teaches patients to distinguish between levels of logical types and that also turns the patient's primary frames into transcribable frames. Discussion of the therapy game, in which the discussion itself is part of the game, teaches log-ical typing, while discussion of the patient's life and her framing tendencies turn these from being unquestionably real into examples of something. As Bateson (1972d) puts it, "By the process of interpretation, the neurotic is driven to insert an 'as if' clause into the productions of his primary process thinking, which productions he had previously deprecated or repressed. He must learn that fantasy contains truth" (p. 192). Bateson also notes that the patient learns that fantasy is not entirely truth, either. Making these distinc-tions teaches the patient metacommunication and how to avoid logical typing errors.

People who find themselves repeatedly making framing errors and there-fore find themselves repeatedly having their performances discredited take defensive action. They avoid discrediting situations by avoiding others, by ig-noring others, by self-discrediting, and in countless other ways. Psychother-apy, then, is more than intimacy exposure; it's also an opportunity for expo-sure to being discredited, where the patient can learn that being discredited need not be disastrous. The therapist "breach[es] the frame of ordinary face-to-face dealings at just those points" that protect people from "influence and relationship formation" (Goffman, 1974, p. 385). The therapist does this largely by commenting on the information in the disattend and concealment channels (which is also what parents do with infants). "You say you feel sorry for your brother, but you look kind of excited."

Lively psychotherapy enhances teamwork and engrossment by getting se-crets, treating normally disattended communications as subject matter, and encouraging the patient to breach standards of decency and modesty (Goff-man, 1974). These objectives are facilitated by the rule of free association (saying whatever comes to mind, holding nothing back), which is explicit in psychoanalytic therapy and implicit in other approaches. Free association also gives the therapist the opportunity to create a relationship devoid of reprisals. To fully clear a relationship of reprisals, it must also be cleared of praise since the potential for praise makes its absence a sort of reprisal, and the instances of praise define the relationship as a judgmental one.

The therapy pair creates its own concealment channel by developing an exclusive relationship (Goffman, 1974). This too is facilitated by free association—the patient is encouraged to say things about people he would not reveal to anyone else, and this betrayal enhances the therapeutic connection. Goffman also notes psychotherapy's emphasis on resistance as content. In other words, *resistance* designates questions about the game, but in therapy these are treated as communications within the game, as if someone who said, "I don't like chess" were told, "Good move."

Since these characteristics of good therapy also describe successful cults and the presumed difference is only in the motivations of the therapist, it is not surprising that many therapies and schools of therapy become cultlike. As we shall see in the next chapter, another important influence on cultish schools of thought is the shared power among practitioners to form a hegemony that marginalizes patients.

Chapter Three

What Am I Doing to Irma?

Perhaps the key problem in maintaining the loyalty of team members . . . is to prevent the performers from becoming so sympathetically attached to the audience that the performers disclose to them the consequences for them of the impression they are being given.

—Goffman (1959, p. 214)

The plan for transforming the spectator into actor . . . should begin not with something alien . . . but with the *bodies* of those who agree to participate.

—Boal (1985, pp. 126–127)

Many of the concerns of performance theory—power, gender, the place of the individual in a system of categories, and the silencing of voices that would subvert the party line—are intrinsically relevant to psychotherapy, where there is an ever-present power differential, where yang rationality and yin emotionality clash, where the therapist is pushed by her profession to treat the patient as an example of something else, and where the silenced aspects of the self that bring the patient for help turn out to be as disruptive to the therapy as to other relationships in his life. These themes represent the tension between deadly maintenance of the prevailing hegemony within the individual, the therapy, or the profession and lively questioning of its utility. In this chapter, we will see how prominent these themes have been since the dawn of psychotherapy.

In 1895, on the eve of becoming the first therapist in the contemporary sense of the word, Sigmund Freud had a dream about a patient he called Irma. In his breakthrough book *The Interpretation of Dreams*, Freud (1953) treated it as a "specimen dream," implying that any dream would do to illustrate his new technique of interpretation and his new theory of dreams. In fact, however, his ideas coalesced in *this* dream, possibly the following morning when he wrote it down, possibly as he was actually dreaming it. Because of this, the dream has been extensively interpreted over the years (Bosnak, 1984; Erikson, 1954; Grotstein, 1980; Mehlman, 1987; Schur, 1966) although nowhere so searchingly as by Freud himself. Indeed, it is also true that on that night Freud became the first patient in the contemporary sense of the word, modeling for us the courage and humility of subjecting ourselves to whatever we employ on our patients. Unsurprisingly, the utility of that attitude turns out to be the major theme of the dream.

At that time, Freud's practice largely involved the resolution of symptoms that were apparently physical but actually psychological by explaining them to patients. Much of psychoanalytic theory revolves around the effort to understand what must be going on in the mind to create symptoms and how it's possible to eliminate them by explaining them. But one need not accept psychoanalytic explanations to accept his successes. The behaviorist sees interpretation as a kind of exposure, where labeling the symptom highlights its function, making it clear that it's futile to avoid punishment by disguising behavior through metaphor. Behaviorally, interpretation reveals the disguised behavior, and analytic neutrality keeps from punishing it, allowing it to extinguish. Systemically, symptoms may be viewed as examples of Watzlawick, Bavelas, and Jackson's (1967) metaphor of a passenger who anticipates being bored by a seatmate. The passenger would normally pretend to fall asleep to avoid conversation, but, feeling too guilty about the implied dismissal of the other person, the passenger solves the conflict between wanting to escape boredom and not wanting to seem heartless by actually falling asleep. Watzlawick sees symptoms as versions of such self-deceptive compromises. Metacommunication about the purpose of the sleep robs it of its finesse, and the passenger has to find some other solution to the conflicting demands of his roles. However explained, Freud found that many patients relinquished their symptoms once he explained them, but many did not. In 1895, he felt— understandably but defensively—that his job was done when he offered the explanation, not when the patient got better. His dream about Irma changed his thinking about this and led to a century of ideas about the therapist's role in the therapy.

On the night of the dream, Freud wrote out a long case history on Irma for Dr. M (Josef Breuer), the senior physician in the group that was exploring talk therapy. This request for consultation was spurred by events of the day. Freud's wife was pregnant (with Anna Freud) and her own birthday was a few days away. At her birthday party, Freud expected to see Irma, who was a friend of the family as well as a patient (this was before Freud discovered the inadvisability of treating friends). Irma's anxiety had improved, but her somatic symptoms had not. During the day, Freud entertained another family friend, Otto (actually Oskar Rie), who was not only one of Irma's other physicians but also the pediatrician for Freud's children. Otto had seen Irma recently, and he reported to Freud that she was better but not quite well. Freud wondered if he had missed something in the treatment and diligently appealed to Dr. M for consultation. Freud's interpretation of that night's dream was that he took Otto's report as a reproof, that he really wrote out the case history to justify himself rather than for consultation, and that he used the dream to avenge himself on all who had injured his narcissism, especially Irma for not getting better and the other doctors for knowing it:

> A large hall—numerous guests, whom we were receiving.—Among them was Irma. I at once took her on one side, as though to answer her letter and to reproach her for not having accepted my "solution" yet. I said to her: "If you still get pains, it's really only your fault." She replied: "If only you knew what pains I've got now in my throat and stomach and abdomen—it's choking me"—I was alarmed and looked at her. She looked pale and puffy. I thought to myself that after all I must be missing some organic trouble. I took her to the window and looked down her throat, and she showed signs of recalcitrance, like women with artificial dentures. I thought to myself that there was really no need for her to do that.—She then opened her mouth properly and on the right I found a big white patch; at another place I saw extensive whitish grey scabs upon some remarkable curly structures which were evidently modeled on the turbinal bones of the nose.—I at once called in Dr. M., and he repeated the examination and confirmed it. . . . Dr. M. looked quite different from usual; he was very pale, he walked with a limp and his chin was clean-shaven. . . . My friend Otto was now standing beside her as well, and my friend Leopold was percussing her through her bodice and saying: "She has a dull area low down on the left." He also indicated that a portion of the skin on the left shoulder was infiltrated. (I noticed this, just as he did, in spite of her dress.) . . . M. said: "There's no doubt it's an infection, but no matter; dysentery will supervene and the toxin will be eliminated." . . . We were directly aware, too, of the origin of the infection. Not long before, when she was feeling unwell, my friend Otto had given her an injection of a preparation of propyl, propyls . . . propionic acid . . . trimethylamin (and I saw before me the formula for this printed in heavy type). . . . Injections of that sort ought not to be made so thoughtlessly. . . . And probably the syringe had not been clean. (Freud, 1953, p. 107)

Freud reports his associations to each element and development in the dream in a display of self-scrutiny that is shockingly honest even by today's standards. He concludes that the dream, through wish fulfillment, reinstates his pride by exacting revenge on Otto and other doubting doctors by having them do and say foolish things; by injuring Irma and recalling better patients; by dropping reminders of what a helpful, skilled, and compassionate fellow he really is; and by conjuring his friend Dr. Fliess, who sees Freud as he would like to be seen. (Fliess was a brilliant wacko who thought many problems could be fixed by internal nasal surgery; Freud and Fliess ran a powerful mutual admiration society.) Freud's interpretation would fit any work-related narcissistic injury: "It's not my fault." His interpretation ignores the fact that the dream was about a therapy patient.

Erikson's interpretation is, well, Eriksonian. He reminds us that Freud was 39 years old at the time of the dream, in the midst of a midlife crisis about whether his sixth child and his entry into middle age meant that he would have to relinquish his dream of conquering the psyche and becoming famous and instead resign himself to the full-time practice of neurology. He was in a conflict of generativity versus stagnation, a conflict exacerbated and complicated by his culturally and personally bound definitions of generativity as masculine and stagnation as feminine, definitions particularly difficult to sustain in light of his wife's repeated success at giving birth and his own stalled career.

Freud's narcissistic concerns about success are evident not only in his own associations to the dream but also in his having written to Fliess about that night. In the letter, "Freud indulges in a fantasy of a possible tablet which (he wonders) may someday adorn his summer home. Its inscription would tell the world that 'In this house, on July 24, 1895, the Mystery of the Dream unveiled [enthüllte] itself to Dr. Sigm. Freud'" (Erikson, 1954, p. 7). This letter justifies our treatment of the dream as more than a specimen, but it also suggests an interpretation in which Irma represents the Mystery of the Dream. Erikson says the dream starts as a twosome, a union with his wife, that is disrupted by concerns about the appearance of the mystery of the dream. Freud exerts masculine authority over this mystery by reducing her to a mouth ("the mouth opens" is the correct translation) and then to a point where she no longer speaks at all. His allegiance is to the doctors, not to the mystery, and his concern is for his reputation, not for his patient. Erikson also informs us that when Freud wrote, "I noticed this," meaning the infiltration in Irma's shoulder, he meant that he felt it physically in his own shoulder. The conflict is also about identification with the patient, which is painful, and identification with the doctoring, which is above pain but lonely—a conflict recapitulated in the stereotyped role of father. Erikson (1954) concludes that dreams are not just naked wish fulfillments; they also "lift the dreamer's isolation, appease his conscience, and preserve his identity" (p. 55).

Grotstein (1980) does not offer a new interpretation of the dream, but he does provide some important background information. Freud had referred

Irma to Fliess for a consultation, writing to ask him for his "authoritative advice" (p. 26), much as he had asked for Dr. M.'s advice the night before the dream. Fliess recommended nasal surgery (having already operated on Freud's nasal passages) but accidentally left over a foot of gauze in Irma's sinus, which led to disgusting complications. Freud, also a surgical patient of Fliess's, could have identified with Irma, but instead, he wrote to Fliess, "The fact that this mishap should have happened to *you*. . . . Of course no one blames you in any way, nor do I know why they should" (p. 26).

Grotstein also rounds out Freud's association to looking into Irma's mouth. Freud tells us that he was thereby substituting for the unsuccessful treatment of Irma a successful treatment of a different patient named Mathilde. Freud also thought of his daughter, Mathilde, who had survived a frightening battle with diphtheria 2 years earlier. Grotstein recalls that she was under doctor's orders not to eat for fear of choking, but she pleaded so longingly for a strawberry that Freud gave her one. "When Mathilde tried to swallow it, she had a fit of coughing which dislodged the obstructive membrane and thus saved her life" (Grotstein, 1980, p. 28).

Bosnak (1984) emphasizes the iatrogenic issues in the dream. He informs us that it was the selfsame Otto who discovered Fliess's malpractice with Irma so that Otto's imagined reproach of Freud the day of the dream was bound to remind Freud of Fliess's botched surgery. Bosnak, a Jungian, identifies four archetypal doctors in the dream. Freud is the innocent do-gooder, Dr. M. is the one who limply pronounces the diagnosis without the power to help, Leopold is the careful observer, and Otto is the cause of the problems. Bosnak interprets the dream as the "creation myth" (p. 105) of psychoanalysis, an imperfect situation in which the therapist's personal agendas and confusion lead to an impure intermingling of self with the patient, which stimulates the patient's capacity for self-healing. Bosnak notes that the word for "syringe" in German is *spritze*, which also means "squirter" or "spritzer" in the colloquial sense. To him, the needle is dirty because it is human, and this humanity is what makes therapy work despite the therapist's discomfort with it. While I see much merit in humanizing psychotherapy, it's very difficult for me to applaud a kind of humanizing that's based on an indefensible and utterly avoidable kind of being human, such as leaving gauze inside a surgical patient.

Mehlman (1987) analogizes the conflict in the dream to Freudian psychology, in which the ego strives for autonomy and omniscience at the expense of the self. Mehlman cites an important footnote (as does Erikson) that Freud added in 1925 that chides clinicians not to overemphasize the hidden meanings of dreams but instead to focus on the process, the dream work, by which meanings become hidden. The Freudian ego is much like Freud in this episode: narcissistic, imagining a false autonomy, defensive and regretful about having a body, and clever. Mehlman locates this conflict in the dreamer's substitution of the chemical formula for trimethylamin—a molecule involved in sexual functioning—for the substance itself. The ego, the narcissistic doctor, prefers the formula for sexual substances to sexual imagery because it distances him from the body. Mehlman wisely cautions us to consider this conflict afresh every time we make an interpretation. Suspect also is Freud's ready acceptance of blame for believing in 1895 that the analyst's job was over when the truth was spoken because it rejects and diminishes the 1895 Freud while lionizing the Freud in 1899 who writes about him.

Dreams, like early memories (Karson, 2006), are road maps for negotiating different kinds of situations, road maps that usually have useful information in them about how the dreamer's world works but that also have some errors based on idiosyncratic preferences or misleading life experiences. I interpret the Irma dream as a road map for conducting psychotherapy, complicated by Freud's personal history. The dream, which occurred either the night before or in real-time concurrence with Freud's becoming the first therapist and the first patient, tells us the importance of thinking about gender, power, teamwork, and humility as therapists.

Among them was Irma. This is not just a dream about therapy; it is a dream about what happens when therapy is made public (Irma is received in a large hall with other guests) and about what happens when the patient is viewed as an example of psychopathology rather than as a unique individual (Irma is introduced as a person among others). Therapy is made public not only when we breach privacy—it is also made public every time we imagine what others would say about what we are doing, every time we hear a story from a patient and think what a good example it is of something, and every time we feel pride about an intervention. The patient's individuality isn't obliterated merely when we diagnose or when we consider using a preexisting therapy regimen rather than developing each therapy specifically for each patient—it's also obliterated each time we label a behavior, even to ourselves, rather than unpack the behavior by exploring its functional relationship to its occasioning environment. The dream tells us that we are most likely to breach privacy and obliterate the patient's individuality when our pride is at stake, whether our pride is stimulated by an outside audience (the other doctors, the dual relationships), enhanced by a good intervention (the solution Freud invented), or subdued by a lack of therapeutic progress (Irma's not getting better).

If only you knew. Like a normally patient and accepting parent whose child misbehaves in a public place, a restaurant or church perhaps, Freud's patience evaporates. He scolds Irma, and it is this scolding that introduces her pain and her suffering. Irma arrives in the dream apparently functional and healthy, but Freud's pride turns him into a reproachful parent, and his reproach of her has the same effect as Otto's reproach of him: it hurts. Freud's reproach is a performance for his buddies, which makes it clear to Irma that their relationship is subordinate to his allegiance with other doctors. Irma replies by appealing to his narcissism about knowing, hoping that his narcissism about knowing will overcome his narcissism about showing off. She (i.e., this part of Freud) was on the right track because as narcissistic as Freud was in public, he still stands second to none in his willingness to listen to patients—taking supervision directly from Anna O. on how to conduct her therapy, for example. His presentation of his own dream also shows his willingness to listen to the marginalized parts of himself. In the dream, her appeal pays off: Freud gets alarmed and shows us what we need to do when patients' agendas are cast aside by pride. He looks at her.

I must be missing some organic trouble. When writing about this, Freud humbly confesses his wish that she should have had an organic illness, sacrificing her physical health to preserve his status as not being wrong in his solution. To me, the major import of this sentence is his switch from a doctor who blames his patient to a doctor who is not omniscient. This switch was occasioned by his willingness to look at her—inside her, even—rather than to look for approval from others.

Dentures. Irma behaves self-consciously and like a person with no teeth. The dream tells us to expect such behavior from patients whose therapists are acting pridefully and for a public audience. However, the authenticity of his interest and their moment of privacy helps the therapist see that the patient can act again as one with teeth—as one with privacy.

Remarkable curly structures. Engrossed in his patient's performance of her pathology, Freud is confronted with a sight that both makes him question his competence to help her and, more important, reminds him of the harm he has done to her. Every therapy—every session, if we are paying attention—confronts us with information we have never heard before, feelings we have never felt before, and terrain for which we have no maps. Therapy at these moments requires faith in the patient's guidance, but, like Lewis and Clark following Sacajawea across the Rockies and back, we are not entirely sure the guide is working for us. It is a tricky decision whether to seek consultation at such moments since the therapist must balance the utility of a second opinion with the intrusion on the relationship. Second opinions are least intrusive when they come purely psychologically ("What would Horney say?") or when the opinion can be sought nondefensively from a colleague whom we can trust to perceive us not as infallible but as competent and good despite our mistakes.

In the dream, Freud calls in his colleagues because he is confused but mainly to eradicate his sense that he has hurt Irma. We all do this. The patient comes late for a session, and, while waiting for her, we remember something we once read about patients' inherent ambivalence about change, and we force this distant writer into agreeing with us that the patient's lateness is her own fault (or her mother's). Or we mention the lateness to a supervisor or colleague in a way that induces the other person into advising us to make increased demands on the patient's punctuality. The worse the patient's behavior, the more likely we are to disown responsibility for it—suicide is always the patient's fault, while coming late might be a response to something we said. In between, responsibility varies according to the therapist's courage.

Confirmed it. When we call in colleagues not to assist with competence but to justify our conduct, it vitiates their ability to improve us, making them limp, pale, and beardless (which at the time meant unauthoritative). It also enhances the teamwork among professionals, leaving the patient stranded in a passive and helpless version of the role of patient.

I noticed this. Freud's empathy saves the day. Just as the doctors are bonding in superiority at the patient's expense, Freud feels what she feels in his own body. His empathy opens the door to reframing her problem (dysentery) as health—a self-preserving, "supervening" response to misused authority. That is, once he identifies with her, her response becomes understandable and restorative rather than troublesome and defiant.

The origin of the infection. In his associations, Freud acknowledges the revenge the dream takes on Otto for reporting that Irma was not quite well—and, presumably, for discovering Fliess's incompetence. He places a dirty syringe in Otto's hand while congratulating himself on never having caused such an infection. But the actual infection was the infection of the awareness of iatrogenic disease into the Freud–Fliess and Freud–Freud mutual admiration societies. Is such an infection a good thing or a bad thing? When the occupational goal is to attain an elevated, even Olympian apotheosis of rational insulation from suffering, then the introduction of imperfection and humanity feels like a bad thing. When the occupational goal is to help, facilitate, engage, and see, then the introduction of imperfections and humanity is not an infection at all: they are already present. The German word *spritze* can mean "syringe" or "squirter." In a frame of clinical sterility, humanity dirties; in a frame of human relatedness, it does not. When it's a syringe, humanity sullies it; when it's a breast, it's already human.

In every session, I can pull rank on the patient and declare my framing of the relationship to be the true frame, or I can collaborate with the patient around discovering how we are jointly framing things. This is the heart of intersubjectivity (Buirski & Haglund, 2001) as I understand it—the therapist's commitment not to pretend that he has no backstage. Intersubjectivists call this two-mind versus one-mind therapy, whereas I prefer calling it four-mind versus three-mind (two-mind therapy to me would be advice between both parties' front-stage functioning; three-mind therapy would involve the patient's front stage and backstage and the therapist's front stage; four-mind therapy involves two front stages and two backstages). In every session, because we are human, some conflict will arise, and I will either deny my contribution to it, thereby declaring my team allegiance to doctors, or explore my contribution to it, thereby declaring my team allegiance with the patient.

One thing I have always enjoyed about doing therapy and about raising children is that they can be done only so well. Because they are just human relationships, they cannot be perfected. I can't boast about therapy and parenthood, but I also spare myself from being haunted by the idea that I could be doing a much better job. A few geniuses occasionally make me jealous — Milton Erickson and Chloe Madanes come to mind — but I think each of us is a genius now and then: Erickson and Madanes just act geniusly more often than most of us do. I have my faults as a father, but there is no father so much more gifted than I that I must contend with the idea that my own children would have been better off with him. Indeed, they would not be themselves if they had been with him. And I feel pretty much the same way about other therapists. A few are just dreadful and should not be allowed to practice, but most of us are just slogging our way through human relationships, trying to help, sometimes making messes and sometimes cleaning them up.

That strawberry says it all. When Freud the physician confronted his daughter's diphtheria, he properly refused to feed her. When Freud the father confronted his dying daughter's plea for one of the freshly picked strawberries that the other children were enjoying, he gave it to her, and it saved her life. The human frame makes such kindnesses restorative; the clinical frame makes them deadly.

Chapter Four

Status Games

It is true that Grandcourt went about with the air that he did not care a lan-guid curse for any one's admiration; but this state of not-caring, just as much as desire, required its related object—namely, a world of admiring or envying spectators: for if you are fond of looking stonily at smiling per-sons, the persons must be there and they must smile—a rudimentary truth which is surely forgotten by those who complain of mankind as generally contemptible, since any other aspect of the race must disappoint the vo-racity of their contempt.

—Eliot (1995, pp. 585–586)

I don't myself see that an educated man in this culture necessarily has to understand the second law of thermodynamics, but he certainly should un-derstand that we are pecking-order animals and that this affects the tiniest details of our behaviour.

—Johnstone (1981, pp. 73–74)

HUMAN AGGRESSION

I find it a bit suspicious, looking at the array of species in the animal king-dom, that there are a zillion different kinds of bats and beetles and horses that look like zebras and deer—indeed, every animal has some near neighbor on the tree of life, but there's only one of us. Oh, I recognize that chimpanzees and gorillas are distant relatives, but where are all of our close relatives? Where are *Australopithecus* and *Africanus* and *Neanderthalus*? Our place on the evolutionary bush reminds me of a lifeboat that washes ashore carrying only one survivor and a lot of bones under the seats and blood in his beard.

Think about it. You're camping in the woods, the sun has set, and you are miles from the nearest civilization. You hear a noise nearby. What's the *last* animal you want to run into under these circumstances? Maybe a bear, maybe a mountain lion, but probably a man. It just seems to me that human beings are easy enough to get along with if you act like a puppy, but otherwise, well, I wouldn't want to run into *Homo sapiens* in a dark alley.

Getting along with humans often requires acting like a dog—knowing when to be docile and when to be aggressive. Churchill said the Germans are always at your feet or at your throat, commenting on what he perceived to be their obsession with dominance and authority. But we are all obsessed with dominance. Without even realizing it, most people orient themselves to the dominance hierarchy in their immediate environment, and they quickly figure out when to act dominant, submissive, or equal. This hierarchy is necessary because we have been both blessed and cursed with an abundance of aggression—blessed in our survival advantage, cursed in how hard it is to get along with other people. People learn their place in the pecking order so that role definitions need not be established by constant fighting—too much fighting is not conducive to survival. A primary, possibly *the* primary, cause of death in nonindustrialized societies was—and still is—homicide (Diamond, 1997). All of civilization (according to Nietzsche, 1967, and Freud, 1961) can be thought of as a method of organizing a vicious species to keep its members from killing each other.

PECKING ORDERS

Insights into the nature of our various pecking orders can be gleaned from the study of chickens, who invented pecking orders. Chickens get food and access to nests according to their pecking ability—their ability to fight. If a chicken knows that every chicken in front of her could beat her up, she'll wait her turn and not try to cut in line. If a chicken knows that every chicken behind her knows her place, she doesn't have to pick on them. Pecking orders reduce violence. But how does the chicken know which chickens can beat her up and which she can dominate?

Chickens, like humans, can tell each other apart. They determine their pecking order by fighting each other and remembering who beat whom, and then they line up accordingly. There must be some difficulty when Adelaide beats up Bessie and Bessie beats up Cornelia and Cornelia beats up Adelaide. They wouldn't know what order to stand in. But generally speaking, remembering who beat whom will put them in a pretty organized line. It would be even better to have some nonviolent way of assessing fighting ability, say, a strength test, or a résumé, or a bank account. This would allow all the benefits of a hierarchy without first making each chicken fight every other chicken.

Crickets cannot tell each other apart. Instead of remembering who beat whom, they stand a little taller when they win a fight and hunker down a bit when they lose a fight. This way, they can get some idea of how good a fighter each cricket is by looking at posture. Animals that lack the brainpower to tell one from another also lack the brainpower to lie about their fight records—otherwise, some deviously resourceful cricket could stand very tall and march to the front of the line, regardless of actual prowess in battle.

Humans act like both chickens and crickets, keeping track of who beat us and whom we beat but also carrying ourselves like champions or bums depending on our overall record. Of course, things are more complicated for us than for chickens but not complicated beyond all analysis. The main complexities stem from three sources. One, our status issues pertain to many more resources than the birdseed and sex that interest chickens. We have status hierarchies for everything from how long we can speak at the dinner table to where we will sleep at Grandma's house. Two, we have many more ways than physical prowess to organize status hierarchies, including income, heredity, intellect, and musical ability, to name a few. Part of what makes us so fascinating is our ability to invent new status hierarchies that leave us peculiarly well placed. A man whose efforts have come to naught at work and at home, for example, can still stand on the top of the heap when it comes to Most Reformed Drunk or Star Trek Trivia Buff. Three, we're a bunch of liars. I don't mean this in a moral or disapproving sense. I mean that one of the main things about us is our ability to emit signals rather than signs, to use our capacity for language to invent ourselves as we would like to be. Chickens may not know enough to put on a nice suit and act important, but we sure do, whether the suit is literally good clothing or metaphorically a representation of the self to others.

GOODNESS

Nietzsche (1966a) thought that one of the main dynamics in Christian history was the redefinition of status from masterful (accomplished, competent, good at doing things) to slavish (meek, humble, good in the moral sense). Christians had redefined *good* so that it no longer meant to them the opposite of *bad* (as in I'm good at fighting) but instead meant the opposite of *evil* (I'm good for not fighting). Nietzsche called this *slave morality* because it organizes status in a way that compensates the slave for not being in charge. It replaces geographical power (the ability to exert your will on your environment) with social power (the acquisition of social approval for being unable to exert your will on your environment). Nietzsche's point was that condemning power is not a productive way to resolve social problems that arise from power discrepancies. Whatever you may think of that view of history and of Christianity, surely we all know a few individuals who resent other people's competence, revile it as "pride," and implicitly extol their own virtuous humility. There's even a name for this: acting "holier than thou." It happens in psychology when a practitioner's accomplishments are disparaged as a pathological need for recognition. (Anyone with less training than me is not competent to practice, and anyone with more training than me is masking her insecurity with unnecessary credentials.)

PERFECTION

Horney (1950) theorized that pathological behavior stems from the difficulty with managing the discrepancy between perfection and how we really are. Some neurotics hate themselves for not being perfect, some accept themselves as they are and stop striving to improve, and some claim to be perfect already and ignore contradictory data. Horney writes about three main kinds of neurotic perfectionism: competence (I should be capable), lovability (I should be appreciated), and freedom (I should be unfettered). I think that each of these has a shadow perfectionism as well. Nietzsche said that people who enviously reject strength as a virtue present themselves as humble pacifists; likewise, those who resent the friendliness and freedom of others can make a status success out of being unfriendly or trapped. They don't call themselves unfriendly or trapped any more than those obsessed with not being powerful call themselves weak or impotent. Instead, people who resent the lovability of others glorify their own ability not to be swayed by the approval of others: they show us how *truth* and *honor* are more important to them than being loved. They say things like, "The mass of men lead lives of quiet desperation." (I don't know enough about Thoreau to say whether this observation was the fruit of insight or the spoils of resentment about not being well liked, but it sure sounds like the latter to me. It sounds like, "I feel sorry for people who get along with others.") People who resent the freedom of others applaud their own ability to endure the rat race. They call themselves *mature* and go on about how immature and childish and impulsive it is to enjoy one's freedom. They cluck about people who are still having fun, even when the fun they are having is not at anyone else's expense. "I just don't think that's necessary," said one woman to me, as proud as I would be if I won a Pulitzer Prize—but she was proud of not masturbating. "THAT'S NOT NORMAL!" screamed a school psychologist after I said I saw a behavior management problem but not psychopathology when a teenage boy stood on a table in class and sang show tunes.

Waiters in French restaurants provide common examples of redefining status to your own benefit. The clients are typically people who can afford to eat there, while the waiters are often lower in socioeconomic status. More important, the waiters are there to bring our food, dig their tips out of the sauce béarnaise, and dust our crumbs off the tablecloth. But often the waitstaff redefine status by ignoring servitude and finances and emphasizing the ability to pronounce the menu items correctly or to choose the correct wine. "Very good, sir," they will say, as if to compliment you on your ordering ability, but the compliment itself creates a role relationship in which they are the teacher and you are the student. Patrons of such restaurants usually divide into two groups. One group is boorish enough to trumpet money as the measure of a person; the other group defers to the waitstaff. Both end up playing low status, either by being boorish (you act like a pig, and you end up eating their spit without knowing it) or by being deferent. The only way to play high status in such a place is to out-French them ("You only have the '85? Well, then, we'll just have the beer"), which also ends up with you eating spit.

PLAYING STATUS

In addition to being good at inventing new definitions of status to suit us, we are also very good at pretending to have power that we do not. That's why Keith Johnstone (1981), the theater director, says that status is what you *do*, not who you are. Johnstone analyzed why staged scenes do not look as lively as real life looks, and he found that offstage interchanges always carry a subtext analogous to Goffman's directional channel or to Bateson's metacommunicative definition of the relationship—status was *always* being played. Every effort to define the relationship also defined the status transaction between the players. He demonstrated this by having actors play high status or low status and showing how much that single difference changes a scene. You can experiment in your own life by alternating between high-status maneuvers and low-status maneuvers and seeing what happens. This kind of acting is complicated but for most purposes can be broken down to a few behaviors. High-status maneuvers include keeping your head and hands still, moving apace but not quickly, speaking clearly and with conviction, standing upright, and maintaining eye contact. Playing high status also involves carefully monitoring your position relative to the other person and declining to be cast as a subordinate. Playing low status is shown by nodding your head, fidgeting with your hands, touching your face, hurrying, saying "er" and "um" between words, speaking uncertainly, hunching down, and breaking eye contact. Low status also involves carefully monitoring your relative position and sidestepping opportunities to cast the other person as an equal or as a subordinate. Even more simply, low-status behavior includes what children can't help doing, while high-status behavior includes doing what children can't.

POWER, STATUS, AND POSITION

Power is the potential to affect another person. I have virtually no power over the president of the United States; he has fairly extensive power over me. Outside our roles as president and citizen, as two persons, I suppose I could try to hit him with a rock, but the cost would be greater to me than to him when I lost my job and was thrown in prison. He could try to sic the FBI on me, but the risk to him would be great if he were found out (I would hope). Within the roles of president and citizen, he can issue executive orders and adopt policies that affect my world in a variety of ways that are important to me. My boss's boss has great power over me. I have some power over him too, but if I exert any that affects him adversely, I may find myself in a showdown with someone who can have me fired, so my own power in the situation is constricted. A waiter can make a patron's meal more or less pleasant, and a patron can treat the waiter well or poorly and leave a large or small tip.

In ongoing relationships, all parties have the power either to foster or to derail the definition of the situation and the power to make others feel good or bad. Family therapists usually view a power imbalance between partners as their way of defining the relationship. Rather than seeing the putatively less powerful person as a victim, the therapist often sees an actual equal in co-constructing a relationship that looks like a power imbalance. Notable exceptions include relationships where one partner wants out, where there's physical violence, or where there's an imbalance in some other feature of the relationship—money, fame, able-bodiedness, even looks—that make one person more dependent than the other on the relationship's continuance. These imbalances are sometimes correctable by ceding power to the less powerful member, but often the power imbalance suffuses the relationship permanently.

Children and patients have power in relating to parents and therapists because the parents and therapists care about them. Child abuse laws and ethical codes also provide children and patients with some power. But parents and therapists ultimately have the power advantage not only in affecting their subordinates but also in their enormous power to define the relationship. When a parent dismisses her child as cranky and thereby excludes her own unreliability from consideration or when a therapist frames her patient's uncooperative response as pathological, both are using power to define the relationship. Another source of power for therapists (and parents) is the breadth of their commission: "None of a patient's business, then, is none of the psychiatrist's business; nothing ought to be held back from the psychiatrist as irrelevant to his job. No other expert server with a system to tinker with seems to arrogate this kind of role to himself" (Goffman, 1961, p. 358).

Regardless of your power in a situation, you can play various status transactions. You can play lower, equal, or higher status in relation to the other people there. Successful trial attorneys and expert witnesses play very slightly lower with the judge, equal with the jury, and higher with the opposing attorney. In the movie *Arthur* (Greenhut & Gordon, 1981), Dudley Moore plays low status, while his servant, John Gielgud, plays high. It is funny because the audience constantly flip-flops on which is the master.

Power and status also depend on position, or role. The waiter and patron could have met at the patron's place of business—say he is a stockbroker. The waiter has made an appointment to discuss investment options for his retirement savings, and the position of potential investor changes the stockbroker's perception of the waiter's high-status moves. This example illustrates one solution to problems with a status hierarchy—to remind people that the shoe may someday be on the other foot. Sonny Bono ran for mayor of Palm Springs so he could fire the city employee who made it hard for him to clear his liquor license for the restaurant he wanted to open. Many people in this country are constrained in their status maneuvers and power plays because they know they will have to face the recipient and the community in church on Sunday.

Monitoring your position is a useful precursor to status maneuvering. A female professor teaches a class, and a male student raises his hand in a careless, indolent manner. The gesture communicates that he does not really care if he is called on but that if the professor chooses to allow the class to benefit from his insight, he is willing to contribute it. If the professor ignores the student, the student can play the scene as if the professor feels threatened by the student's superior insight. If the professor calls on the student, the student can have free rein to demonstrate that he already knew everything that the professor is saying. What is going on? The student finds the positional subordinate role as student aversive and is doing what he can to recast the student role in terms that are not subordinate. The professor finds the role of superior somewhat aversive as well because of misplaced fantasies of democracy and concern about turning into her father, who gave superiority a bad name by misusing it to stifle his children. So she plays low status because she wants her class to like her without realizing how playing low status also causes them to disrespect her. She monitors the position she is being put in by the arrogant male student, and she has an opportunity to play professor, but she declines it. Instead, she calls on the student and lets him put her in the role of colleague or even student. (There is nothing wrong with a professor playing colleague as long as she is merely visiting the role to demonstrate that the exchange of ideas is between equals and that scholarly status should depend on the power of the idea, not the power of the proponent.) The student plays high status because he always feels humiliated or ignored in the subordinate position. The student monitors the situation and sees that the professor's lecture is going well and finds himself cast in the role of student. He avoids this role by raising his hand and acting like an expert who happens to find himself there. Even licensed psychologists behave this way. In some states, they are required to attend workshops to maintain their licensure. You often see audience members trying to make clear to everyone else that they have greater expertise in the subject matter than the presenter. While it is frustrating for them to know more than the presenter, they might simply seek workshops in subjects about which they know little, but that would not solve the conflict between professional status and student role.

The student's power over the professor might be hidden. Perhaps his father is the dean. Perhaps he is respected by his classmates and can influence her course evaluations, which she needs to be positive for an upcoming tenure review. Perhaps she is intimidated by his intellect on a personal level. The same two people in slightly different positions will interpret each other's status moves differently. If she is supervising his senior thesis, they may interpret her power as having the potential of protecting him rather than as having the potential to hurt him. Without an audience, she may interpret his high status as confidence rather than as a challenge. All three—power, status, and position—come into play in all interactions.

STATUS AND SOCIAL CAPITAL

Status depends not only on how we act but also on our social position—what other people make of us. A social scientist showed that a stranger standing on a street corner looking up will induce more passersby to look up if he is well dressed. I know: duh. (My favorite social science finding ever was captured by this headline in the official newsletter of the American Psychological Association [2001, p. 10]: "Study relates desire for death in the terminally ill to depression, hopelessness.") So, okay, social science often tells us what we already know dressed up in numbers and citations, but my point is that what you wear, not just what you do, affects your status. I was involved in a different social science project where I was introduced to three different college classes as a visiting professor, a graduate student, and someone applying to graduate school. After I left, all three classes guessed my height (among other things), and sure enough, the more social capital attributed to me, the taller the college students thought I was. Even science itself dresses up to appear high status by using proper-sounding prose.

Our status is affected by what people make of us—not by what's true of us. It doesn't matter in face to face interaction whether you're rich and powerful if people think you're a working slob like the rest of us. And it works the other way, too—you can play high status even when you're not powerful because what matters is what people think. If you play high status, people may not like you (unless they are also inveterate high-status players), but they will respect you. If you play low status, people will like you, but they'll doubt your competence. It's not too hard to spot the degree to which boys are trained, in general, to play high status and girls low status.

STATUS FLEXIBILITY

One of the mistakes I made as a parent was not demanding that my kids respect me. I always thought that parents were wrong to demand respect from their children solely by virtue of their position as parents. I thought parents should earn their children's respect. In truth, I still think this. But I also think I did my kids a disservice by not teaching them how to play low status, which, I think, is what children actually learn when parents demand respect. My older son once asked a teacher in high school to sign a routine administrative form. The teacher called us at home, angry and insulted, saying, "I have never been spoken to by a student in such a manner." When she told us exactly what my son had said, there was nothing even remotely offensive in the content of his request. The complaint was the way he said it, and the way he said it was as if he were speaking to a peer. My younger son had similar encounters.

I personally don't like deference, but I should have taught my sons how to play it. People find it irritating, even enraging, to be accorded lower status (to be confronted with higher status) than they are expecting. They usually respond by trying to repair the status hierarchy, raising their own status or lowering that of the miscreant. This can lead to violence, but more often it leads to intimidation, bragging, or denigration. "Do you know who I am?" demanded the congressman of the security guard. Sometimes, status repair involves a further lowering of the injured party's status in order to elicit solicitous, status-raising conduct from the other person. This is called pouting.

BODY AND STATUS

Having a body is low status largely because we like to think that we are minds or spirits merely inhabiting our bodies—a fantasy that allows us to sidestep any implications of imperfection, mortality, or ordinariness. Much of what passes for good manners is really disguising the fact that we have bodies and that those around us do too. Belching and farting are, I'm glad to say, frowned on. But why am I glad? Probably because I have been trained to associate having a body with being embarrassed. If I pass gas, my status is lowered by my failure to control myself. How people respond depends largely on how they feel about having the higher ground: they can compound my humiliation by snorting, disguise their schadenfreude by being solicitous ("Are you well?"), or pretend they did not notice. When someone else farts, I have the same options. Close friends may not appreciate it when it happens, but they continue to play equal status. At a poker game, you can expect loud complaints about the potential odor, but the complaints are good-natured and not demeaning.

Death is horrifying not just because it is the end of what is known—death and the deterioration preceding it make it impossible to sustain a bodiless performance.

STATUS AND COMMENTING ON OTHERS

One extremely effective status move that may cross geographical and political lines is to comment on other people's behavior in a calm voice, which puts the other person in a child's role. Therapists love this maneuver. In a case conference, a therapist makes a point about her colleague's presentation, and the presenter responds by opining as to why the commenter "felt a need" to criticize him. The commenter retaliates by chiding the presenter for being "defensive." The defensive presenter returns fire with "I see you have a need to psychoanalyze me." This may seem like checkmate since the commenter must now shut up or confirm the hypothesis. However, in this game, there is always a higher metalevel of communication to step up to: "Is that how you see psychoanalysis? As a power ploy?"

The content argument is the least of their concerns. Of far greater importance is the status they are accorded and the role they are placed in. Politicians learn early on to avoid being cast as job applicants and to strive for the role of statesman. Early in his first presidential campaign, George W. Bush answered a reporter's question that challenged him to name the foreign minister of Mexico. Whether Bush knew the minister's name or not, his status was diminished by answering the question and accepting the role of pupil. After he was president, a reporter asked him how September 11 had changed him. Another curve ball—if it changed him, then he is just a man and not a statesman, but if it did not change him, then he is inhuman. Bush responded, "You'll have to ask my wife; I don't spend much time looking in the mirror except when I'm combing my hair." (That is, I cannot be described or characterized, but I am still a regular guy.)

GETTING OFF THE SEESAW

Two important things I did manage to teach my sons are to listen differently and to get off the seesaw. To listen differently, we must attend not only to the content of what is said but also to the role the speaker is casting us in. Often by merely observing the subservient role we are being cast in, our feelings of outrage can be quelled. If not, then we can usually comment on the situation in a way that retrieves our status in the transaction.

If you present a new idea at a conference, you can learn a lot about status. Some colleagues will weigh the idea, either privately or publicly, and evaluate it independently of the status concerns inherent in potentially learning something from someone else. Some will respect you for presenting the idea regardless of their evaluation of it. But some will dismiss you out of hand, playing high status, and they'll imply that it is not conceivable that a good, new idea could come from a source such as you. Most dismissers can't be engaged as equals—you can try citing their work as the foundation for your own, but groveling only makes high-status players content: it does not get you off the seesaw.

A few dismissers can be engaged as equals but only if you can set aside the anger that you feel on having your status lowered. This happened to me not too long ago when I presented a paper explaining why Minnesota Multiphasic Personality Inventory (MMPI) code typing is not statistically viable (Karson, 2005). My reasoning is not important for this discussion; what matters is the drubbing I received for questioning this established way of categorizing MMPI profiles. Some audience members, including some who are nationally known for interpreting MMPIs, were privately congratulatory afterward, although as one of them told me, he did not want to speak publicly for fear of being hit by the verbal rotten tomatoes aimed at me. None of the public scoffers spoke to me privately, and for the remainder of the fairly intimate conference they even avoided eye contact, presumably to keep me in my place as an uninformed interloper rather than to raise my status to colleague.

One psychologist approached me later that day and told me I didn't know what I was talking about and that he had a lot more confidence in Hathaway and Welsh (famous MMPI psychologists) than in me. Anger that in my youth would have produced a retaliatory put-down was met instead with a moment's reflection. Why did he bother to tell me this? Why not just ignore me as others were doing? I found a way to identify with him: "When it first occurred to me that code typing is not statistically defensible, I was pretty upset." "Damn right," he replied, suddenly a confidante: "It means I've been doing it wrong for thirty years." "I hate it when that happens," I said. We parted on friendly terms because my energy was directed at getting off the seesaw rather than at raising my stature on it. Lao-Tzu (1988) writes, "Since the Sage does not contend, no one can contend with the Sage" (No. 66). I think that a steady diet of disparagement showed me that I would never ascend that conference's status ladder, which helped me find a sagelike response.

STATUS CONFLICTS

Some conflicts are about the seesaw itself. This is rare, but it happens. The player of loud music may actually enjoy it at that volume, but it is also likely that he enjoys imposing himself on those around him. The sap in the next room, inundated by the loud music, initiates a conflict, and the conflict may be about status rather than noise. The recipient of loud music might not like the music, but it is also likely that the motivation for the complaint is her awareness that she is being subjected unwillingly to it. A better example might be the conflict when her neighbor leaves his garden hose barely in her yard. If she senses friendliness (if when face-to-face with the neighbor he plays equal or lower status), then the hose does not bother her. If she senses an air of entitlement or superiority (if when face to face he plays higher status), then the garden hose is infuriating. When siblings argue over whether one has encroached on the space of another, the conflict is purely over status. Another pure status conflict is the classic bar fight where one man brushes another as he passes and does not apologize. The brushed man is being treated as if he were a potted plant, and he reclaims his status with aggression: "Watch it, asshole." Since the brusher is now being treated as a low-status weakling, he must escalate to regain his own status. At this moment, either person could get off the seesaw by asserting his own status *not* at the other person's expense, and the conflict would likely dissolve. The brushed man could say, "No problem," and adopt the posture that it is up to himself to let it go, without putting the brusher in a down position (Smith, 2003). This drama also plays out in traffic when people treat each other as obstacles rather than as people and *cut each other off*, a locution that is enough in and of itself to make a normal person a Freudian.

Even conflicts that start off about some substantive issue quickly become about status, and the substantive issue recedes into the background. Many domestic squabbles end up not being about wasting money, flirting, or emptying the dishwasher—instead, lovers' quarrels almost always end up being about status. My partner's repeated failure to empty the dishwasher is annoying not because it means I have to do it but because it means I am unimportant. Even outside of romance, most conflicts become either energized or deflated depending on how the metaconflict is managed. By *metaconflict*, I mean the conflict over how we are going to manage the underlying substantive conflict. Is one party going to try to overpower the other? Is one party expected to be subservient and grateful? A commitment to resolving conflicts as equal-status partners in conflict resolution often makes conflicts evaporate since the resolution process itself soothes the status concerns of the parties.

STATUS GAMES

A fairly common negotiation technique, especially at higher levels of finance and law, is to play on people's tendency to confuse status and power. By wearing expensive clothes, keeping the opposition waiting, sitting in leather chairs, and meeting in walnut-paneled conference rooms, one side uses the trappings of power to communicate that it has actual power (Meltsner & Schrag, 1974). Another trapping of power is the way status is played behaviorally: each side is emotionally reserved and demonstrates ownership of space. You can play high status regardless of your power or position. If your opponent offers you rich coffee in expensive china, complain about how quickly it cools and ask for a Styrofoam cup. If it is served with a variety of creams and milk products, ask for a soy latte. In other words, if your opponent tries to intimidate you, reject the underlying premise of the intimidation.

We can make an informed choice about whether to raise our status or to try to get off the seesaw by attending to the metaconflict (the conflict over how the conflict will be resolved) and addressing it. Toward the end of the Vietnam War, the North Vietnamese and the Americans agreed to engage in peace talks in Paris. A great deal of time was spent negotiating the shape of the table and the seating arrangements. Although this was largely a delaying tactic, as both sides hoped that new developments would strengthen their bargaining positions, it was also a dry run on a trivial issue in which both sides could discover how the real issues would be handled. Would one side be making concessions? Would one side make unreasonable demands? Could both sides count on the other to stand by offers and acceptances? You can test the water with equal status to see if it will be met with equal status before resorting to high-handedness. Biologists call this strategy tit for tat.

STATUS MANEUVERS

Johnstone (1981) writes that many people become status *specialists*, generally playing high, low, or equal. He adds that an effective actor must learn how to play all three, and the same might be said for an effective social actor. Here is a list of status moves (many of which were appropriated from Johnstone). The equal-status version of these moves is, typically, simply to do what the other person does. Notice the extent to which low-status moves are what children do and high-status moves are what adults can do that children can't.

High-status maneuvers	Low-status maneuvers
Head still ("I already know")	Nod ("I'm listening")
Hands still	Touch face; fidget
Stand tall	Hunch over
Emotionally reserved	Emotionally expressive
Indirect bragging ("When I was in school, in New Haven . . .")	Direct bragging ("I went to Yale")
Smirk	Smile
Comment on other	Comment on self
Tell (lower inflection even for questions)	Ask (raise inflection even for statements)
Stride	Run or trudge
Maintain eye contact	Break eye contact
Expand personal space (jacket on next seat)	Restrict personal space (jacket on seat back)
Speak in complete sentences	Er, um, ah (short, interruptible ers, not long ones that hold the floor)
Declare facts ("Paris is lovely")	Offer opinions ("I like Paris") or ask questions ("What was loveliest?")
Ignore defeats	Worry
Arrive late	Arrive early
Get even	Get angry
Relax	Sweat
Primp subtly (before seeing others)	Primp a lot or not at all

All these behaviors are on a continuum. To play slightly higher or slightly lower, do them just a bit more or less than the other person. To play equal status, imitate the other person and constantly think, "Me too." If they say, "I made a million-two last year" and you only made forty grand, thinking "me, too" leads to saying, "Yeah, it was a banner year all around." To play high status, you should be thinking, "That's nothing" (as in, "That's nothing, my daughter's at Yale") or "That's too bad." For example: "I made a million-two last year." Response: "Oh dear." When Mr. $1.2m gets offended, just apologize: "I sincerely regret having offended you." You're in the position of offering condolences and apologies, not in the position of seeking them. To play low status, you should be thinking, "I only," as in "I only went to the University of Colorado" or "I only drive a Ford Escort." If you drive a Hummer, "I only get twelve miles a gallon." If you went to Yale, "I only have book smarts."

If you get pulled over for speeding, should you play high status or low? It depends. Basically, status comes down to whether you communicate having something they need or needing something they have. If you have something the cop wants or needs, then you can play high status effectively. I know three people who never pay tickets. Neal is an ex-cop, shot in the line of duty. He keeps his Purple Heart propped in his glove compartment, so when a cop asks for his registration, it sort of pops out. Cops want friendliness from cops with Purple Hearts. Neal doesn't want the other cop to think he knows he has a free pass, so he pretends to hide it. A colleague of mine, Daniel, always plays on the cop's boredom with lame excuses. He says, "If I tell you an excuse you've never heard before, will you let me go?" The cop invariably says, "I've heard them all." Once, Daniel said, "I have an illegal radar detector because I love my grandmother." He went on to say that he drives her around and uses it to avoid microwaves that can affect her pacemaker. Cops like stories, and Daniel trades stories for speeding tickets. I was driving with a friend, Jane, in Boston when she ran a red light to make an illegal left turn up the wrong side of a busy street. A cop pulled her over and, as he approached the car, Jane told me, "Open the glove compartment." I opened it expecting to see her registration, but the only thing in it was bright red lipstick. She quickly applied it and unbuttoned the top two buttons of her shirt. The cop let her go with a warning.

At a workshop with Keith Johnstone, he told us that the secret of getting the job (once you manage to get an interview on merit) is to play equal status. If you play low status, people will think you are nice, but they will question your competence (this happened to me frequently). If you play high status, people will think you can do the job, but they won't want to work with you. By playing equal status, people will see you as fitting right in. I tried this at a job interview, and it went smoothly until I was being interviewed by two people at once, one of whom was playing high status, the other playing low. I wish I had a videotape of myself. I would look left, utterly stone-faced, speak in complete sentences, and communicate indifference. I would look right, nod my head enthusiastically, blurt out humorous comments, and touch my face.

Recently, a psychologist on my listserv asked us what she should do about a prosecutor she had irritated by her response to his subpoena. Instead of accepting service by mail, she exercised her legal right to make a deputy bring the subpoena to her office. A number of us suggested she call the prosecutor and make nice since he could make her life miserable if he wanted to. Others congratulated her on teaching him a lesson in manners and reminded her that if he got too feisty, she could report him to the judge. The first group was a bunch of low-status players, and the second group was a bunch of high-status players. High status incorporates and communicates a sense that the world will yield to you; low status communicates that you must yield to others. (First children—who create their families by being born—play high status more comfortably than later children—who adjust to preexisting families.) High-status players sometimes run afoul of reality and suffer the consequences; low-status players sometimes miss out on opportunities and rewards they would have gotten if they had demanded them. It is high status to be an optimist—why shouldn't things go well for such a deserving soul? It is low status to be a pessimist—to settle for whatever is offered.

STATUS IN PSYCHOTHERAPY

Therapists are supposed to be honest, upright, and true. Goffman tells us the only way to become the front that we present to the world is to believe it ourselves. In other words, nobody is honest, upright, and true because everyone has a backstage—but you can play these virtues by believing thoroughly that you have them and ignoring your backstage. So the real choice is not between honesty and dishonesty but between self-deception (believing your mask is your face) and self-acceptance (wearing a mask). When strategic family therapists manipulate the family to achieve therapeutic goals, some observers recoil at the manipulation involved. But the truth is that all therapists manipulate their clients, and I see no virtue in doing so accidentally or unconsciously rather than strategically. Thus, what I am really asking here is not whether and how therapists should play status but rather how thoughtfully and deliberately therapists should play status. Thoughtless and reactive therapists play status in a manner that suits their own familial roles and their feelings about power, while thoughtful therapists play status in a manner that furthers the therapy goals.

A therapist, like a good actor, must learn to play different status transactions fluidly so that she can subject this central aspect of lively relating to deliberate decision making. If a therapist is incapable of or uncomfortable with playing high or low status, such choices are constrained. Women often have trouble playing high status—they bob their heads, constantly smile, and stream mm-hmms while listening to others. I asked one trainee to knock it off for a week, and she reported that a disconcertingly large number of friends and relatives asked her if she was depressed or angry. Some men have the same problem, but girls are more likely than boys to be trained to play low status. Conversely, men often have trouble playing low status or even equal status. They adopt an imperious, emotionally blank attitude when approached by students, waiters, or employees—what Shakespeare called the insolence of office. They do not like intersubjectivity or radical behaviorism because it is low status to have a psychology. Inflexible therapists who refuse to play equal status with patients cannot truly engage them; those who refuse to play higher status with patients cannot replicate the hierarchy to which most patients need nonpunitive exposure. Both types waste patients' time and money.

JOINING AND HOMEOSTASIS

Some family therapists advocate a *one-down* (slightly lower status) position with clients, presenting themselves as ignorant and clumsy. They are concerned about joining and homeostasis. Joining means the process by which one enters a system, which is especially touchy with reluctant patients. Usually, we join by playing equal status, by letting the client know we share certain experiences or values or by demonstrating an ability to speak their language. In film, Judd Hirsch's therapist in *Ordinary People* (Schwary & Redford, 1980) starts with Timothy Hutton's patient by exhibiting his incompetence with his own radio, and Claude Rains's psychiatrist in *Now, Voyager* (Wallis & Rapper, 1942) comes to meet Bette Davis's neurotic in her own home and asks *her* for help.

Homeostasis means the tendency of a system to right itself. If a pattern does not have self-regulating and self-perpetuating (homeostatic) functions, it will cease to be a pattern. Some family therapists worry that a high-status move will push for change and the family will push back. Playing one-down, both positionally and in presentation of self, can diminish the threat of forced change and reduce the system's homeostatic response.

STATUS AND THE ROLE OF THERAPIST

The meaning of a status maneuver depends on the definition of the role relationships involved. A doctor who plays low status sends a very different message from a waiter who does it. The individual therapist's job is to capitalize on the power differential in therapy, not to disavow or disperse it. One exception to this may be a situation where the therapist does not have much power to begin with. For example, a patient attends sessions to get her partner to stop bugging her, and the fee is paid in full by health insurance. Or a person with a lot of social capital seeks treatment at a training clinic where the therapist has little social capital, the fee is reduced, and the therapist's role is defined as student rather than doctor. In these situations, the therapist must use her lack of power, rather than her power, therapeutically—often by demonstrating her comfort with powerlessness.

Using one's power doesn't mean a continual display of it. Once the relationship is defined as fundamentally hierarchical, the therapist can visit equal and even slightly lower statuses without endangering the definition of the relationship, just as a reliable and authoritative parent can profitably act goofy and impulsive at times. But these episodes must be a play within a play, with all the framing operations necessary to set them off as episodes. A therapist caught looking nervous must frame the situation as a momentary stumble rather than as a discrediting backstage glimpse of her essential insecurity. The main difference is how the therapist plays status when her nervousness is exposed. If she maintains her composure and reflects wisely and maturely on her own psychology, her nervousness need not be discrediting. If she ignores it or otherwise treats its exposure as dangerous, her ability to maintain her therapeutic face will be seriously compromised.

If status moves can be broken down into lower, slightly lower, equal, slightly higher, and higher, I don't see any advantage to playing lower or even slightly lower in the typical individual therapy. The "me, too" quality of equal status is enough to engross the patient in a mutual moment and create a team. Again, I am not talking about admitting ignorance or foibles or personality; I am talking about *how* one does so. Even equal status transactions must occur in a larger frame of a power differential—otherwise, they will define the relationship as nonhierarchical. And the status hierarchy in therapy must itself be an episode—therapy—in a larger frame of equality. The handshake at the start of therapy, whether expressed metaphorically in the therapy contract or literally in the waiting area the first day, is to me an agreement that our human equality will be put into the background and that the frame of the power differential will be treated as primary for the duration of the contract.

Chapter Five

Gender Is Something We Do, Not Something We Are

Twas the Greeks love of war
Turnd Love into a Boy
And Woman into a Statue of Stone
And away fled every Joy

—William Blake, *Why Was Cupid a Boy*

Gender is one of society's main categories and one of its main sources of behavioral expectations. To study rules, categories, and expectations is to consider alternatives, and to consider alternatives is to enhance liveliness. The study of gender subverts power because it raises questions about who is behind the party line and to what purpose. To be curious about gender is to question the hegemony and its sex role rules.

GENDER AS A PERFORMANCE

Performance theorist Judith Butler (1990, pp. 43–44; 1993) describes gender as "the repeated stylization of the body, a set of repeated acts within a highly rigid regulatory frame that congeal over time to produce the appearance of substance, of a natural sort of being." The performance bent is critical to her approach: "There is no gender identity behind the expressions of gender; that identity is performatively constituted by the very 'expressions' that are said to be its results" (1990, p. 33). She (2004) tentatively defined gender as "the cultural significance that the sexed body assumes" (p. 275), a definition she did not fully adopt because it did not acknowledge that sexing the body is itself a cultural act, but this definition (with that caveat) is still useful. Most emphatically, by *cultural significance*, Butler means socially constructed as opposed to biologically determined meanings. Gender is not only communicated but also created by performed acts, whose fate in the relevant culture determines their endurance. Skinner would say that people try out all sorts of gendered behavior and find that some efforts are allowed and some are not allowed, with nonallowance expressed as violence, scorn, ridicule, disapproval, and guidance.

Also explicit in Butler's approach to gender is a recognition that the link between maleness and masculinity and the link between femaleness and femininity are socially and politically constructed. These links are not entirely arbitrary in the sense that they serve a reproductive purpose by separating the sexes, by constellating sexual attraction between them, and, biologists would add, by creating an organizational structure for managing access to the uterus. Butler's point is that gendering is not arbitrary, but its specific attributes are.

Like many evolved practices, gendering could be replaced by a different practice constructed by us to enhance political goals if we wanted to. An analogy is the way technology has changed the definition of maladaptive traits by supplementing what formerly were deficits. Medical theory has replaced selection pressures against poor eyesight with glasses. Political theory could replace management of uterine access with some scheme other than patriarchy, for example, by leaving it up to the individual woman.

The term *sexed body* is also central to the performative approach to gender. It emphasizes that framing people as male or female is not a fundamental fact of life but a social construction. Yes, there is a real difference between male and female (and there are people who are neither), but this one difference need not be a fundamental frame. If we constructed a society in which life's roles were as bifurcated by earlobes as they are in our culture by genitals, then the first thing parents and grandparents would want to know at birth would be attached or unattached, not boy or girl. Sexing the body is something that we do, not something that must be done.

Goffman (1959) summarizes his approach to the socially constructed self: "The self, then, as a performed character, is not an organic thing that has a specific location, whose fundamental fate is to be born, to mature, and to die; it is a dramatic effect arising diffusely from a scene that is presented, and the characteristic issue, the crucial concern, is whether it will be credited or discredited" (pp. 252–253). When crediting or discrediting a performance is based on the sex of the performer, we call that performance gender.

Masculinity is the set of performed acts under specific conditions that society accepts in males, *femininity* those it accepts in females. The term *society* in that phrase bears scrutiny. Goffman (1963) is clear that a stigmatizing society can be as small as a single person and as evanescent as a moment.

When big brothers chide little brothers but console little sisters for crying at school, they are teaching gender.

GENDER LABELS

Gender is a function of its stigmatizing environment. I use *yang* and *yin* instead of *masculine* and *feminine* because *masculine* and *feminine* sound necessarily linked to their respective sexes, while *yang* and *yin* sound arbitrary. Indeed, much that passes for femininity has little to do with being a woman and has much to do with the way those not in power appeal to those in power. Butler (2004) is also concerned about reifying gender expectations using the traditional labels *masculine* and *feminine* and even extends that concern to the labels *man* and *woman*. An analogous concern arises in psychiatry with the noun *schizophrenic*, which not only elevates the stigma into a definition of the person concerned but also focuses our attention on the wrong question. Turning diagnoses into nouns makes us ask who is and who is not schizophrenic. Even the politically correct *persons with schizophrenia* only makes us ask who has and who does not have the disease. The more useful question is when—under what circumstances does the person behave schizophrenically (or compulsively or hysterically or what have you)? The preferred (though awkward) term would be *persons who behave schizophrenically*, a term that gladly includes everyone. Instead of *women* or *men*, we might use (in light of discussions defining sex by external genital appearances) *persons who behave vaginistically* or *persons who behave penilely*—that is, people using their genitals and reproductive systems and people in situations where not to sex their bodies would be biologically unreasonable. I mean situations such as deciding whether to do a pap smear or a prostate exam or deciding whether to prepare your child for wet dreams or menstruation. This terminology, unwieldy and amusing as it seems at first blush, allows for the idea that nobody is always a woman or a man and the vast majority of people are women or men only rarely.

SEXUAL CATEGORIES

Butler (1999) writes, "I continue to hope for a coalition of sexual minorities that will transcend the simple categories of identity. . . . I would hope that such a coalition would be based on the irreducible complexity of sexuality" (p. xxvi). But we are all sexual minorities, as anyone knows who has looked at his or her own sexual proclivities. The only majority in sexuality is the pretense of not having a backstage, a pretense that makes our sexuality seem uncouth and disruptive, which leads the party line to condemn it. Condemnation is facilitated by categories, just as racial categories facilitated apartheid. The result is a public posture alienated from pleasure, passion, and joy. The culture in an individual therapy may have a different agenda from the larger culture, but the important thing is not what is marginalized in the therapy relationship but how the margins are treated by the prevailing party line. Deadly therapy teaches us to live in the mainstream, a mainstream that is a fiction of polite hegemony. Lively therapy teaches us to live on the margins, with ourselves.

GENDER AS A THERAPY TOPIC

Like status, gender is a useful therapy topic because it's pervasive, hidden, and usually played thoughtlessly. Its pervasiveness assures its relevance to any transaction described by the patient. Its hiddenness means that in addressing gender, one also helps the patient learn to consider what else is hidden from view. Discussing gender can be a laboratory for the "invisible made visible" (Brook, 1968, p. 41). Its usual unconsciousness can make gender considerations a training ground for performing the self deliberately instead of reactively.

When I was doing college counseling, I could make do in a pinch with only three interventions. The first was, "Sounds like you're having some feelings about leaving home." The last was, "Sounds like you're thinking about stopping" (because the therapies were time limited and patients often had to be prompted to think about leaving). The third intervention was, for women, "Sounds like your version of being a woman doesn't fit precisely with your parents' version," and, for men, "So, how's that definition of manhood working out for you?"

Goffman (1963) says that we all seem to know how to play the stigmatized and normal roles, judging from the speed with which we adopt them when our performances are discredited or restored. One training ground for learning these roles is gender since all of us have been trained how to play boy or girl, with unexpected or deviant actions stigmatized. When gender expectations are consistent, we simply place our discrepant behaviors backstage. Punished behaviors do not lose their strength; they merely wait until the punisher is not present for expression. Sexual fantasies frequently show gender's backstage. The cowboy fantasizes about wearing women's underwear, the captain of industry loves being dominated, and the stay-at-home mother imagines meaningless sex.

Another reason to tackle gender in psychotherapy is to further a conception of health as androgynous (Kaplan, 1976). "Know the male, maintain the female," advised Lao-Tzu (1988, No. 28). Psychological health requires both yin and yang in goodly measure, so people find themselves stymied when effective behavior is constrained by gender considerations. Common examples include women who need to learn how to express their opinions without excessive concern for the effect on other people's feelings and men whose families are falling apart for want of affection. A vast array of therapy goals are easily within the patient's behavioral repertoire, but achievement of the goals contradicts some precept as to how the patient is supposed to behave, and often these precepts are gendered.

PLAYING GENDER AS A THERAPIST

Whether or not androgyny is central to healthy functioning in all areas of life, I certainly believe that good therapists are androgynous. I would like to write that we should be good mommies and good daddies both, but out of concern for reifying what is expected of mothers and fathers, I will say instead that in a fiduciary position of power, we must provide all of what many parents divide between them, such as warmth, curiosity, reliability, stability, guidance, limit setting, challenge, and support.

Sexing the body is high on our list of priorities when we meet someone new. *Sexing* in that sentence means sorting into males and females. Sexing's presence in virtually every culture is evidence that it is human nature, although this does not mean we should continue to do it, any more than we should indulge our homicidal genes. Anyway, we are aware of the patient's sex, and he is aware of ours. Along with his awareness comes a host of expectations about how we will and won't behave.

Underlying gender studies is the recognition that certain stereotypes perpetuate simply because they are stereotypes—they define what is acceptable in gendered behavior, they are followed, and they become true. When both patient and therapist share a sex role stereotype, it remains unspoken and can constrict the therapy. This was brought home to me at a workshop I attended long ago to hear Sal Minuchin teach therapy. His approach resolves role ambiguities largely by imposing clearer role relationships on families. I asked him if his blueprint for a functional family had changed over the course of his career, and he said the greatest changes were influenced by feminism. He used to cajole and push for very stereotyped roles for women and men, but by examining his own sex role expectations, he broadened the array of possibilities open to his client families.

In individual therapy, certain behaviors often play better when performed by men than by women. When a man embodies Albert Ellis's scoffing disputation, it comes off as playful, but when a woman does it, it can come off as hurtful. Women in power are often expected to act tender and soothing—"nice"—rather than to put their arm around our shoulders and give us a playful slug. When a man embodies Kohut's tender concern, he is showing his affectionate core, but when a woman does it, she is abdicating her authority. When a man utters the classic Kohutian line, "I've disappointed you," it's understood that he is acknowledging the harm done but not asking for forgiveness or consolation. Coming from a woman, it can seem like an apology. When a man ends a session on time, he's firm; a woman is heartless. Sometimes, adaptive behaviors play better on women than on men but usually not when she is in power. A woman who carries out her supervisor's exact instructions is cooperative, but a man who does so may feel and may be perceived as submissive (unless he compensates with a uniform and a firearm). Because women are generally expected to play lower status than men, special problems arise when they are expected to play high status as a therapist. Women surgeons, investment counselors, professors, and mechanics face the same problem.

Generic solutions to these problems won't do, but finding specific solutions is facilitated by seeing them as performance problems. If an actor has trouble playing a part because she's the wrong age, sex, or race, she needs to create a different frame for the production from the let's-pretend-you-are-looking-in-on-reality frame. If a young woman plays Lear, she can signal to the audience that they are to accept her as Lear, and then she need not even wear a beard. The other actors can help by muttering, "The King, it's the King," as she approaches and bow before her. The audience, then, is in on it, not asked to accept her as *old* but asked to accept her as *playing* old, just as when an old man plays Lear, the audience is not asked to accept that he is the King but only playing the King. When Olivier played Lear late in life, the audience was asked to disattend to much about him that breached a framing of the play as real, not least of which was the fact that he spoke, however intimate his sentiments, in a voice loud enough to be heard throughout the theater. A young woman cast as Lear must ask the audience to disattend to even more things, but as long as they have been asked and as long as the woman does not appear to think she can pass for Lear without their help, her youth and femininity need not discredit her performance. The young therapist who requires patients to accept her as genuinely wise, tempered, and authoritative will be discredited, but the therapist who includes the patients in her casting problems benefits from whatever goodwill they bring (and if they do not bring enough goodwill for this, she cannot help them in any event), and the resulting frame keeps her casting problems from discrediting her.

It is a good idea to metacommunicate when the therapist's body is sexed. "You seem conscious of me as a man," I told a patient who looked hesitant to nurse her new baby in a session. As a result of the pregnancy, birth, and nursing, her own body was more sexed than it had ever been in her life, and the ensuing discussion gave her a chance to reflect on her gender expectations of not only me but also herself. Metacommunication is trickier for female therapists when the patient is male because "you seem conscious of me as a woman" has a sexual connotation since sexing the female body is so often in our culture combined with lowering its status by also sexualizing it. She may need to start one level higher, metacommunicating about metacommunicating: "Let's talk about your expectations of me."

PLAYING GENDER OPPOSITE EACH OTHER

A woman unbuttoning her shirt to nurse the infant in her arms isn't sexy to me, so I could innocently, if implicitly, suggest she do so. I think patients sense any prurience in the therapist, so if it's there, it can't be disguised, and if it's not there, there's no need for caution. Even patients I find attractive out of context lose their attraction once I define the relationship as caregiving and hierarchical. Therapists who are attracted to people in a subordinate position probably have a more difficult time of it.

Sexiness nearly always sexes the body, perhaps needless to say, as lust has a way of making both persons' sex salient, and once the body is sexed, gender expectations abound. How can the therapy relationship be kept from constellating a sexy frame, when in so many ways it looks like something lovers do? We intimately discuss the patient's life and our mutual interactions in a way that most men experience only, if ever, with lovers. Some women (and a few men) achieve this level of intimacy in friendships, and this makes it harder for female therapists to resist defining the relationship as a friendship. But both male and female therapists must be careful to distinguish the therapy frame from a romantic frame, especially since the sessions have certain earmarks associated with assignations: they are often clandestine, it takes only a few seconds to make the transition from social to intimate, they can occupy the imagination of at least one of the parties throughout the week, and they offer the same kind of soothing and acceptance found with sexual vulnerability and warm embrace. Analogous problems face doctors who do to patients things that look very much like sex acts, framed differently by demeanor and set design. Although therapists do not palpate, insert, or thump, we do have conversations that could easily be framed as romance.

We frame our doctorly or teacherly presence as more fundamental than our sexed body by responding therapeutically or educationally when we could respond either sexually (which is unethical) or as sexed (which is not unethical but which can challenge the frame). However, it is not entirely up to the professional to define the frame. A female friend of mine went with her husband to see her attractive male doctor and told him that she had been having headaches and needed a pap smear. He conducted a pelvic exam first, and when he put his gloved fingers in her vagina, she quipped, "Hey, my headache went away." Even though the quip was protected by the presence of the husband—the usual nurse had not been included because the husband was present—it ruptured the clinical frame, and suddenly the doctor was just a guy with his hand in her vagina. He started to remove his hand, realized that once it was removed the frame would not be reconstructible, blushed, and continued the exam. The doctor's youth, physical attractiveness, and air of confidence evoked a sexual frame for my friend. If he had spent more time discussing the medical implications of a pap smear and if he had deprived her of her audience (her husband), he would probably have maintained a clinical frame.

Other examples of the clinical frame faltering in the face of the gender frame are not hard to find. I treated an Orthodox Jewish woman who would not shake my hand in the waiting room because contact between the sexes is forbidden. A disturbed man masturbated semisurreptitiously while discussing his attraction to me. I worked with a disturbed woman for many months before she let it slip that she thought we were dating.

Usually, such faltering is a function of the therapist's lapses in framing the relationship clinically. My headachy friend's doctor may have already keyed a social frame by responding to her and her husband in a myriad of ways that implicitly recognized that they could easily be friends, not the least of which was his decision to dispense with the regular nurse, whose purpose is precisely to avert such framing conflicts. When therapists socialize with patients, in the name of democratizing or warming the relationship, they weaken the clinical frame. By *socialize*, I do not mean going out for tea, although goodness knows some therapists make such dates with patients; I mean chatting on the way to the office, asking how they are, commenting on the weather, and so on. Once a clinical frame is firmly established, it operates like any other authoritative frame in that it can sustain some minor departures. At the beginning of the relationship, however, it is important to nail it down. Since we live in a world that sexes women's bodies more than men's, this is a greater challenge for female therapists than for male therapists.

If yin stumbles in therapy by making the relationship too social, yang stumbles by making it too much about the therapist. I call this shining versus polishing—men are trained in yang modes of self-expression, shining at the expense of group process, while women are trained in yin modes of polishing or facilitating the shining of others. When I do therapy, my ideal is for patients to leave therapy thinking of *themselves* rather than of me as insightful, creative, and socially adept while thinking of me as merely reliable and trustworthy. (I had the same goal with my children.) Working against that ideal is a lifelong history of reinforcement for showing off.

One way we cope with social anxiety is by trying to look our best, especially when we are young. *Our best* often translates to our sexiest, whether brazen or refined, plucked or natural, done up or undone. Every year, a colleague of mine takes a group of forensic psychology graduate students to tour a local prison, every year she admonishes the women to cover up, and every year, despite their best efforts, several of them wear outfits that male inmates would find so provocative that the guards don't let them in. (My colleague brings bulky sweaters for last-minute repairs.) Psychotherapy trainees are told to dress professionally on days they see clients, but professional dress tends to exaggerate sex differences and unnecessarily genders the relationship. Choice of their own clothing is just the kind of thing that therapists prefer to ignore, but it need not be a big problem if the therapist is willing to discuss it. After all, to the extent that the patient's problem is a gender problem—and, according to gender theory, that is a much larger extent than one might otherwise think since psychopathology is so often a function of stigma and role inflexibility and so many of the roles one could successfully play in life are restricted by gender concerns—placing gender concerns in the foreground of the therapy can be an opportunity to explore them. Analogously, cross-sex casting is less of a directorial problem when the play is about gender. But even when the problem is framed as a gender problem, therapists frequently fail to capitalize on the gendered therapy either because they have failed to establish a strong enough clinical frame to sustain discussions about sex roles or because they do not see their own gender performance as a performance and instead see it as just the way they are—a perspective that makes gender hard to discuss. When the patient's problem is not a gender problem, unnecessarily sexing the relationship is just a distraction. Often, it is a defensive maneuver that avoids intimacy, either by establishing a power differential (let's seat our intimacy in the context of the fact that you want me but can't have me) or by substituting a titillating but superficial topic for what is more pertinent (let's talk about sex rather than the fact that I disappointed you).

Therapists and patients play gender opposite each other when the patient can choose to act yin or yang in relation to the therapist. For example, a patient who notices that her therapist is tired may facilitate the relationship by tactfully ignoring it or may express herself by stating how it makes her feel unimportant. The therapist's interest in keeping his tiredness backstage will miss an opportunity to facilitate the patient's yang expressiveness. The therapist is especially likely to miss this opportunity if he defines the relationship as a doctor–patient

one where he must live up to a superhuman role and the patient is not authorized to be strong. Yang and yin therapists alike should take care not to define
their male patients as overcoming their hardships and their female patients as
needing support.

GENDER IN A SYSTEMIC FRAME

Some gender theorists have pointed out the paradox inherent in claiming that
men subjugate women (Lerner, 1986). They see patriarchy as systemically
created, impressed by the collaborative effort required. In fact, many marginalized men—especially those who want something from the patriarchy—act
with as much yin as mainstream women do, suggesting that what is called
feminine is actually an adjustment to powerlessness. Women in power seem
to start as many wars proportionately as men in power, suggesting that yang
is actually an adjustment to having power. Indeed, whatever you might think
of Derrida's and Chuang-Tzu's emphasis on the way a term constellates its
opposite, it seems pretty clear that the words *male* and *female* and *man* and
woman have no meaning except in the context of the duality.

Beyond the logical problems with viewing men and women as operating
independently of each other, there are political problems as well. If men subjugate women, then the political power is held by men, and there is little
women can do about it. If the system subjugates women, well, women are
part of the system. Janoff-Bulman (1982) found that victims often fare better
when they blame themselves because even though self-blame is upsetting, it
enhances an internal locus of control and a sense that the victim can do something about it. Women who view themselves as part of the problem construct
a world in which they can do something about the problem. In this section, I
intend to analogize the battle of the sexes to the individual's psychology and
to analogize the feminist agenda to the therapeutic. I have begun that analogy
by claiming that both sexes are part of a system, as are the functions of an individual's psychology, and are irretrievably interlinked.

THE REPRODUCTIVE SYSTEM

In sexual reproduction, gametes that happened to be larger competed well because they contained more nourishment for the developing embryo. But their
large size meant that other gametes could compete not by providing more internal nutrients once combined but by proliferating at a smaller size to increase the chances of mating. Big gametes mating with big gametes did well,
but they had trouble bumping into each other. Small gametes could easily

bump into each other, but they did not contain many nutrients between them. Eventually, large gametes reproduced only with small ones. You might say the small ones exploited the large size of the big ones. The name for the gametes selected for large size is female; the name for gametes selected for motility and profusion is male. (Because allusions to biology often seem to justify its effects as natural, let's be clear that the fact that some of our sexual urges evolved in a certain way does not make them preferable any more than it is preferable to die naturally at the age of 30 or 40.)

In the reproductive sense, women are occupied with gestation for 9 months, and usually with nursing for a few months after. Men are occupied for a matter of minutes. This ratio corresponds to the egg–sperm ratio: the human egg is about 50,000 times larger than the human sperm, and there are about 50,000 10-minute intervals in a year. Geographically, there are many important resources for human survival, including food, water, and shelter. It's widely accepted among evolutionary biologists that the most important sexual resource by far is womb time. Just as societies organize access to geographical resources, they have organized access to sexual resources. As the object of that organization, women were put in an objectified role. (If reproduction seems not to be that central to your own self-concept, consider that whatever your own attitude toward children, you are here because well over a billion generations of your direct ancestors reproduced successfully. You have more ancestors than you can imagine, and not one of them failed to have children. In the evolutionary game, you come from an amazing string of reproductive winners, with no losers among them. Surely, that common trait of all of them has something to do with you.)

The existential dilemma—the paradox of living with an infinite mind in a finite body—can be considered in gender terms. The brainpower that makes us capable of imagination, communication, problem solving, and abstraction also makes us aware of death. We identify with thought because it seems like thought controls nature (Blake, 1794), and given a choice between dominant and submissive roles, we prefer to identify with the dominant, controlling, immortal abstraction rather than with the submissive, mortal corpus. All of us are introduced to this drama in the role of corpus, as infants, as that-which-is-controlled. All of us switch sides as soon as we can and believe that we own rather than are our bodies.

THE PORNOGRAPHIC MIND

Griffin (1981) offers an account of what she calls "the pornographic mind," a term she attributes not to individuals but to a cultural worldview. She describes the pornographic mind as a way of looking at nature that subdues and

even humiliates it to prove that nature's powerful, chaotic dyscontrol is be-
neath us. In our society, that worldview has largely distilled into patterns of
men turning women into humiliated and physical objects while themselves
playing the role of puppeteer, although a fairly common variant reveals the
backstage of the patriarchy and has women in the dominant role.

In pop culture, perhaps nobody plays with this theme better than Madonna,
who, for example, in "Open Your Heart," turns the role of humiliated victim
into one of power. In the music video, she is an exotic dancer but a powerful
one whose audience is caged in glass. Instead of being humiliated by their interest in her body, she sings, "You're afraid to look in my eyes. You look a little sad, boy." Another variation on the theme is the character of Hannibal
Lecter, who is to men what men are to women, only more so: he controls,
kills, and even eats them. Both exemplify a famous use of performance in
psychotherapy—Cloé Madanes's (1981) techniques of either pretending to
have the symptom or exaggerating it. Both techniques demonstrate that the
symptom can be under the patient's control. Both allow the patient to perform
the symptom without the usual conviction as to its sincerity. Both let the patient observe its effect on the relevant system. Madonna's pretense works
well, and it's a way of owning a role otherwise forced on her (Irigaray [1985]
advises women to own their sex roles; Nietzsche [1977], with the concept of
amor fati, advises everyone to own everything). Hannibal Lecter's exaggerations do not work well (accepting for a moment the novel's frame as primary—his exaggerations work just fine as entertainment) because there is no
level of dominance that satisfies him. One would not prescribe symptom exaggeration for a batterer, either.

Griffin's pornographic mind is contemptuous of nature, joy, and the
body. Those who embody roles that are natural, joyful, or corporeal become receptacles for the projective identifications of those who would be
supernatural, transcendent, and spiritual or intellectual. Disdain helps the
projectors disown and repudiate the physical, like a self-righteous moralist
preaching against sin. A desire for immortality needs to assign intimations
of mortality to others. Women seem almost to invite this bodily assignment
as they get pregnant, menstruate, and excite men's lust. When an angel gets
turned on, it makes him wonder if he really is an angel—it's easier to
equate the stimulus with deviltry than to consider his own humanity. Children, too, have a way of embodying the natural, the joyful, and the corporeal that just makes you want to cluck your tongue. It's not yang or even
masculinity in this view that triumphs; it's transcendence, abstraction, and
immortality. Facticity, quotidian concerns, and mortality are repudiated,
not yin or femininity. The confusion of transcendence with masculinity and
facticity with femininity stems from how easily women (and children) are

assigned to bodily roles, an ease that has prospered in the context of evolved strategies for uterus management.

The excitation of lust has been especially problematic for women. In the 15th century, discouraged by the fact that absolute political power had not produced a paradise on earth, the Church came up with the *Malleus Malefi-carum*, a treatise that blamed the Devil and his minions, that is, witches, that is, women. If it were not for women, men would not be troubled by lust. Only a couple of monks could invent such a thesis, but it soon became doctrinal: male sin is blamed on women. She made me eat the apple. (I'm not taking a profligate swipe at monks, by the way. I'm noting how backstages look so often like inverted front stages. When morality is pursued by repudiating sin, slips will be sinful. Adjustment to Thou Shall Not produces a backstage of licentiousness. When celibacy is pursued by condemning lust, lust will haunt it.)

Lust takes us out of our angelic persona, as do wrath and greed. When therapists feel sexy, angry, or pecuniary, we are quick to accuse patients of arousing these feelings in us because they are not well. We do this because we can get away with it. Internally, we all have a penchant for doing this—we blame our bodies or our emotions or our impulses in an effort to sustain a purchase on our identification with the righteous, the rational, and the holy. Underlying this tendency are the usual privileges of power but also the fear of death. The body dies, the mind lives on—we prefer to identify with the mind. Although the mind is phenomenologically reducible to the things that go through our heads, we convince ourselves that these thoughts and images exist on a mental plane, that they are more than acts of hearing and seeing, because we take solace in believing that in the mental plane, we transcend mortality. But the mind turns out to be only what Goffman (1974) calls "a box of sentences" (p. 527). I would add images and other sensory behaviors, but the point is that the mind is textual, abstract, immortal, hegemonic, and deadly in the sense of not lively. Only something devoid of life can keep from dying. Mark Twain (1968) makes this point by reflecting on how boring the mainstream conception of Heaven is.

Thus, the pornographic mind and its disdained object bear a strong resemblance to Freud's ego and id, to Beck's rationality and irrationality, and to Horney's (1950) idealized self and real self. Horney clearly advocates liberating the real self, while Freud and Beck can easily be misread as advocating the colonizing of the id and irrationality. What Freud really advocated was taking ownership of the id, and what Beck really advocated was to dispute *detrimental* irrationality, or what might better be called unreasonableness. An important idea in performance theory is the way the liminal opposes the status quo (e.g., Turner, 1969), the way Dionysius makes the party line seem deadly (Nietzsche, 1966b). Good psychotherapy creates a place for the liminal, for its celebration and embrace. Society tries to eradicate it, but we cannot live without it, or we turn into Melville's (2004) "cadaverous" copy clerk, Bartleby, or Friedan's (1963) unfulfilled housewife.

One of the pornographic mind's greatest critiques was Homer's *Iliad*. Achilles' embodiment of the yang fantasy of invulnerability is contrasted with Hector's androgyny. Hector is a great warrior, but he is also beloved by his wife, his children, his father, and his people. Achilles' invulnerability translates into an emptiness that cannot be filled with accomplishment. Achilles' heel is his affection for Patroclus, and when Patroclus is killed in battle, Achilles restores his sense of invulnerability by converting his agony into rage. After he kills Hector, he refuses to hand over the body for burial, but Hector's father comes to Achilles and begs for the body in a simple display of fatherly affection that finally allows Achilles to act like a man and not like a "man." Achilles hands over Hector's body for burial, and the *Iliad* ends. The message is a feminist message—vulnerability is better than invulnerability, love is better than rage, humanity is better than godliness, and doing the right thing is better than standing on principle. The performance of yang without yin is an empty performance, backed only by rage and fear.

This is the reason macho performers—"real men"—get so angry at gay men: by their occasional burlesques and their openness about their backstage preferences, gay men out masculinity as a performance. Other men attack them to prove it is more than that. Dorothy Parker once said of the Hollywood he-men of her day, "Scratch an actor, find an actress." Her point was that John Wayne and Randolph Scott were not *cowboys*; they were *actors*. (The same insight may have changed psychotherapy from a man's profession to a woman's: scratch a therapist, find a caregiver, not a doctor.) Real cowboys may become violent if one communicates to them that their garb is a costume or that their swagger is a show. Why do so many sports figures hate reporters and camera operators? Because the reporter and the camera remind everyone that sports figures are not athletes but entertainers, paid not because of their prowess but because of their ability to sell tickets and advertising.

The pornographic mind was also critiqued by Shakespeare, Goethe, and Tolstoy. Think of Angelo's mistreatment of Isabella in *Measure for Measure* and the strength Shakespeare shows us not in Angelo's dominance but in Isabella's capacity to forgive him. Think of Faust's empathy for Gretchen as the ruination of the devil's plan to use and discard her. Think of how Tolstoy's *War and Peace* demolished the fantasy that history is the work of great men pulling strings. I mention these writers only partly to show how well read I am; I mention them also because they are men—some men have always been aware of the toll that the pornographic mind takes not only on women but also on men. The poem *Invictus* captures the more traditional yang attitude: Henley claims to be "the master of [his] fate, the captain of [his] soul," even under "the cruel bludgeonings of chance." The poem inadvertently shows us how the performance of the self as having an "unconquerable soul" converts chance into a cruel bludgeon.

Henley died in 1903. The inevitability of death also discredits—eventually—all performances of invincibility.

The pornographic mind shows itself in therapy whenever we exploit our power to define the relationship in a way that emphasizes our transcendence and disdains the patient's facticity, whenever we make the patient an example of something, and whenever we consider it an embarrassment to have a psychology and attribute psychology only to the patient. Perhaps the worst example is the psychiatric grand rounds where the patient, costumed in a revealing johnny, is paraded before an audience of doctors in white coats. These exhibitions don't really teach interns to recognize psychiatric conditions—they teach interns how to relate to psychiatric conditions. Almost as pornographic is a supervisor's behaving like an attending physician, that is, actually meeting with the patient, supposedly to enhance the supervisor's assessment of the case, but actually to ensure that the therapist–patient teamwork remains subordinate to the doctor–doctor teamwork. While these extreme examples clearly show the negative effects of a pornographic attitude, it's important to recognize that it also occurs in common and mundane interactions in which the therapist makes the patient an object of scrutiny.

Lest there be any confusion, by the way, I want to be clear that I'm *for* sex and *for* the objectification of the body during sex. I've treated men for impotence (erectile dysfunction) and women for painful intercourse (vaginismus) who were under the lamentable impression that the cure for their conditions was to relax during sex. Relaxation is not sexy. I've encouraged women to take charge, to grip rather than relax. I've encouraged men to stop thinking about their performance, their masculinity, their relaxation, and their situation and to think only about their partner's body. Thus, I advocate objectification of the body during sex, but the frame of that objectification should be playful rather than contemptuous, mutual rather than one sided, and invited rather than imposed.

STANDING ON PRINCIPLE

When therapists stand on principle, it is often at the expense of their patients. It can foster yang feelings of honor and pride, but it also leads to inflexibility in the face of new information. The whole point of acting on principle, of rule-governed behavior, is that it frees the actor from the vicissitudes of chance and idiosyncratic situations. "Look both ways before crossing" is a good rule because, even though it is usually a waste of time, on balance its net effect is positive. "Double down with 11" at blackjack is a good rule because, even though it might not have worked last time, on balance its net effect is positive. *Acting* on principle is a good thing, as long as the principle was derived from situations similar to the present one. But *standing* on principle implies that one is no longer questioning the applicability of the principle, no longer open to the idea that the current situation is different enough from those from which the principle was derived to invalidate its present use.

Principles, like all rules, seem to come from the top—handed down to the individual to use in a given situation. This is a yang conceit, that one is an instrument of something higher. Contingency-shaped behavior, which is non-principled and responsive only to what works in the moment, is yin. Confucius represents yang thinking with his insistence on respect for rules and authority. Chuang-tzu represents yin thinking, making a folk hero of the butcher who never needed to resharpen his knife because he let the carcass guide his cutting decisions rather than a plan. Kohlberg's (1958) version of moral development, criticized by Gilligan (1982) as applicable more to boys than to girls, peaks with abstract principles. Gilligan proposes a different scale for a different morality that she labels feminine, in which relational and incidental issues are weighed for all sorts of costs and benefits but in which principles are neither appealed to nor applied.

Glorification of rules is tempting because it smacks of honor and holiness and because it idolizes and thereby appeases the source of the rules, but it is a wise course only when the rules are carefully tailored to the kind of situation before us. Sometimes, we just have to wonder if there is something wrong with the map, even if it is a Hammond or a Rand-McNally, even if the only thing wrong with it is that the terrain has changed since it was drawn. Operating by trial and error is not glorious, but it is often more effective. The history of chicken sexing is a good example of rules just getting in the way. Before chickens were bred specifically to enable people to easily distinguish the pullets (females) from the cockerels (males), the ability to sex chickens was quite valuable to chicken farmers. Since it only pays to raise the pullets, accurate sexing saved farmers a lot of money. Sadly, very few people were able to do it accurately. Rules were developed to describe the differences between pullets and cockerels, but they were ineffective. However, one useful method was to capitalize on one man's ability to sex chickens with a high degree of accuracy. He made a 3-hour film of day-old chicks going by on a conveyor belt and simply said "male" or "female" in a voice-over as each one passed. A colleague of mine who grew up on a chicken farm watched the film as a young girl, and afterward she, too, was able to sex chickens with a high degree of accuracy. But to this day she is unable to state a rule to differentiate the sexes. My point is that we glorify rules and principles, but they are often not only deadly but also downright ineffective compared to experimentation and trial-and-error learning.

According to cognitive therapists (e.g., Beck, 1976; Ellis & Harper, 1975), all our psychological problems stem from using outmoded rules (i.e., beliefs). In fact, every approach to therapy has some way of expressing the idea that the patient is using an outmoded map (Karson, 2006). People get overly attached to their rules for a lot of the same reasons they don't like critical thinking—they want to feel there is an order to their world, their faith is in the rules and not in the process, they feel stupid if they question their rules, and they want to show respect for the originator of the rule. In addition, rules can lead to glory. "Ours is not to reason why" and all that.

Oliver Wendell Holmes (1881) addresses this problem in his masterpiece *The Common Law*. Darwin showed that speciation is not a top-down process of design but a bottom-up process of adaptation, and Holmes applied the new idea about causality to the law. He saw a pretense that laws are handed down from the top based on abstract principles and then applied to specific situations, but through his examination of the history of the law, he found that the law actually evolves on a case-by-case basis. The law pretends to have Kohlberg's morality but actually has Gilligan's. Where evolution selects characters according to their survival value, law selects rules according to "considerations of what is expedient for the community concerned" (p. 35).

Similarly, the nomothetic (from the Greek for "law giving") tradition in science, which seeks lawfulness by testing hypotheses, is seen in many circles as more scientific than the idiographic (from the Greek for "one's own") tradition, which inspects individual cases and accounts for them. The result is a current fashion in psychological science where a study showing how most depressives do in a particular kind of therapy is privileged over a minor and unpublishable study that shows how my particular patient does—the former is useful for developing general ideas about depression and treatment, but the latter is where I will discover which ideas are useful for my particular patient. Instead of trying stuff and developing a method for determining whether it's working, we pick an approach based on research done on strangers and stick with it.

When my colleagues and I were reading Langs (e.g., 1976, 1978) in the early 1980s, we were fascinated by his attention to patients' metaphors as guides to what works with them and what does not. We also felt constrained by his many rules for conducting therapy: never chitchat, start and end precisely on time, never self-disclose, never accept insurance, and so on. Langs had abstracted across situations, understanding what worked for several patients under specific circumstances and deducing rules that he said applied to all patients under all circumstances. (John Stuart Mill says that is where all apparently deduced rules come from—induction.) Eventually, we realized that instead of feeling constrained by Langs's many rules, we could feel free to operate without rules (except as a general starting point) because we had also learned a method to tell if what we did worked. That method was to understand the patient's ensuing speech as a commentary on what we did, that is, to understand the functional relation between the patient's behavior (talking) and its occasioning environment (what we did). Whether or not one accepts Langs's methodology (which was actually articulated by Bateson and his colleagues in 1956), one can see the advantages of basing therapy decisions on relevant and unconscious feedback from the patient rather than on a set of rules and policies.

GENDER AND INTIMACY EXPOSURE

Much psychotherapy is really intimacy exposure—patients previously hurt in intimate relationships now avoid and escape them, and they need to be exposed to intimacy in such a way that aversive reactions extinguish. This requires a therapist who allows and fosters intimacy and who allows extinction of fears to occur. These skill sets combine yin and yang. Intimacy is enhanced by the particularity of the relationship and by its emotional responsivity. Extinction is fostered by stillness—resisting social pulls to reassure or praise. Therapists too much in yang mode who need to shine, strut their stuff, and make good points tend to deflect intimacy. Therapists too much in yin mode create their own problems by self-disclosing, expressing affection, and framing the relationship as unique in a way that prevents extinction and keeps the intimacy exposure they provide from generalizing to other intimate situations. The patients conclude not that intimacy is safe but only that intimacy with this particular therapist is safe and only because this therapist is so tender, caring, and nice.

Chapter Six

Deadly Multiculturalism

[Alice:] "But little girls eat eggs quite as much as serpents do, you know."
"I don't believe it," said the Pigeon. "But if they do, why, then they're a
kind of serpent."

—Lewis Carroll, *Alice's Adventures in Wonderland*

The hand of Vengeance found the Bed
To which the Purple Tyrant fled
The iron hand crushed the Tyrants head
And became a Tyrant in his stead

—William Blake, *The Grey Monk*

CATEGORIES MARGINALIZE

One solution to the problem of marginalizing voices that are out of line with
the prevailing ideology is to learn more about different kinds of voices. At its
best, this endeavor teaches us that our way of thinking is just a way of thinking, not the way things are. At its worst, it merely replaces the current hegemony with a new one. This new hegemony is often called political correctness, but I don't like that dismissive term because I think that political
correctness—using mild aversive control to monitor expressions of racial,
ethnic, religious, and sexual hatred and insensitivity—has taught a lot of people to perform better and has made the world a better place. The real problem
is the use of categories to understand people, and any system of categories
will become a dismissive hegemony.

MISGUIDED SOLUTIONS

Multiculturalism has become a major force in psychotherapy training. Often, it is presented to trainees as a statement that they may not be competent to treat people with different ethnic and cultural identifications from their own. Thus, the psychologists' ethical code states,

> Where scientific or professional knowledge in the discipline of psychology establishes that an understanding of factors associated with age, gender, gender identity, race, ethnicity, culture, national origin, religion, sexual orientation, disability, language, or socioeconomic status is essential for effective implementation of their services or research, psychologists have or obtain the training, experience, consultation, or supervision necessary to ensure the competence of their services, or they make appropriate referrals, except as provided in Standard 2.02, Providing Services in Emergencies. (American Psychological Association, 2002)

The American Psychiatric Association (1994) takes special care to avoid mistaking "culturally sanctioned" responses as disordered responses and cautions psychiatrists working with patients from cultures other than their own. The party line is that if you are a white man, you may not be qualified to treat a black woman, and, even more alarmingly, if you are a black woman, you might not be qualified to treat a white man. Special training is advised for relieving this incompetence, but I get the impression that what is meant by special training is really just stereotyped platitudes about what other people are like. The dominant view of multiculturalism, then, is that we have to be cautious in working with people who carry some label that does not include ourselves. The absurd culmination of this brand of multiculturalism is that I am qualified to work only with myself since every other human being can be distinguished from me in some important categorical way.

I understand what the dominant view of multiculturalism is a reaction to—there has been a lot of harm done in the past by clinicians who mistake culture for pathology. For example, early in my career I came across a case of a psychologist who recommended that a man lose custody of his children because of his paranoid psychosis. The evidence for this psychosis consisted entirely of the man telling the psychologist, via a translator, of a period in his life when he dug up graves and reburied the bodies—this turned out to be a true story about his summer job moving a cemetery rather than a delusion. These harms can't always be prevented by simply seeking consultation with someone who carries the same label as the patient. These harms were caused by using erroneous or outmoded templates to evaluate individuals, so it's a natural reaction to refine or update the templates—but that's not the answer. The answer is not to use templates at all. The assumption that my Haitian colleagues know what it's like to be a Haitian in Boston because they are Haitian ignores how a particular Haitian man is coping. I wish I could count how many cultural specialists have told me, in serious and expert intonations, that the men of their particular culture feel a deep need to provide for and control their families, as if this distinguished the men under consideration from other men. This approach to multiculturalism also invites me to make unwarranted assumptions about people who do happen to share some labels with me. My problem has always been the opposite of the historical one. When I meet someone who seems not much like me in some important away, I'm inclined not to make assumptions about her. I tend to make unwarranted assumptions when I meet someone who *is* like me in some important way.

MULTICULTURALISM AS A LEVEL OF ANALYSIS

I think there is a much better place for multiculturalism in psychotherapy training than a system of categorization that apparently has no natural basis (see, e.g., Helms, Jernigan, & Mascher, 2005) and a network of workshops on various cultures that, if framed only slightly differently, would be exercises in racism. Rather than seeing multiculturalism as an *area* of psychology, I see it as a *level* of psychological abstraction. Most clinical courses either teach a language for understanding psychological phenomena or teach details about psychological phenomena. Multicultural training should transcend language and topics to metacommunicate about the languages we use and the topics we discuss in psychology.

In multicultural training, we have a chance to emphasize two great truths about psychology (numbered for your convenience): one, we are all the same, and, two, we are all different. By discussing people and problems that look very different from us and ours, we learn that we are all the same in the ways covered in other areas of training because so much of what is taught in the other areas of training applies to so many different kinds of people. Then, by demonstrating the ineffectiveness of lumping people together by category, we teach that we are all different. Analogously, it has been estimated that all humans share 98% of their DNA molecules in common (we are all almost the same) and that 97% of all human genetic variation can be found in even the most isolated New Guinea tribes (even people who seem utterly similar to outsiders are almost as different from each other as people can be).

MULTICULTURALISM AND IDENTITY

Multicultural training should be freighted with the task of challenging students to consider the nature of identity—its centrality to human experience, its social construction, its defensive functions, its performative quality, and whether it can be transcended. People abstract from their experiences a construct of self that facilitates successful behavior, soothes anxiety, and unfortunately limits growth. Identity facilitates successful behavior because in planning ahead for any person, it helps to know something about the person one is planning for—identity is shorthand for what a person thinks she knows about herself. Facilitating successful behavior by articulating an identity also soothes anxiety. As Skinner said, anxiety is the feeling of not knowing what to do, and knowing the kind of thing that I like to do or that I am likely to do reduces my anxiety. However, anxiety is often provoked by choices, and sticking with what I like to do or what I typically do keeps me from exploring alternatives. Identity, then, can be a defensive posture that limits growth and constricts behavioral alternatives, and I think the exploration of the typical dimensions of identity in a multiculturalism class can familiarize students with this important concept. Identity should be revealed for study in multicultural training in the same way that a culture is revealed in a comparative literature class, for identity consists not only in what one is but also in what one is not. These *nots* should be remembered and explored in multicultural training.

OTHER BENEFITS OF MULTICULTURAL TRAINING

Multicultural training should challenge us to think about how the canon became the canon, how the program of psychology became its program, and how the methods of psychology became its methods. The shadows and margins of psychology's culture must be examined to understand it. This process can be facilitated by multicultural training simply because it is the kind of people discussed in such training who were ignored or wrongly vilified in much of psychology's history. More important, multicultural training should facilitate the process of looking behind psychology's curtain because its topics raise perennial questions about the relationship between the powerful and the powerless and about the privileged, unreflective elite that assumes that its definition of situations—of psychology itself—applies to everyone. The test of a psychology is its ability not to fit the problems on which it was derived but rather to fit new problems—different people in different situations. Thus, I want multicultural training to be a workshop for critical thinking about the suitability of our premises for new situations and for inspecting our ideas for hidden, self-serving purposes.

DIFFERENCES BETWEEN SELF AND OTHERS

Skinner said that much of what you believe about human behavior stems from your up-close and personal observations of one particular human—yourself. Most major theorists have made the same point. Much of what is taught in the clinical curriculum can be thought of as a process for determining which beliefs about yourself apply to others generally, which to others in particular circumstances, and which hardly at all (i.e., which are idiosyncratic to ourselves, our families, or our groups). This process can be made explicit in multicultural training if students practice questioning ideas about human behavior regarding their suitability for other people and other situations.

DEADLY MULTICULTURALISM

Deadly multiculturalism is labeling people and treating them according to those labels. It's deadly because it categorizes people and forces conformity within the category rather than unpacking labels and encouraging responsiveness to situations. Further, it is often difficult to say whether a given person is inside or outside a category: Polish? Polish American? Polish extract? American with Polish grandparents? Grandparents who were born in Poland but considered themselves Jewish while living in a town that became part of Lithuania during their adolescence? Which of these categories applies?

Each of us knows that the labels we bear do not do justice to our behavioral variability. Each Catholic is Catholic in her own way. Each cognitive-behaviorist practices uniquely. It's easy to dismiss a lot of what I say as the self-serving opinions of a man, of a white, of a psychologist, of whatever label I carry that anyone who disagrees with me doesn't. Labels are indeed useful for understanding groups of people but not for understanding any particular person. They are much more useful and much more widely used as reasons not to listen to others.

Deadly multiculturalism hides the arbitrariness of labels and takes them as fixed entities when in fact you can draw a circle around any group of people and call them a culture. All psychopathology is culturally sanctioned, but the culture that sanctions it—often a culture of only three or four family members—is different from the culture that considers it pathological. A given practice—gay sex, say—could easily be culturally conforming in one's home but not in one's neighborhood, yes in one's city but not in one's state, and so on.

Lively multiculturalism is a process of examining where categories come from and what good they do and exploding them. Cultural competence is achieved not by finding out about another culture but by finding out about our personal norms and their potential inapplicability to other people. To become culturally competent, we have to learn about *our* people, not *other* people (even if we get perspective on our people largely by comparing them with others). Lively multiculturalism asks questions about claims and situations that often go unasked, such as, "Does it matter that all the subjects in this study were boys?" and "Would the story mean something different if the patient were black?"

You can tell if your multicultural training was lively—were these sorts of questions asked of the training itself? All too often, the trainer acts as if she has a free pass from the arbitrariness of power and blindness of privilege, a pass awarded to her categorical label as lesbian, Latina, or woman. She then fails to examine the power dynamic in the classroom, the local norms established there, and the marginalization of voices that are out of line. Instead, she should capitalize on the availability of the very problems she is discussing and use them as cases in point (Goodwin, 2001; Robinson, 2006).

GOFFMAN'S VIEW OF STIGMA MANAGEMENT

Multiculturalism tries to manage stigmas, and psychotherapy patients seek help with stigma management. In Ossorio's (1983) felicitous phrasing, multicultural training teaches us not to view other people as "defective versions of ourselves," while patients often come for help because they feel like they have become defective versions of *them*selves. Goffman's (1963) book on stigma is subtitled *Notes on the Management of Spoiled Identity*, so stigma is the condition of having—and having to manage—a spoiled or discredited identity. Identity elements become spoiled by their failure to live up to group expectations (norms). These norms are central to our dramaturgical human nature because they tell us which aspects of our performance of self will be credited and which discredited. In any group with any sort of stability—even people standing in an elevator—normative identity elements will dictate whose performance as an authorized elevator user will be credited and whose will be discredited. Every human being is sometimes stigmatized and sometimes not.

Surpassing normative expectations is called *prestige*. Nietzsche (1966a) wrote extensively about the tendency of groups to redefine prestige as stigma by turning yardsticks upside down. A rich woman is considered to be a Marie Antoinette, or a prolific writer is considered by colleagues to be ambitious. Despite this tendency, there will always be individuals who exceed group norms in a way that the group endorses.

In a group that stigmatizes a person—that holds identity expectations the person falls short of—the individual has certain choices available. A crucial aspect of Goffman's analysis is that stigma is ubiquitous and that none of the choices are good ones. People often avoid groups that stigmatize them—a relatively benign alternative, but it doesn't work for everyone for economic and practical reasons. While white people can conveniently avoid black groups in America, black people who avoid white groups will probably find themselves economically disadvantaged. (By *white people*, I mean people who are perceived as white and who can sustain that perception in the eyes of the relevant group.) The distinction between actual and perceived characteristics leads to Goffman's second relatively benign alternative, which is to hide one's stigma, if it is the sort of stigma that can be hidden. In a group of behaviorists, I can choose whether to reveal my psychoanalytic bent—but in a group of behavioristic women, I can't choose whether to show that I am a man. But I do have control of how I play gender, and I may elect to hide my interest in action movies from a group of women or to hide my interest in tearjerkers from a group of men. I may elect to hide my entire psychology from the public, from my colleagues, and from my patients in situations where having a psychology is stigmatized. A gay person may pass as straight. Choosing to hide a stigmatized identity element is a benign solution only if it is not experienced as a kind of treason to the group of stigmatized people and only if it is not experienced as a kind of treason to yourself.

When a stigma is obvious to the group in which it falls short or when the stigma has been revealed to the group by the individual or by others, problems in stigma management change. These situations are related to the development of psychopathology because most stigmas are known to the families of the individuals involved. In other words, psychopathology can be seen as an unproductive management of spoiled identity. Situational disorders involve secondary identity elements or central ones spoiled by new groups, and characterological disorders involve central identity elements spoiled by families of origin.

Psychopathology is more likely to develop when a family stigmatizes an identity element that is unavoidable rather than an identity element the person can do without. For example, if a girl is caught masturbating in a family that stigmatizes public sex, which presumably she can do without, she will productively learn to hide her sexuality. But if she is caught masturbating in a family that stigmatizes *all* sex, she will develop a pathological attitude about this identity element. Psychotherapy helps because it is a group of two people whose norms are carefully chosen so as not to stigmatize identity elements that people need for love and work.

The stigmatized individual whose stigma is known must learn to cope with the group's treatment of her. It matters whether she accepts the norm—whether she also stigmatizes herself—or whether she merely recognizes that she has been stigmatized but does not accept that definition. For example, a woman who does not like to socialize faces a gender problem that depends on whether she accepts the idea that women are supposed to enjoy socializing. In psychotherapy, I see far more problems arising from the patient's agreement with the stigma than from the mere recognition that others think badly of her. A tricky problem for us arises when we ourselves stigmatize the patient—this puts her in a conflict between membership in our little group and the cost of such membership, namely, acceptance of her stigma. This occurs most frequently when we identify certain behaviors as pathological—explicitly with labels or implicitly with extended discussion of them.

Goffman mentions another important way of coping with stigma: the individual exaggerates the stigmatized identity element in order to gain a sense of control over the stigmatization and in order to divert the group's attention from the self to the exaggeration. This strategy was used by gay men in highly stigmatizing social environments with clothing, speech, and affective displays and is currently seen in marginalized groups who behave angrily to divert the disapproval from the self to the anger. Many psychological symptoms may be productively viewed as coping mechanisms of this sort. For example, the girl who cuts herself may gain control of her sense of not belonging and may lessen its impact by doing something that explains her stigma and keeps the interaction about the behavior and not about the self.

Stigmatized people are not authorized to behave in certain ways. A black woman may be treated well enough at work, but the group may not authorize her to be ironic, to engage in critical thinking, or to be interested in certain kinds of music. A white man may not be authorized to express opinions about race or multiculturalism in a group of black women or a group of psychologists. Coping with stigma often means constricting one's conduct to meet group expectations. People who don't accept this are usually angry; people who do are usually depressed. Metacommunication about the impossibility of successfully managing the situation may help. The role of patient can be examined for the authorizations that various therapies do not condone. Psychoanalytic therapies, for example, sometimes refuse to authorize the patient to make interpretations about the therapist. Cognitive therapies sometimes refuse to authorize the patient to express fear, helplessness, and sadness.

If a stigmatized individual learns to pass by hiding his stigma or if he learns to cope with the stigma by passing as the sort of person who does not insist on a full range of conduct, he is likely to develop ambivalence about himself. Either he accepts himself as stigmatized or he feels bad about his decision to cope. He feels shame about being stigmatized, according to Goffman, and, if he feels there is nothing really wrong with him, he feels shame about being ashamed. Most stigmatized individuals who cannot afford to avoid the stigmatizing group find themselves in a paradox. For example, we think that honor dictates that we behave authentically and that we resist minstrelization (Broyard's [1950] term, originally for blacks, for going along with the group's expectations). Then, we are told that those who are resisting minstrelization are still responding to it since they are trying to fight the stereotype. Thus, we are damned if we do and damned if we don't. A flurry of opinions that only make us feel bad are always available from people that Goffman labels *professionals*—people who cope with a stigma by telling other people how to cope with it.

Goffman reports that although there may be some variation in how a group expects a stigmatized individual to cope, it usually amounts to an expectation that she will gracefully and cheerfully accept the constrictions on her conduct—especially the fact that her presence sometimes makes things awkward for normals—and that she will tactfully and gently educate the group about the nature of her identity and her predicament. The fact that this expectation comports with what may be in her best interest does not make it any easier to accept since the knowledgeable performance of stigma management feels shameful, as if the identity element is accepted as spoiled. One thing we can do as therapists to help patients manage spoiled aspects of their identities is to avoid putting them in a position where, when they have been stigmatized by us, they are expected to remain cheerful, apologetic, and tactful.

ARBITRARY CATEGORIES

As a lesson in multiculturalism, Goffman's approach has much to recommend it. A lot of racism can be described as responses to people's categories rather than to what Martin Luther King Jr. called "the content of their character." By being clear that the categories we use are socially constructed and otherwise arbitrary, Goffman's articulation of stigma avoids endless arguments about black–white or gay–straight differences and instead asks why the group is focusing on skin color or sexual orientation. Once a category is settled on as a source of stigma, Goffman also focuses attention on the individual's options with respect to the category, which keeps us from fusing the category and the person. Instead of saying, "He is faced with these identity management problems because he is black," Goffman teaches us to say, "because he has been categorized as black by a group that stigmatizes that category." The flexibility of categories and the focus on options enlivens the problem of stigma management.

UNIVERSALITY OF STIGMA

Goffman also enlivens the problem by focusing on situations rather than on societies. It is in situations that people have options. Stigma and privilege are functions of situations, not of personal characteristics. This approach helps us see the universality of the problem of stigma management. While I would much rather face the problems that beset a nonstigmatized individual who is sympathetic to a stigmatized person than the problems that beset the stigmatized person, they are essentially the same problem. Sympathy to people identified as racial minorities or as possessing any other stigmatized identity element is itself stigmatized—not as brutally, but it still discredits group membership and usually must be managed in the same ways as racial identity. I find this universality appealing.

The facility with which we adapt to becoming stigmatized and unstigmatized also implies universality (Goffman, 1963). When we are suddenly stigmatized—when we suddenly find that we are the only behaviorist in a room full of analysts or the only Jew in a room full of Baptists—we immediately know the landscape we are in and the options we have. We know how to play the role. As Goffman says, "The painfulness, then, of sudden stigmatization can come not from the individual's confusion about his identity, but from his knowing too well what he has become" (pp. 132–133). And we are equally adept once a stigma is removed. When we suddenly discover that a group already has a lot of Jewish or behaviorist members, we immediately relax and play our nondiscredited role with ease.

Women will recognize this feature of stigma when they reflect on any occasion in which they realized that the group believed that they got something because of their being a woman. This impression was communicated via direct accusation, rumor, innuendo, or a simple smirk. Suddenly, their position in the relevant group is stigmatized, and they obsess about what happened, take clarifying steps that are interpreted as angry or pathological, and wind up either accepting a marginalized role in the group or loudly refusing that role, both of which make their identity as a woman more prominent than it needs to be, confirming the group's stigmatizing impression. When group membership or group identity norms change and women are perceived as acquiring their position on merit, they act affably, generously, and calmly and rarely obsess about work. And the same is true for men. When groups smirk about men's comfort with expressing themselves and attribute their positions to their maleness, and men feel as women do, it is easy to see that we are all adept at playing stigmatized and at playing normal.

The advantage of recognizing universality is that it implies a common bond. I'm not suggesting that the pain of being marginalized as a Skinnerian is equivalent to the pain of being marginalized as a black man any more than touching a hot stove is equivalent to being branded. But I am suggesting that the latter are both burns and that the former have the same parameters if not the same dimensions. The common bond is that none of us like it, we avoid it when possible, and avoidance often occurs at the expense of others when we trumpet our situationally normal identities and stigmatize those who don't or can't.

IMPLICATIONS FOR TREATMENT

Several schools of therapy share the idea that psychopathology is a matter of navigating current terrain with outmoded maps. These maps may be the organizing principles of self psychology, the paradigms of object relations, the homeostatically preserved patterns of interaction from systems theory, the rules of rule-governed behavior, or the schemas in cognitive theory. Verbal descriptions and conceptual categories are kinds of maps, reducing information for efficient processing at a higher level of abstraction but susceptible to drawing people's attention away from the problem in front of them. Conceptual categories also have a way of becoming the party line, a text that resists new information. In this view of pathology, anything we can do to question or even demolish categories is generally therapeutic (except with patients whose identity functions are so diffuse that some categories can serve as temporary building blocks). Many clinical problems break down into this unspoken formula: it would be good for me to do that, but I am not the type of person who does that. Typing the self constricts behavioral flexibility—freedom. One of the great harms of stigma is that the individual, while resisting the stigma, accepts the category, and her behavior becomes a function of managing that category instead of a function of what she wants and what the situation can offer.

And yet, it has become the fashion in clinical report writing to begin with a list of categories. X is a Filipino American, nonpracticing Catholic lesbian seeking help with her sleep disorder. I hope this trend reflects only the demands of writing a report and not an approach to patients. Although report writing conflicts with lively psychotherapy, it's a necessary compromise for other purposes, including patients' rights, insurance companies' expectations of documentation, and the occasional clinical needs that arise when consultation is sought or the therapist is unavailable. Once we are in a position where we have to write things down, we don't want to create an impression that the default patient is a white, Protestant heterosexual, so there is some merit to detailing these other labels. But in both reports and treatment, the identifying labels should not arise until critical thinking about situations requires them. Stating them up front tends to ossify both our and the patients' expectations about the type of people they are.

Even worse than rendering these categories in reports is the tendency to impose them on people in the clinical process. One clinic I know of asks people *on the phone* to classify themselves ethnically, racially, and sexually, and many therapists feel they cannot proceed with helping someone until they nail down their categorizations. This is the opposite of therapy. Therapy is helping people who think of themselves as heterosexual to see that it's more complicated than that. Therapy is helping a black man think about when, under what circumstances, he is black, when he's a biologist, when he's a professor, when he's a big brother, and how he can more adroitly and satisfyingly manage these situations. The opposite of therapy is to establish that he is always a black biologist when his presenting complaint may be that he knows exactly how to be black and exactly how to be a biologist but does not know how to be both—as if it is incumbent on him to think about the feeding habits of fruit flies as a black man and to listen to jazz as a biologist. There are bound to be situations where a true conflict emerges for us to work on, but it is the opposite of therapy to make that conflict ubiquitous.

Instead of classifying people, we can ask them on the phone at a clinic whether there is anything they want the clinic to know about them for assigning a therapist. In a private practice, we can ask people whether there is anything we need to know about them to understand why the problem is a problem for them. If there is evidence to support a more direct inquiry, we can ask if there are religious overtones to the situation. What we don't want to do is to conclude that lesbians are specially stigmatized in Catholic, Filipino American families and ignore her claim that she is sleepless because she has to decide whether to stick with her safe job or take an exciting job that may end abruptly. While it may develop that she is really rehashing her decision not to pretend to be straight and to try for the more gratifying but unsafe lesbian life, to presuppose it is to stigmatize her. It says that as a Filipino American ex-Catholic lesbian, she can't have normal problems.

Chapter Seven

Therapeutic Privilege

When a contest occurs over whose treatment of self and other is to prevail, each individual is engaged in providing evidence to establish a definition of himself at the expense of what can remain for the other. . . . Insisting on a desirable place is thus covered and strengthened by insisting on one's rightful place, and this is further hardened by the obligation to do so, lest the whole pattern of rules deteriorate.

—Goffman (1967, pp. 241–242)

The key factor [in social encounters] is the maintenance of a single definition of the situation, this definition having to be expressed, and this expression sustained in the face of a multitude of potential disruptions.

—Goffman (1959, p. 254)

Nearly all men can stand adversity, but if you want to test a man's character, give him power.

—Abraham Lincoln

Along with our power over patients comes the power to define the situation. Everyone defines situations, but when definitions clash, a lot of what it means to say that someone has power is that his or her definition of a situation will prevail and become the official or party line, while a lot of what it means to say that someone does not have power is that his or her definition of a situation will be suppressed, marginalized, or ignored by the mainstream. According to systems theory, we define situations—we name the play we're putting on—so we'll know what roles are available. This knowledge tells us which role to play, which enables us to keep things running smoothly. In behavioral

117

terms, we don't define situations—they define themselves according to the way discriminant stimuli in the immediate environment have been associated with reinforcement contingencies in our learning history. Both theories agree that we behave according to cues in the environment that define the environment, and the latitude in inferring the sort of environment we are in from the cues available allows us to impose certain preferences on that definition. These preferences include a tendency to define situations in a manner that includes roles we have already mastered, in a manner that makes us look good, and in a manner that advantages us in some way. Advantageous definitions of situations tend to become a party line: self-justifying definitions that maintain power among the current hegemony that promulgated them.

Performance scholarship investigates the tendency of a party line to resist change by defining efforts to change things—signs of liveliness—as threats to the status quo and dealing with them accordingly, whether they are silenced, demonized, ridiculed, or pathologized. This is what Brook (1993) meant by writing, "The characteristic of all forms of dictatorship is that culture is frozen" (p. 110). It's what Read meant by saying that theater "is worthwhile because it is antagonistic to official views of reality" (quoted in Carlson, 1996, p. 50). It's what is meant by the old saw that good art is a hammer, not a mirror, shaping rather than reflecting society.

Every major school of therapy addresses the issue of empowering the marginalized, whether it's Freud's recovery of the repressed, cognitive therapy's disputation of the party line, behaviorism's suspicion about language and rules, systems theory's investigation of oppressive or paradoxical role relationships, humanism's celebration of the tyrannized, or intersubjectivity's care not to blame the patient for the cocreated relationship. Every major school is also hindered by becoming a party line itself. The power differential in therapy tempts us even when we are at our best and want to recognize and avoid mismanaging it. Despite our best intentions and despite our explicit agreement with patients to do otherwise, we ignore the performances—symptoms and metaphors—that they produce to challenge the therapy's official party line.

There are two kinds of therapists: those who, when something goes wrong, try something else and those who, when something goes wrong, enhance the diagnosis. There are two kinds of therapists: those who, when the patient gets miffed or angry, think they must have done something wrong and those who, when the patient gets miffed or angry, think the patient's parents must have done something wrong. Each of us is sometimes one, sometimes the other. When we act defensively, blaming and egotistical, we do it partly because it's natural to reject responsibility for setbacks and partly because it's natural to hide anything that discredits our performance as benign, wise helpers. But when we blame patients for setbacks and define ourselves in such positive terms, we do it mostly because we can get away with it.

To counter our deadly tendency to define reality in a self-serving manner and dismiss alternative definitions of the situation, we must attend to the patient's theatrical performance of metaphor as a source of liveliness.

POWER DIFFERENTIALS

Whether oppression is human nature or merely a function of the hierarchical distribution of resources is not a matter of concern to us. In any society likely to support a psychotherapy practice, resources will be distributed hierarchically, and child-rearing practices will train children to function in hierarchies by using the parent–child hierarchy as a model. When the power differential in the parenting relationship is mismanaged—exploited for the benefit of the parent at the expense of the child—pathologies ensue. As Adler (1937) teaches us, exploitation boils down to mismanaging power in order to control (abuse and excessive punishment), to ignore (neglect), and to avoid conflict (indulgence).

To the extent that pathology arises from the misuse of a power differential, the inherent power differential in therapy can be used remedially. This remediation is conceptualized differently by different schools of therapy, but they all amount to the same thing. The patient's expectations of exploitation are evoked by the power differential in therapy and disconfirmed, the patient discovers different roles to play in power differentials, the patient receives developmentally important interchanges from a parent figure and enhances self-cohesion, or the patient learns to use critical thinking as a liberating rather than marginalizing tactic. The great obstacle to using the power differential in therapy remedially is that the therapist is all too human and will inevitably exploit his or her power over the patient.

THERAPEUTIC INDULGENCE

Some therapists reject a power-driven view of humanity and imagine a bucolic society where oppression is not a factor, trying to reproduce a miniature version of this in the consulting room. Even if such a society did exist, on a tropical island, say, where food is plentiful and shelter unnecessary (Bateson, 1972a), it's hard to see how it serves *our* patients to train them to live in such a world. Therapists who repudiate their power to control also repudiate their power to help. These are the therapists who are dismayed to learn that hunter-gatherers often kill each other, that the Bantu committed genocide and engaged in slaving, and that women in power act just like men. The attitude that exploitation is unnecessary—or a residue of white men—ill prepares such therapists for managing power differentials. They are so uncomfortable that they indulge patients to avoid conflicts over power.

As with all such psychological categories, it is more productive to think of *therapists uncomfortable with power over patients* not as a category of individuals but as a category of individuals-in-situations. We are all that therapist at times. We are especially likely to become that therapist when the situation has made it seem neglectful or abusive to withhold gratification. A parent normally comfortable with setting limits may be indulgent at a family gathering if the family construes discipline as mean ("Aw, let her play," says grandpa).

If an interchange with a patient recalls incidents in which parents, teachers, or therapists (our own or our patients') were cruel, we are likely to repudiate our power in order to distinguish ourselves from those aversive representations. It's difficult to realize we have erred when we act indulgently because that's when patients (and children) are especially grateful, admiring, and easy to get along with. Therapeutic indulgences include extra time, fee waivers, praise, agreeing with patients' construction of events, and any other behaviors whose purpose is to avoid upsetting the patient rather than to achieve the therapeutic goals. To the extent that the therapist's self-evaluation depends on the patient's approbation or overt statements of gratitude and relief, the therapist will overindulge the patient. The analogy in theater is the risk of being pulled away from "truth, reality, and creativity" by audience laughter and applause (Brook, 1993, p. 29). In the theater, as in therapy, there is nothing wrong with pleasing the audience, but there must be some other way to gauge success. Otherwise, the pursuit of conscious pleasure will dominate other agendas—actors will be reduced to cheap sex jokes and therapists to saccharine reassurance.

THERAPEUTIC NEGLECT

Therapeutic neglect occurs when the therapist puts her own needs ahead of the patient's. This too we all do occasionally. A common example is how we capitalize on a boring stretch by indulging our own imagination. I'm not talking about the highly desirable ability to access our own imagination as a reflection of what is going on in the room—I mean the moments that are analogous in parenting to plunking the kid down in front of the television while we pay bills or answer e-mail, except the analogy breaks down because the child knows exactly what is happening. A better analogy would be pretending to play with a child while worrying about something else, a combination of activities that leaves the child confused and tentative. And it's usually not the patient's boring monologue that drives the therapist's attention out of the room—it's the therapist's wandering attention that trains the patient to talk superficially.

Neglect also occurs when the patient needs to talk about something and the therapist ignores it in favor of a topic that is easier for the therapist to discuss. A parenting analogy would be when a child is obviously upset or unexpectedly remote and instead of pursuing the child with quiet questions and lots of conversational space in which to respond, the parent asks, "What's wrong with you?" and quickly adds, "Well, I guess you don't feel like talking about it, but I'm here for you if you do," and leaves. One therapist asked a client, "You're not feeling suicidal, are you?" signaling that suicidal ideation would disrupt the therapist's agenda. These kinds of moments happen in therapy when the patient is feeling something unpleasant and the therapist is focused on some other agenda. If the patient had power over the therapist, the therapist would be extremely aware of the other person's affect—but with a subordinate, she can afford to ignore it.

At a workshop I attended with Keith Johnstone, he showed us how improvised scenes between actors often leave the audience knowing exactly what needs to happen next, while the actors who created the scene are clueless. For example, one actor was instructed to play a man walking through the woods and the other to improvise a talking frog he comes across. The frog mentioned her condominium with an indoor pond in a way that left us all feeling strongly that the scene should switch to the condo, but the actors did not see it. Analogously, a frequent occurrence at my poker game is that the players who have already folded their cards can see exactly what a player is doing, while those still in the hand can't. When a therapist neglects a patient's affect, it's not necessarily because she isn't interested. It usually happens because it's harder to see what's going on from the inside.

Therapeutic neglect can also mean that the therapist's personal agenda trumped the patient's needs in a way we can't simply chalk up to understandable human frailty. At their worst, these mismanaged displays of power have outside-of-therapy effects. Breaches of confidentiality, missed or tardy appointments, self-disclosures that serve the therapist's needs, and ill-considered value judgments are examples on the relatively mild side, while more egregious instances include sex with clients, abandonment, and failure to take action when suicide is imminent.

THERAPEUTIC ABUSE

Punitive therapy occurs when the therapist shapes the patient's behavior by emitting punishers—by acting aversively. The worst example is probably lobotomy. To appreciate the sway of the unconscious mismanagement of power over even well-intentioned practitioners, all you need to know is that the mutilation of people who did not conform to societal expectations of behavior once won its promulgator a Nobel Prize in medicine. As another example of outrageous aversive control, Haley (1965) discusses nice therapists talking to mental patients during the day and attendants beating them into compliance at night.

Most punishers in the therapist's repertoire are more subtle than laceration or battery. Deadly conformity is achieved via aversive control of the patient as a child—parents construe self-expression and natural pleasures as unnecessary and unwanted. We are unlikely to be of much help with the ensuing problems by creating our own systems of aversive control. Aversive control often begins with labeling the marginalized behavior as problematic rather than with labeling the system of marginalization as problematic. In this way, we may pathologize depression rather than self-hate, or we may pathologize anger rather than dissociation. In the latter example, I am thinking of the many foster children who enter foster homes dissociated—spaced out and freaked out but obedient and quiet—who are viewed as high functioning until their histories and feelings catch up with them. Then their improved functioning and new sense of safety produces inconvenient outbursts, recriminations, and suspicions, and they are viewed as low functioning. Indeed, Rank (1936) worried early on about psychotherapy's "secret ideal of the much prized adaptation to reality, which breeds patient, docile Philistines" (pp. 200–201). His concern was that toeing the party line would take precedence over health. Rank was more concerned about society's party line than the therapist's, but the point is still valid.

I'm not against letting patients know what I think is healthy and what I think is pathological. In fact, I'm against pretending that I can disguise my opinions on these matters, and I am especially against pretending that I have no opinion on these matters. I don't think it's possible to conduct a therapy that is free of my values, which means the only real choice is whether to impose my values on patients wittingly or unwittingly, openly or underhandedly. Regardless of my personal values, I will respond to the patient's stated goal by saying, "I'm not sure I really understand why that bothers you," but I have no doubt that the patient can tell the difference between my unstated "because that seems perfectly fine to me" and my alternatively unstated "because there must be something in your world maintaining such destructive behavior." Presenting my values wittingly and openly allows both of us to scrutinize them critically. The most overused word in psychology is *inappropriate*, a word that attempts aversive control without even acknowledging whose agenda is being satisfied. What I can do instead of trying to hide my values is to be someone whose values evolve with input from different people and broad reading.

Therapists also maintain aversive control of patients by expressing the same kinds of anger, disapproval, and disdain as anyone else, although they often convince themselves that they have disguised it. Since people operating in a less powerful position are good at hiding their reactions to aversive control, for fear of evoking even more punishers, it's easy for the powerful person to convince herself that her expressions went unnoticed.

A special form of aversive control occurs in psychotherapy that is particularly insidious and hard to stop. Comforting therapists often create conditions in which neutrality is experienced as aversive. An analogy would be the way the expectation of a warm greeting from a loved one makes a blank look seem like a harsh look, producing behaviors in the recipient that attempt to fix what seems to be a bad situation. Praiseful, smiling therapists turn neutrality into harshness and drive their patients to seek praise. This is counterproductive because neutrality is needed to extinguish aversive expectations of intimacy — comforting therapists dispel fears of intimacy from the therapy, but the effects do not generalize to neutral parties. In this respect, praise and punishment are alike because they introduce or highlight a gradient of approval and disapproval. This is what Lao-Tzu (1988) meant by writing, "Is and Isn't produce each other" (No. 2).

Just as actors can get off track striving for immediate audience approval and just as therapists can get off track striving for immediate patient approval, patients can get off track striving for therapist approval. Actors must condition audiences to suspend their reactions long enough for a decent narrative to emerge, or else they won't even be able to perform a complicated joke, much less tell a meaningful story. By the same token, patients need extended periods of silence in order to develop their narratives, explore their imaginations, and give voice to their marginalized selves — but the nodding, approving, praising therapist occasions sound bites and pronouncements of improvement.

PRIVILEGE

I have been using *power* to mean the ability to affect the other person and *position* to mean the role relationship between the parties. Both patients and therapists play two roles at once. One set is defined by the societal frame of therapist and patient, with the therapist, despite certain legal and ethical safeguards, having much more power than the patient (assuming the patient is not willing to resort to slander or physical assault). The other role relationship is defined by the therapy frame rather than by the societal frame and depends on the patient's psychology, the patient's expectations of therapy, the therapist's orientation, and the therapist's psychology. I am using the term *status* for the way both parties manage hierarchy and face within the relationship. *Privilege* will be used to refer to luxuries of power, position, and status.

The issue of race provides many examples of privilege. *White privilege* refers to the luxuries of being perceived as white in many situations. When a restaurant with outdoor seating puts me far from the entrance where I could easily walk away before paying, I wonder if a black customer would have been seated in a spot where it would be easier to keep an eye on him. Once I visited a Department of Social Services office in Boston, and the new black receptionist buzzed me right in. A black colleague of mine who actually worked at that office every day was required to show his identification. But white privilege is not primarily about getting good tables in restaurants or easy admittance through security—the great luxury of white privilege is not having to think about such things. The black restaurant patron, seated by the kitchen or restroom, wonders if the poor seating was because of his skin color. The lack of privilege is not just in the occasional bad table but also in the pervasive wondering about it.

Yes, of course there is such a thing as black (and other minority) privilege. There are situations where being black is normal and being white is stigmatized, where being black is an advantage and being white is a disadvantage. Academic interviews and hip-hop concerts are two examples. But in America, even in situations where black skin is an advantage, the luxuries of position run only so deep. The black applicant with a leg up in an academic hiring process is still acutely aware of being black. This awareness puts him in his body even when he does not choose to be a body, which lowers his status. Further, it makes him "situation conscious" (Goffman, 1963, p. 111) as opposed to being free to operate within the situation, one of the great burdens of being stigmatized.

Situation Consciousness

In America, a white therapist may become self-conscious with a black patient and may not be privileged to hear intimate details of the patient's experience of race, but the white therapist still enjoys the privilege of not having to specially prove that he knows what he is doing. A black therapist must wonder if his authorization to play the societal role of therapist will be questioned because of prejudicial expectations of black people or because of assumptions that affirmative action underlies his credential.

Good theater and good therapy require that the audience and the patient not be too situation conscious. The audience must accept the theatrical frame and ignore the societal frame—Coleridge's (1985) suspension of disbelief is a suspension of other frames. In the societal frame, the audience member is a paying theatergoer, and the people on the stage are actors; in the theatrical frame, the audience member is an engaged onlooker with a peculiar vantage point, and the people on the stage are characters living out their relationships and interactions. In the societal frame, the patient is a mental health consumer; in the therapeutic frame, he is a neglected child or an irrational reactor or what have you. Good technique reduces the audience member's and the patient's situation consciousness by highlighting the theatrical and therapeutic frames. In the theater, the house lights are brought down at the start and up at the end, the actors keep pretty much to their own space, and they stay in character. Dispersal of situation consciousness allows engrossment.

In therapy, mandated reminders of the social situation, such as disclosures regarding the limits of confidentiality and negotiation of the fee, should be managed in as circumscribed a manner as possible. The circumscription should be clearly stated—"We have to put the therapy on hold while we discuss your suicidality." This makes it clear that the therapist is not alarmed and unempathic within the therapy frame, just that the frame has switched. That said, however, it is also important to note that many therapists abandon the therapy frame too readily when suicidality, scheduling, and fee arrangements are discussed. Usually, the therapy frame can be maintained—like actors staying in character despite a disruption in the house—with curiosity about suicidality, what changing the fee would mean, and so on. The therapy frame is also strengthened when the therapist communicates only in the consulting room with the door closed, when privacy is enhanced, and when the clock controls the starting and stopping of sessions. In a good therapy, the burden of the patient's stigma is removed by creating a relationship in which stigma is impossible. This is partly because every secret and every element of "spoiled identity" (Goffman, 1963) is treated as nonstigmatizing, but it's also because the therapist remains situation conscious throughout the therapy, allowing the patient to explore the experience of being engrossed.

Male Privilege

Men are frequently privileged by financial advantages (again with many exceptions that do not adequately compensate women), by not having to prove themselves, and especially by not having to think about being men. Patients may be fearful of male therapists because of a history of bad experiences with men, but even then the therapist need only demonstrate his nonpunitiveness and lack of arrogance without usually having to prove his general competence. A patient's consciousness of the therapist's maleness is usually taken as relevant to the patient's history with men and sexes the therapist but does not sexualize him—it doesn't put him in his body. A patient's consciousness of the therapist's femaleness is often accompanied by sexualized awareness of her body, which is status lowering because it puts the woman in her body without her consent. Men put women down by putting them in their bodies, aggressively with catcalls and leers, more subtly with compliments about looks and clothing.

Reality Defining as Privilege

The greatest privilege of all and the one that drives performance theory and feminist theory as forces of change is the luxury of defining reality. Politically entrenched forces in every social group, however large or small, define reality in self-serving ways that constitute a party line. When reality talks back in the form of evidence, the hegemony in charge can incorporate the new evidence in its view, it can deny the existence or import of the new evidence, it can change its view, or it can fall in favor of a new view. Recent investigation on how science works (e.g., Longino, 1990) demonstrates that while it is supposed to be constantly revising its view in light of evidence, science is actually much better at incorporating new evidence into its preexisting view—big changes typically await a new generation that is not entrenched in the dominant view.

But reality almost never talks back. That's because most pronouncements defining reality can't be tested against reality. When low income among blacks is justified by defining blacks as intellectually inferior to whites, no empirical evidence can refute the definition. Instead, whatever evidence that seems to refute it is interpreted by the hegemony as idiosyncratic or irrelevant. The same is true of the definition of Israelis as marauding invaders who steal land from Arabs and the definition of Palestinians as anti-Semites who cannot recognize Israel's right to exist. Indeed, the definition of blacks as inferior, presumably created to justify enslaving them, has lasted through many phases of reconsidering what is meant by inferior. Whites used to claim that blacks were physically inferior until Jesse Owens won all those gold medals in 1936, at which point physical superiority became a kind of animal sign, connoting intellectual or spiritual inferiority. Evidence of superiority in minorities will never topple the party line that they are inferior. When blacks outdo the white hegemony on vocabulary, the definition of superiority retains *intelligent* but excludes *well spoken*—an adjective that likens the black person's verbal facility to a stunt. Asians outdo whites on many intellectual tasks, so they are reframed as obedient, compulsive, and nerdy.

DEFINING PATHOLOGY

The definition of reality is a self-serving function of political power, and therapists have much more political power than patients in both the societal and the therapeutic frames. In the societal frame, the privilege of defining what is sick or well is beyond the scope of this project, except to insist that such definitions must be critically examined. Psychology and psychiatry have gone from pathologizing homosexuality, its pathologization being a classic case of heterosexual privilege, to normalizing pedophilia and transsexualism, their nonpathologization being a classic case of liberal privilege: The hegemony of liberalism in psychology and psychiatry has made it technically incorrect to pathologize pedophilia or transsexualism unless the person in question also experiences subjective distress or functional impairment (American Psychiatric Association, 1994). The establishment rejects the cultural absolutism inherent in saying that a behavior is sick even if it doesn't upset the person doing it. But if your definition of psychopathology doesn't include lusting after 6-year-olds and cutting off your own penis, then you need a different definition of psychopathology.

How the term *pathological* became a put-down rather than a signal for caregiving is also part of the story of privilege. Self-serving definitions of reality include self-correcting mechanisms for managing doubters, or else they wouldn't last very long. Depending on the constructs used to build the definition of reality, doubters may be satanic, ignorant, immature, irrational, unpatriotic, or sick—so anyone who questions the party line is doing the devil's work; suffering from misinformation, childishness, or stupidity; giving aid and comfort to the enemy; or succumbing to an emotional disturbance. It was an attorney general of the United States who is supposed to uphold the Bill of Rights, who construed civil libertarians as unpatriotic by saying, "To those who scare peace-loving people with phantoms of lost liberty, my message is this: Your tactics only aid terrorists, for they erode our national unity and diminish our resolve" (Ashcroft, 2001). In the United States, organized psychiatry has not been as active in demonizing—pathologizing—reformers as in communist states where "delusions of reform" has reportedly been accepted as an actual medical diagnosis. In the United States, diagnosis has served to control and explain deviance (homosexuality being a clear case in point) rather than to directly attack dissent (for which we rely on patriotism). However, I think it is fair to say that if one does not quit protesting when accused of being unpatriotic, authorities end up believing that only a wacko would keep at it.

The therapist's definition of what is wrong with the patient—the basis for the entire relationship—is steeped in privilege deriving from the power differential. Performance theory teaches us that the patient's definition of the situation will be hidden from the party line and revealed in discrediting slip-ups. For example, a therapist lets sessions go on a minute or two after the allotted time is up and defines the situation as a kindness. The patient defines the situation as a weakness but disguises his insulting view until he forgets to bring up a difficult issue until he is on his way out of the room. The therapist's job is to credit such slip-ups as furthering the patient's definition of the situation (you don't see me as someone who can help you in the normal course of therapy) rather than to use them to further the therapist's own agenda (you exploit my kindness with doorknob disclosures). Performance theory also teaches us that the patient will resort to metaphor to complain about the therapist's dominant definition of the situation. For example, he complains about his mother's inability to get him ready for school on time when he was a child. The therapist must overcome the natural tendency of privilege to console the patient for the bad mothering he received if she is going to attend to the metaphor and solve his predicament.

THERAPEUTIC PRIVILEGE

Another major privilege in defining reality, besides fail-safe mechanisms to manage dissent, is to deny that reality is being defined. The powerful hold out their definitions of reality as just the way things are, or they cite irrefutable religious or moral codes.

Within the therapy frame, we therapists naturally, routinely, and deadeningly exercise our privilege to define reality, to deny we are doing it, and to construe the patient's dissent as pathological. Political hegemonies concentrate on their legitimacy, whether from the divine right of kings or Jefferson's consent of the governed, and ignore questions about how they are *using* their legitimately acquired power. Therapeutic hegemonies concentrate on their legitimacy, whether from credentials, training, or benign motivations, and ignore questions about how they are using their power. In my experience, the lifelong pursuers of social justice are just as likely as the stuffy establishment types to be the worst offenders, for once a government or a therapist proclaims itself to be so good as to be incapable of tyranny, self-monitoring ceases. Madison (1945) said that if we were governed by angels, we would need no checks and balances on government, and some therapists (and some government officials) believe themselves to be angels, at least in the sense that their awareness of their benign motivations blinds them to their petty tyrannies.

Our tendency to pull rank on patients in defining reality runs through every conflict that arises, and conflicts are ubiquitous because we all constantly define relationships, and no two relationship definitions are precisely alike. A patient begins our second session by saying, "What you said last time made a lot of sense to me." This I take at face value. I don't examine the statement at all because it conforms with my definition of the relationship as helpful and wise. I am rolling up my sleeves and getting down to work when I say, "Which thing I said?" She replies, "Well, just all of it." This now is too much. This is laying a burnt offering at the feet of an idol. I must be perceived as wise and helpful but not *that* wise and helpful. Eventually I will interpret her sense that she must compliment me to avoid my wrath, but I will do it in a way that subtly denies that I have any wrath. I'll define her obeisance as a function of her learning history and not as an adaptation to me. My own aggression is kept backstage, and I'll require her not to notice it. Intersubjectivity and systems theory tell me to include it, but I override them. I don't admit that I'm overriding them simply because I can, because I prefer to be seen as wise and helpful rather than as merely human. Instead, I tell myself that research has demonstrated the importance of inspiring faith in the therapy process, and she needs me not to acknowledge discrediting emotions right now. She has staged a countercultural theater piece that burlesques the dominant culture, and I am accounting for it but not validating it. The lively thing to do would be to chuckle at its accuracy.

Of a million examples, here's another. A boring patient is telling me a story about some minor narcissistic injury—a waiter who did not bring the check quickly enough—and I am paying close enough attention to get the gist, but I don't really need to listen carefully to know what he is going to say about his sense of insignificance disguised as righteous indignation. I glance at the clock to discover that only 15 seconds have elapsed since my last glance at the clock. He can't possibly have noticed my glance at the clock, right? Like my own therapist, I keep the clock behind the patient where I can easily see it to promote my own situation consciousness and to free him to become engrossed. It's not like I have to stretch my arm and look at my watch or turn sideways to see the clock. He can't possibly have noticed, and even though it would make plain sense of his story and his indignation to acknowledge that it was I who had ignored him—not the waiter and not his father—I discreetly draw a curtain over my backstage boredom and describe him to myself as narcissistic. I am a perfectly good therapist saddled with a mediocre patient. He has staged a small poetry reading commenting in what poets call a conceit on the source of his conceitedness, but rather than respond to the content of his poem, I critique its technical virtuosity.

The next step toward deadliness, after pulling rank to define reality, is to pull rank to deny that I am doing it. I have intimidated the patients enough so that they can be expected to remain quiet, but my own thoughts about being a perfectly good therapist awaken self-consciousness in me in the voices of supervisors and colleagues. I defend myself by trashing the therapeutic frame and reverting to the societal frame: *he* is the patient here, *he* is the one whose narcissism has wrecked his marriage and threatened his employment, *he* is the one paying me for my superior intellectual and interpersonal functioning. Sometimes, I catch myself at this point and invite a discussion of the situation that is truly mutual.

Whether the conflict continues in my own imagination or whether he finally voices some dissatisfaction with me, I may be tempted to dispense with him by interpreting his dissatisfaction or even my own doubts as elements of his psychopathology. *He* has made me bored—probably to avoid intimacy. *I* am an expert on intimacy, embracing it whenever it presents itself (except now, when it might reflect badly on me), whereas he obviously has problems with intimacy. If he doesn't stop boring me, I may have to consider the possibility of character pathology. If I can sell him on my definition of the relationship, he will not only stop pestering me with accusations of imperfection but also become a long-term therapy payment—I mean *patient*.

DEFINING THE THERAPY RELATIONSHIP

Another major privilege in therapy is the ease of imposing one's own definition of the relationship on the patient. Human beings are highly suggestible—a necessary quality for adapting to social cues and establishing smooth hierarchies. In a power differential, people will sometimes defer to the obviously incorrect perceptions of the group (Asch, 1956; Dvoskin, 1978) and obey commands that conflict with their own values (Milgram, 1963). If the therapist sounds certain, the patient is likely to follow. Experts on interrogation techniques know that subjects are likely to alter their memories to conform to expectations when the more powerful person implies that the answer is already known. Subjects who view a short film and then are asked, "Did you see a bear?" are less likely to visualize a bear and answer yes than subjects who are asked, "Did you see the bear?" (Dale, Loftus, & Rathburn, 1978). The power to lead the patient can be used for good or evil, but of great concern to us as therapists is the potential to use power for good while accidentally rewarding an essentially submissive attitude within the therapy. One way to sound certain is to hide one's own backstage uncertainty (Goffman calls this *mystification*).

The more powerful a person is within a given interchange, the more tact others will generally display in disattending to discrediting information. President Johnson reportedly used the toilet while conferring with aides—only a president could command that much tact. People with little power, especially children, are afforded little tact, and virtually everything is seen and commented on. It is this feature of power differentials that makes it so important for us to husband the power we have as therapists so that we don't lose our license to comment on what is normally concealed and disattended by slipping into a democratic social frame that makes such comments rude. But therapeutic privilege allows us to deny having a psychology of our own and to demand tactful blindness from patients when it emerges. "Pay no attention to that man behind the curtain," said the Wizard of Oz (LeRoy & Fleming, 1939).

I'm not saying that therapists should disclose their personal conflicts, their interpersonal difficulties, or their own symptomatology. I'm saying that we therapists naturally but deadeningly indulge ourselves by discussing our patients' psychologies and what's going on in the office as if we don't have psychologies of our own, like parents remonstrating with their teenagers as if they had been cheerful, cooperative adolescents themselves. Even when we self-disclose—especially when we self-disclose in a tone that claims to be showing the backstage but hides the backstage not shown—we deny having a psychology in the sense of being subject to it. It's like admitting to having a body but still calling it something we have rather than something we are— *my body* suggests that I own it. We are constantly tempted to define our own psychology as something we have mastered rather than as a suitable subject for our curiosity and conversation. We may inadvertently teach patients that having a psychology is as humiliating as they always thought it was, even as we try to expose it and soothe the process of exposure. Lively therapy requires us to acknowledge our psychology when it is relevant to the interchange and not when we condescend to show it or can no longer get away with hiding it.

Another great privilege is the power not to think about things that might be status lowering. There is a folktale about the relationship between the elephant and the mouse. The mouse is an expert on the elephant—her travel habits, when she is likely to walk where, even her defecation. The elephant does not know the mouse even exists. It is status lowering to be concerned about the less powerful, and not thinking about them is a privilege.

A luxury of being a heterosexual white man in America is not often thinking of oneself as white, male, or straight. When I meet a new client, I am "just me," thinking about myself as a therapist and a few of the role relationships that are relevant to therapy (such as father, teacher, and supervisor). In Goffman's terms, I don't expect to depart from the patient's expectations of me, and I don't expect to do anything that most patients won't expect. When a black man meets a new client in America, he wonders if he will be accepted as a therapist or if certain therapeutic behaviors will be viewed as inconsistent with his being black. When a gay therapist meets a new client, he considers how the client might react to this information and whether it would discredit his performance as a therapist. The gay therapist has some personal concerns to put at ease before he can fully engross himself in the therapy frame and put aside the societal frame. When a woman meets a new client, she wonders if her sex will discredit her performance, and she thinks carefully about her costume, wanting to look good but not sexy. All three of them have the skills to manage these concerns, but I don't even think about these things.

I don't think our goal should be for white men to be as situation conscious, sex conscious, and race conscious as black women. Instead, we should all have the privilege of not thinking about race and sex when they are not directly relevant. The question is when, under what circumstances, I am white, male, or straight, and the answer that I always am a white, straight man is deadening. A situational approach to race and sex is more lively and freeing than a categorical approach.

Privilege appears in therapy when clients react to something we did and we don't see the reaction. We miss it partly because the patient is disguising his reaction, just as we disguise our reactions from our supervisors and teachers. If you've ever gone up for tenure in an academic department, then you know what I'm talking about—everyone you meet has some power over you. A few kind souls communicate clearly and believably that they will support your tenure application, setting aside that factor in your relationship with them, and you can relax with them. Others have no idea of the self-scrutiny under which you operate, how you graciously overlook conflicts and tactfully ignore their mistakes. They say things that sound remarkably unempathic— "You can always wait an extra year"—but it isn't a failure of empathy so much as an expression of privilege. They just forget the position you're in. You eventually get tenure yourself and, resolving not to be so heartless, considerately inquire as to your junior colleague's state of mind, forgetting that he must perform for you as you once performed. You would, of course, offer him the same authentic promise of support that a few of your colleagues offered to you, but your record of publication and service merited tenure, and his may not.

SEEKING VALID FEEDBACK

When I was in therapy in college, Dr. M conducted 45-minute sessions with a metaphorical revolving door. As I sat in the waiting area, the door to his office would open at the appointed time, and his previous patient would exit, pointedly not looking in my direction, and not closing the door behind her. A few seconds later, Dr. M would stand in the doorway and nod for me to enter the office, where for 45 minutes I would discuss sibling rivalry, hassled parents, and financial greed, never dreaming I was talking about the therapy. Then I would leave, pointedly not looking at the next patient, and leaving the door open behind me. One day, the patient ahead of me came out of the office literally wailing, and I saw that it was the wife of one of my professors. Ignoring something so blatantly important might have made Dr. M think there was something wrong with *me*, so I asked him if it was hard to refocus his attention after something like that. He acknowledged that it sometimes took a minute or two to fully tune in, so after a decent interval I took to starting every session with a minute of silence, pretending I was collecting my thoughts. Does this mean that the entire therapy was a wasteful charade? Of course not. My parents weren't perfect either, but they managed to do a good enough job overall. I didn't consciously see myself as making a sacrifice for my therapist. It just seemed natural (and it was) to support him in his role as beneficent and wise. We were collaborating, if not on exploring my immediate conflicts, then on exploring my autobiography and performing our roles. I learned a lot about the story of my life, and at least as much about how to collaborate while in a subordinate role. But I could have gotten even more out of the relationship if I hadn't needed to be so tactful.

The knee-jerk solution to the problem of overcoming privilege and tuning in to patients' reactions is to ask patients how they feel and what they think about what's going on. "Does that make sense to you?" "Do you feel better now?" "Tell me how you experienced my being late." "Are you finding the therapy helpful?" These questions are steeped in privilege because they ignore the power differential. They take patients' declarations as valid, thoughtful assessments unaffected by any concerns the patient may have about criticizing the therapist. Therapists often miss this because they focus on their own genuine interest in feedback, ignoring what the situation looks like to the patient.

Worse than interpreting patients' praise as valid is the corollary interpretation of criticism as *in*valid. When the patient denigrates the therapy, it's interpreted as a transference ("you're really angry at your father"), or it's jujitsued into a good sign that they felt they could be honest. Most of us know better than to interpret criticism as positive, but we all tend to interpret praise as positive. I'm not saying the therapist is a vicious schoolmaster standing over the patient with a whip and asking how she likes the lessons; I'm saying that the therapist is a dedicated educator standing over the patient with a ruler and asking how she likes the lessons. Add to the power differential the patient's cognitive dissonance (all this time and expense must have done me good), and there isn't much geographic information in the patient's assessment of interventions or the therapy as a whole.

Reports of progress on treatment goals are of obvious value. If a patient comes for help with her propensity for pairing with narcissistic men, stories she tells about her new lover's generosity and warmth are signs of progress. Or are they *signals* of progress? In other words, are they performances of progress rather than indicators of progress? If she says, "You really helped me; Joe is a great guy," it's much less convincing than if she tells a story about how Joe turned off the television and planned a dinner party with her. The former may be a sop to the therapy, the latter probably isn't (although of course the latter story may have been selected from a host of narcissistic incidents to defend Joe's character to the therapist).

Valid feedback within a power imbalance needs certain parameters. First and foremost is a renunciation of privilege in favor of genuine curiosity about the less powerful person's experience and willingness to subordinate oneself to signs from the patient that things might be done differently. When someone is angry at you, is your immediate reaction, "Wow, he sure is aggressive," or is it, "I must have done something to piss him off"?

Anonymity has some value in generating valid feedback, as in the classic suggestion box. Some clinics attempt to survey patients anonymously, but the freedom of expression afforded the anonymous writer can produce responses that are angrier than what is really felt. Also, any response general enough to preserve the patient's anonymity won't be specific enough for the therapist to make use of it.

We can promise not to retaliate. Such promises will be more believable if we haven't been expressing approval and praise, which define the relationship as judgmental and condition the patient to interpret neutrality as aloofness. We can meet criticism with avid curiosity and explore what might have worked better. This could lead to useful complaining, but praise would always be suspect.

Another way to seek valid feedback in a power imbalance is to identify corollary indicators of psychopathology and monitor them for improvement. For example, a narcissistic woman's posture of superiority and continual high-status maneuvering can be tracked. When we think she is getting better, we can check her reports of improvement against what we can see for ourselves. Here, the problem is that better-functioning patients rarely behave problematically in the office, except for the very behaviors we have to comment on in order to teach metacommunication, work through the transference, distinguish the therapy from other relationships, correct thinking errors, and engage the patient in lively exchanges. This can lead to a change in the behaviors we can see just to look good for us rather than as indicators of improvement. It's hard to tell the difference between enhanced capacity to play the role of therapy patient and enhanced capacity to play life's other roles, and one doesn't necessarily lead to the other.

The patient's conscious reactions can be a valid source of feedback for the therapist if the dyad first establishes their utility as part of the working alliance. An intimate relationship between patient and therapist can generate on ongoing stream of feedback, and the patient can learn from experience that the therapist remains curious and welcoming regardless of whether the feedback is positive or negative. If the therapist hears a wide range of reactions on a regular basis, he can be more confident that positive reactions aren't sops to his power and that negative reactions are attempts to improve the relationship. This is the intersubjectivist strategy for obtaining valid feedback.

Finally, there is metaphor—small acts of theater and poetry produced to critique the therapy's party line. Bateson, Jackson, Haley, and Weakland (1972) suggested that when patients are disappointed in therapists, they find themselves in a power imbalance where it may be dangerous to express themselves. They suggested that *all* psychological symptoms are metaphorical communications developed in risky situations that strike a balance between expression (in hopes of change) and disguise (in hopes of avoiding punishment). They guided our attention to the metaphorical content of patients' speech as a running commentary on the therapy—Langs (1978) has made this the centerpiece of his communicative approach. If you want to know the effects of interventions on patients, look at what they do right after the intervention. Compliance with the treatment plan is desirable, but it may be a sign of fear or resignation rather than progress. Praise from the patient is the same. A good story is more reliable, except once a patient catches on, she can invent good stories at will: I treated a psychology student whose requests for self-disclosure on my part I refused to indulge. One day, she came to therapy delighted to tell me that she had seen a baby bird that had fallen from its nest, supposing (correctly) that this metaphor would make me rethink my decision not to tell her more about myself. But the metaphor lacked sufficient touch points with self-disclosure to be a convincing guide. If she had been arguing against a decision on my part to leave the clinic and transfer her to another therapist there, then the bird's-nest metaphor—even consciously planned as it was—might have convinced me to take her into my private practice.

Therapeutic privilege and its associated power differential interfere with our ability to get useful feedback from patients. Attention to the immediate ensuing consequences of our behaviors should guide us in tailoring our repertoire, but interpretation of these consequences is also rife with problems of privilege and power. Patients' assessments of the utility of interventions and of the therapy on the whole are potential sources of information but are often shaped by issues of performance and tact. Perhaps the best we can do is to remain aware of the performance features of the feedback we get and to work as hard as possible on communicating our genuine and nondefensive interest in feedback. Above all, to the extent that our power and privilege create a self-serving party line that drives the patient's definition of the situation backstage, to be expressed only through small theater pieces called symptoms and through minor poems called metaphors, we should be an attentive, appreciative, curious, engrossed audience for these performances. Peter Brook (1968) gives some guidance when he cites a French term for what the theater audience does—"J'assiste à une pièce." Brook adds, "To assist—the word is simple: it is the key. . . . With this assistance, the assistance of eyes and focus and desires and enjoyment and concentration, [the performance] no longer separates actor and audience . . . it envelops them: what is present for one is present for the other. The audience too has undergone a change" (pp. 139–140). We should assist our patients' performances in much the same way.

Chapter Eight

Is Science Just Another
Party Line?

[Science is a] verbal community especially concerned with verbal behavior which contributes to successful action.

—Skinner (1957, p. 418)

What people understand to be the organization of their experience, they buttress, and perforce, self-fulfillingly. They develop a corpus of cautionary tales, games, riddles, experiments, newsy stories, and other scenarios which elegantly confirm a frame-relevant view of the workings of the world.

—Goffman (1974, p. 563)

Since so much depends on how situations are defined, can't we appeal to some objective method for saying which frame is fundamental, for telling us how things really stand? Science could potentially play that role for us, but the obstacles facing the therapist's quest for objectivity also interfere with the scientist's. There are many reasons to use science to resolve disputes about how to define what's going on, but because it's practiced by human beings, it's rife with power dynamics, self-serving concepts, and performance quandaries.

Science is a human subculture with traditions, norms, and conventions that tend to resolve disputes about the nature of reality accurately. Science is *about* geographical reality, but science itself is all too human. Science happens in a social world, even though it attempts to abstract information about the world beyond social conventions. Science is talk about reality. Because science is a social phenomenon—though it may pretend not to be—it is political and performative.

OPPRESSIVE KNOWLEDGE

Let's face it—none of us want scientists to be right about everything. None of us want to learn, proof positive, that consciousness is an illusion, that there is no life after death, and that we are descended from slime. But none of us has to accept these things, either—we can just dispute the evidence or the argument that leads to conclusions we don't like. We can acknowledge scientists' ability to control and predict what spacecraft will do but question their ideas about where the galaxy came from. We smirk when a spacecraft explodes (when there's no one in it) because it firms up our sense that they don't know it all and that our own pet theory of how the universe came to be is just as valid as theirs. (I personally think the universe has all the earmarks of an afterthought.)

There is one branch of science (meaning, one area of scientific investigation) where we especially rebel against their reducing everything to rules and equations—psychology, the science of human behavior. Nobody likes a smart aleck, but nobody especially likes an aleck being smart about us. In writing this book that you are reading right now (see how annoying it is that I know what you're doing?), I'm trying to be smart about us. We're afraid that self-knowledge will reduce us to machinery. But rather than console myself with the thought that such a reduction is impossible (by dint of my godliness, will, aesthetic appreciation, or creativity), I instead believe that if this is my condition, I must learn to enjoy it—transcendence through facticity is my goal, not transcendence by denying facticity.

This is all by way of saying that the truth about reality may be upsetting. "For in much wisdom is much grief: and he that increaseth knowledge increaseth sorrow" (Ecclesiastes 1:18). Scientific statements can become a party line to protect the scientific establishment and to protect the average Joe from sorrow. Darwin anticipated the use of scientific statements as a form of complacency when he wrote, "If the misery of our poor be caused not by the laws of nature, but by our institutions, great is our sin" (used by Gould [1981] as an epigraph). Darwin was trying to stave off the political use of his theory of natural selection, anticipating that it would be twisted to justify bad treatment of the poor. Within science itself, statements about reality can turn into a party line that preserves the power of the scientific establishment by shutting down new ideas and information. Scientific hegemony produces the often-heard locutions *scientific evidence* and *scientific fact*, where the adjective adds nothing but an aura of respectability.

CULTURAL MYTHS OF SCIENCE

The ultimate scientific fantasy is to be the little boy in *The Emperor's New Clothes* (Andersen, 1993). The story is about clever tailors who dupe a vain Emperor and his courtiers—and ultimately the public—into believing that the nonexistent material with which they are weaving the royal outfit is so fine and elegant that only intelligent and competent people can see it. Everyone claims to see this remarkable material. In my own version of this story, everyone *does* see the material since the existence of the object is only one factor in determining what is seen and the expectations, wishes, and status concerns of the observer are also important factors in determining what is seen. Observers' concern for their own social status ties them to the Emperor's status, whose nakedness requires a level of tact that defies the senses. Then, a little boy, immune to this need for status by virtue of his youth and naïveté, not to mention a degree of insolence and rebelliousness often found in those who, unable to ascend the status ladder, prefer to upend it, says, "But he's naked." Even though the Emperor and his immediate entourage go on pretending that he is dressed, his social-political power can't withstand the effect of this geographical truth, and the people see him for what he is. The scientific fantasy is the triumph of geographical truth over social and political constructions.

In a way, the little boy illustrates the fantasy of every human subculture, namely, to impose and ascend one's preferred status ladder (which in science's case is accuracy about reality), replacing and upending that of the dominant culture. It's partly sour grapes—looks are unimportant, say the unlovely, and money is unimportant, say the unwealthy. But it's more than that. The unimportance of looks or money may be a genuine value in a given subculture, and the members of this subculture will take a certain delight in pointing to public figures for whom money did not buy happiness or whose good looks proved more a curse than a blessing.

SCIENCE AVOIDS PERFORMANCE

In science, the highest value is accuracy about reality, but this value unfolds in a larger culture that has competing values—maintaining a social hierarchy, for example, or protecting the accuracy of religious accounts of reality. When a scientist can state a geographical truth that upends one of these values in the larger culture, she is in the same position as the journalist who gains the respect of her peers by exposing a political leader's sordid past. The scientist's political problem can be summarized by this example about communist

China's agronomists: "Mao personally redesigned China's agricultural techniques, specifying closer planting and deeper sowing to increase yields. Rice planted so closely together could not grow, but party officials, anxious to please Mao, staged shows of agricultural . . . success" (Harford, 2005, p. 221). The phrase "staged shows" is particularly apt and demonstrates how hard it is for scientists—just like the rest of us—to behave nonperformatively.

Science's commitment to an accurate account of reality is not uniform, wholehearted, or exclusive of all other motives. No subculture can claim that kind of devotion. But science is *persistently* committed to this value. When R. A. Fisher, a biologist and mathematician, demonstrated that one of biology's most revered figures, Gregor Mendel, fudged his data to make it look more convincing, many scientists suffered a pang of regret on Mendel's and science's behalf, but no one thought that Fisher should have kept quiet. When church figures or statesmen are caught with their pants down, there is always some question about whether to publish—in science, the truth about reality is the ultimate (if not always the only) goal.

THE FANTASY OF OBJECTIVITY

Science is practiced by people, but it's often presented as if there is a pure science, a sort of Platonic ideal, that could in theory be distilled to its purest form but in practice is corrupted by the psychologies, motivations, needs, and imperfections of humans. This is balderdash since without people, all our foibles included perforce, there would be no science. The fantasy of a pure science is rooted in the deeper human desire to define ourselves by what we're proud of, ignoring the rest or seeing the rest as an appendage to the otherwise perfect self. The Red Sox did not win the World Series between 1918 and 2004, while the Yankees won over 20 times, but a Red Sox fan still thinks that the Red Sox are the best team in baseball history, thwarted only by the fact that the Yankees have had more money and spent that money on acquiring better players. *Apart from* money, the Red Sox are better. *Apart from* my body, I am a better athlete than Carl Lewis. *Apart from* people, science is an engine for discovering the truth. But as Yeats said, who can know the dancer from the dance?

SCIENCE AND GENDER

The conception of science as a human subculture (Kuhn, 1962; Longino, 1990), as opposed to a truth-getting machine, is a yin view of science. Within the subculture, science has fashions, fluctuating between the nomothetic yang (discovering and applying laws of nature) and the idiographic yin (explaining incidents in context). Relations between scientists also run between yin and yang. In yang moments, we are like brothers on opposing football teams, playing aggressively but buddies off the field. We sometimes ignore the goal of understanding reality in favor of winning the competition. Scientists rationalize that in the long run, yang competition will produce the truth because only the best ideas survive—but we all know that's not quite true. The best ideas can die of starvation long before they prove their utility. In yin moments, we are like coauthors, stimulating each other within an envelope of love to refine our thinking. "Two heads are better than one," said one psychologist, celebrating the synergy that can emerge from collaboration. We sometimes ignore the goal of understanding reality in favor of supporting each other. The same psychologist who said that two heads are better than one declined to point out that a colleague had used the wrong statistical test in analyzing her data because she didn't want to make her feel bad. Androgynous integration of yin and yang is the goal in science as it is in life.

SEEKING OBJECTIVITY

Scientists try to eliminate the individual scientist (rather than all scientists) from the truth about reality. One way to do this is by relying on the scientific method's greatest feature—replicability. If enough scientists get the same results, it may be possible to conclude that these results reflect reality and not the expectations of scientists. "May be possible" rather than "must" because the scientists could all be fooled by the same expectation, a political trend could have stifled the reporting of odd results, or all the experiments and observations could have occurred under idiosyncratic circumstances. By making folk heroes and not villains of those who have exploded widely held expectations and lockstep political trends, science makes its members want to sidestep distractions from the truth by uncovering them for what they are.

SCIENCE MAKES UP STORIES

The fruits of science are stories we tell that account for data and follow rules of logic. Science's conventions for stories are analogous to theatrical and television conventions, but science's stories are supposed to be particularly adept at facilitating successful behavior. Dorothy Parker (1978) wrote a story about two Depression-era secretaries in New York City who spend their lunch hour walking up and down Fifth Avenue imagining what they would do if they each had a million dollars. They dream of vacations, mansions, and jewelry, and they make long lists of everything they would purchase, keeping the tally in deadlier earnest than any bookkeeper. One day, they get up the nerve to actually walk into Tiffany's and ask about the necklace in the window that one of them has added to her fantasy shopping cart. The clerk tells them the necklace costs $250,000, and they realize they have been vastly overspending. The women are utterly dejected, and their game is ruined, so they trudge back to work. Suddenly, one of them perks up and asks what the other would do with *10* million dollars.

There are a lot of ways the secretaries could have responded to the new information that demonstrated to them that the story they were telling themselves about being rich was totally inadequate. Their first response was to throw away their story. They were trying to make a theory or a map that guides their conduct and makes them feel good about themselves but that also fits reality as they know it. When information arrives that disconfirms their story, they throw out their map as no damn good, like a driver who suddenly finds that her planned route involves a one-way street going the wrong way. She has a moment of heartbreak in which she realizes she is lost. At that moment, she can turn to philosophy (philosophy being where people turn when they realize they are lost). The secretaries, for example, could question the value of money and earthly goods. They could laugh at the absurdity of their having comforted themselves for so long with something so inadequate, like little girls in a department store who hang on to their mothers' skirts while daydreaming and finally look up to realize that they have been hanging on to a mannequin. They could ignore the new information ("the clerk cannot possibly have meant what he said; he was kidding us; he meant Hong Kong dollars"). Or they can amend their story to take the new information into account. When they did this, they were acting scientifically.

The scientific attitude can be summed up in a single word: *oops*. This conveys the desired relationship with disconfirming data from marginalized voices out of step with the party line.

SCIENCE FOLK HEROES CHOOSE TRUTH

More often than scientists like to acknowledge, personal goals outweigh the cultural value of changing the story to fit the data. This is understandable since scientists' status needs, tenure at major universities, and funding from government grants all depend on which story is told. Of course, *any* value from *any* culture can fall prey to the human foibles of greed, lust, and power.

Most cultures tell stories about heroes who choose cultural values over the temptations of money, sex, power, and even life and liberty. In scientific morality plays, a good example of a hero choosing cultural values over human needs is Galileo, who is portrayed as sticking by the truth that the earth moves—an affront to Catholicism—at the risk of his life and personal freedom.

Scientists much prefer this image of Galileo versus the Church to the story of Ole Roemer, the Danish astronomer who startled the scientific world with proof that light has a finite speed. The idea that light travels at a speed seems obvious to us today, but try to remember the first time you heard the idea from your parents. Probably, it came up with sound rather than light as you heard the crack of the bat a discernible moment after you saw the impact. At that point, your parent may also have mentioned that light, too, travels at a finite speed, and of course, you convinced yourself that you could detect that speed when a friend flashed a light in your direction. But self-deception aside, it now seems straightforward enough to think of light as something that emanates from a source, travels across space, and hits your eyes. (I am not counting the large proportion of people who think that the act of seeing involves the emission of something from the eyes [Winer, Cottrell, Gregg, Fournier, & Bica, 2002].)

But it wasn't always this way. Instead, it used to seem obvious that you saw something when it happened. Given human reaction times, for all practical purposes it is fair to say that light *was* instantaneous. No situation arose between the dawn of time and the 1670s in which the idea of a finite speed for light could possibly make a difference.

By 1676, Galileo and Descartes had been dead for a quarter century, and Newton was the most famous person in European intellectual circles—the scientific method was well established, and scientists would supposedly bow to it. Galileo had tried to measure the speed of light on two Italian hilltops but succeeded only in measuring the reaction times of his assistants. Descartes was on record as believing that the speed of light would prove to be infinite. In 1676, a situation where the speed of light could make a difference at last presented itself. Scientists had accurately and carefully measured the motion of Jupiter's moons, including Io, the third largest of them. Io would pass behind Jupiter and emerge precisely on schedule—except that it emerged precisely on schedule only some of the time and emerged late some of the time. The leading scientists of the day hypothesized that a cloud of dust surrounding Jupiter was slowing down its moon, but it was hard to see how this cloud of dust could slow down Io only some of the time.

Roemer's idea was that Io was moving on schedule, but at certain times of the year it took longer for her light to reach us because we were farther away.

Roemer predicted that on November 9, 1676, Io would emerge from behind Jupiter precisely 10 minutes later than expected. Observatories all over Europe watched, and all agreed that he had been right. In the best tradition of science, he had presented a testable and falsifiable hypothesis, and his experiment had validated his position. But scientists reacted like the people they are—those who stood to lose face pooh-poohed his results. It was decades before the finite speed of light became dogmatic in science. In the short run, scientists were all too human in protecting their stakes and reputations. Ultimately, Roemer went into politics, perhaps realizing that people only pretend to be swayed by the scientific method and choosing instead the more direct course for influencing them. You hear about Galileo but not about Roemer because the scientific subculture wants to advertise itself as a bunch of Galileos questioning the party line, not as the group that disregarded Roemer and maintained their own party line.

SOCIAL VERSUS GEOGRAPHIC SUCCESS

In the quote at the beginning of this chapter, Skinner tells us that the scientific subculture is concerned with making statements about reality that lead to successful action. In this respect, science is like any other party line, promulgating textual rules that define situations and govern behavior. Science is different from other party lines in that it is supposed to be especially concerned with the production of behavior that is successful—but as a party line, it runs into all the same performance problems facing self-serving hegemonies and marginalized voices. Success, then, can mean effectiveness with respect to the geographic environment, or it can mean the performance of effectiveness with respect to the social world, and it's hard to tell the difference.

Science makes statements about reality. The statements are like maps, and reality is like a place that is being mapped. Understanding maps can help us understand the performance problems associated with the practice of science. Maps provide information on which to base behavior, and the utilitarian view is that maps are accurate—statements are true—to the extent that the behaviors based on them are rewarded or at least go as expected. Say you're in a situation where it would be rewarding to get to my house (perhaps you've been invited to a party). I've drawn you a rudimentary map, and you base your driving on it. If you wind up at my house and I ask you, "Did you find it okay," you say, "Oh yes, the map was accurate." (Actually, you say that only if you are a logic professor—what you really say is, "Yeah, where's the beer?" But you get the idea.) Some friends of mine were driving to a wedding reception, using a map the couple provided to get from the ceremony to the party. In drawing the map, the groom had accidentally allowed two extraneous lines to overlap, so one of my friends concluded that these two roads intersected, and they missed most of the reception. From the utilitarian point of view, that was a bad map (assuming the groom really did want my friends to attend and assuming my friends really did want to hear accordion music); it was the same as a statement about reality that is false.

There are two ways that following a map (or instructions or conjectures about reality) can be rewarded. One way is to act accordingly and see if something good happens. The other way is to see what others say about your map-based behavior or just to say you're going to follow the map and see how other people treat you. In other words, behaviors based on maps or words can be evaluated geographically, or they can be evaluated socially. A map that is useless for negotiating reality can be essential for getting a good grade in a class where the teacher is not in tune with reality or for negotiating situations that exist only socially. A detailed map of Heaven, for example, is of questionable utility in the natural sense, but it can get you rewards in the right Sunday school.

Or even a college literature class. Consider the following multiple-choice question in an exam on great books of Western literature: Which of the following can be found in the innermost circle of Hell along with Judas?

A. Genghis Khan   B. Attila the Hun   C. Brutus
D. Herod   E. Hitler

The correct answer is—wait. Correct? Are we actually guessing which of these persons is in the innermost circle of Hell? No, of course not. We don't even know if Hell exists. We're guessing what the teacher thinks is the right answer. We're in a purely social space. Hitler may have been the worst of these persons, and of Brutus, we recall Shakespeare's sentiment that the "elements were so mixed in him that Nature might stand up and say to all the world, 'This was a Man.'" And, yet, with a course on great books as the context, perhaps we recall that in the innermost circle along with Judas, Dante placed Brutus and Cassius. Resolving then to do as the Romans do, we choose Brutus, and later on the teacher tells us we were right. And we *are* right, if not about the navigation of Hell, then about the navigation of great books exams.

This social use of maps was illustrated in the musical *The King and I* (Brackett & Lang, 1956). The English tutor confronts the 19th-century Siamese king's children with a geographically accurate map of the world, and the children are shocked and dismayed by the small size of Siam. The crown prince makes threats, diverted only by the tutor's pointing out that Siam on the map is still bigger than England.

Maps depict reality, but they also have social uses, and the two are often in conflict. If cartographers succumb to social pressure, this conflict could lead to overestimating your own strength compared to that of a neighboring country. Thus, the truth—successful action based on verbal and visual beliefs— has two major relevant arenas, one being geographic (what happens when people base their conduct on a statement) and the other being social (how other people react to conduct and statements). Scientific maps become party lines when the two are conflated.

There are many arenas in which a map can be useful. Some of these arenas are primarily geographic, some primarily social, and some a combination of the two. A street map is useful in geography. If someone thinks the map is wrong, it's easy enough to test it against the actual streets. Someone might not like the map because it's hard for them to read or is drawn with ugly colors— even the most geographically oriented map has social aspects, in other words, a communicative function. J. R. R. Tolkien's map of Middle Earth has purely social functions. Behavior based on it will succeed or fail only in the social sphere, perhaps as an aid to following the story or as a basis for resolving disagreements between students of Tolkien.

A road map is useful in a geographical setting, but it's the geography of getting someplace in a car. Another map might be geographically useful for drilling oil, deciding where to live, or following a history book. Indeed, the history map will usually distort the geographic features to highlight them in order to facilitate communication, making it less useful for navigation. Even road maps distort geography by making highways disproportionately large and easier to see. Thus, maps, like statements, are more or less useful in a variety of relevant situations, some of which are primarily social and some of which are primarily geographic. Even purely geographic maps have a social, communicative aspect, and even the maps designed or used primarily for social reasons can be construed as geographic, where the relevant geography is the navigation of the social sphere.

*   *   *

Here's another approach to social versus geographic. Say you're taking an exam for a class, and there is a question your professor has covered in detail. You are certain that her version of this topic is incorrect. This happens more frequently than we would like to admit. On the exam, do you write down the correct answer or the one she thinks is correct? Many statements about the world are almost never acted on—few behaviors are ever based on them. These range from statements about subatomic particles to statements about faraway places to statements about obscure mathematical functions. Very few people, a very small proportion of those who study photons in school, are ever in a position to alter their behavior according to what they understand. The rest of us are just flicking light switches. Even photographers can make do with an idea that photons are little billiard balls. So if two theoretical physicists are debating whether photons are particles or waves or whether they are in a particular place or merely in a potential place, the rest of us are probably never going to base any behavior on what they say. I mean, behavior other than saying things about photons.

DO STATEMENTS MATTER IF WE DON'T ACT ON THEM?

In class, the desire for a good grade competes with the geographical truth of a statement. If my teacher tells me that cold *always* makes things contract, I'll end up with some cracks in the foundation of my house if I build it under his influence. If he asks me on an exam if this is true, then I may say yes just to get the better grade. Outside of class, there are all sorts of competitors with geographical truth, like social approval, status, and funding. The less likely I am to act on a statement, the less harm I'll suffer in acceding to social demands and expectations. Thus, it may be perfectly clear that Darwin was right, but what good does it do? The only actions most of us ever base on Darwin occur in classrooms or cocktail parties, where we are merely demonstrating our mastery of the theory. Since it doesn't matter if Darwin was wrong or right, why do we care? Why not just get along with religious folks who do care and agree that God made us as we are?

The answer is that while it may not matter whether Darwin was right, the thinking process by which he came up with his theory does matter. When we defend Darwin, we're defending logic, critical thinking, and the ability to change one's mind according to evidence. The same impulse makes us balk at acceptance when other people talk about astrology, ghosts, and psychic powers. What difference does it really make to us if someone finds it comforting to believe that she knew that the planes were going to crash into the towers or that the ringing phone meant her father was dead? What makes a difference is the way of thinking, not the content. It's not our place to cross-examine the poor woman who only wants to feel a modicum of control over her father's death, leading her to forget the million times over the past year when she thought of him dying and nothing happened. Not to mention the million times something bad happened and she hadn't thought of it beforehand. It's not our place to tell her that her dreams of him are only dreams and not visitations. But we are entitled to resist her explanations and claims because we are entitled to resist wishful thinking, illogic, and a faith that never yields to evidence and logic.

SEXUAL AND NATURAL SELECTION

This distinction I am drawing between *social* and *geographic* mapmaking appears in other contexts. Consider the difference in evolutionary theory between sexual selection and natural selection. Natural selection means that a randomly developed trait must be useful out in the world, or else animals or plants with that trait will not be as successful as their counterparts, and the trait will not be passed on. Thumbs presumably arose by a genetic accident, but they've proven so useful that eventually only apes with thumbs survived to pass on the structure of their hands.

Sexual selection means that randomly developed traits are passed on not because they are useful out in the world but because they are appealing to members of the opposite sex. The peacock's tail is most likely a hindrance out in the world, but it's so exciting to peahens that it gets passed on. Presumably, peacocks with little tails had an easier time of it getting dinner and avoiding predators, but they had too hard a time of it getting laid (and the eggs of their future heirs were not laid at all). To help compensate for the burden of carrying around that tail, peacocks whose tails happened to look like eyes had an advantage over peacocks with small tails and peacocks whose tails were merely pretty. The size and colors of the tail attracted peahens, while the eyes may have discouraged enough predators to compensate for the inability to flee.

Another level on which selection occurs, by the way, is the "intragenetic" (between genes) level. A new gene has to get along with other genes before it can ever get a chance to be tested in the environment or among members of the opposite sex. If a new gene kills the embryo, it doesn't matter much that it would have benefited the animal if only it had not killed it. The analogy in mapmaking is that a map has to make sense on its own terms before it can be used geographically or socially.

TRUE MEANS SUCCESSFUL

If you agree with a statement—if you think the statement is true—then it means you would endorse, approve of, or advise actions based on it. If you disagree with a statement—if you think the statement is false—it means you would not endorse, approve of, or advise actions based on it. This clarifies what *truth* means, but it complicates things, too, because now we have to spell out what we mean by "actions based on it." Does that include actions such as talking and thinking? Take the statement "God has an inscrutable plan for me." A wise person who advises rationally weighing important decisions rather than praying for a sign would probably consider the statement false, while an equally wise person who advises using mistakes and setbacks as opportunities for education and personal growth would probably consider the statement true, especially if it prompts a spiritual calling to examine mistakes and setbacks.

Does "based on" mean that the action must be a *logical* consequence of the statement? Or just an *actual* consequence? In other words, do I evaluate a statement as it is understood by the ideal, intelligent, educated listener or as it was understood by the person who actually heard it? There was a rumor not too long ago of a scurrilous politician claiming in a campaign that his adversary was a "heterosexual." The politician was supposedly relying on the ignorance and bigotry of the electorate, so he could say something that was technically true and yet tar the adversary nonetheless. If the story is true and if the electorate did think that "heterosexual" meant some kind of perversion and therefore did not vote for the adversary, there is a question of whether the statement "My opponent is a heterosexual" was true. It's a true statement if only logical, educated reactions are considered; it's a false statement if all reactions are considered and someone actually refused to vote for the opponent on its basis (false with respect to that particular listener). I assume it's obvious that statements can be true or false depending on the listener or the circumstances.

The example of the "heterosexual" politician is rather simply dealt with by defining terms. A more complex example is the statement "There is a 70% chance the cancer will kill you within 3 years if you do not have the operation and a 10% chance you will die on the operating table." Unless the patient is so old that she is unlikely to live for 3 years in any event, she should logically elect to have the operation (because having the operation will increase her life expectancy). But if most patients who hear this statement elect not to have the operation, then what good does it do a doctor to say the statement is true but poorly worded? Health care is better served by focusing on the statement's effects—by assigning a truth value according to its actual consequences rather than only its logical consequences. A doctor can then consider how to make the statement more true rather than the daunting agenda of making patients more logical.

Analogous to natural selection, in science's search for truth, it wants to make statements that generate behaviors that are well tailored to geography, the infamous and so-called real world. In other words, we try to say things that produce actions that work. Like sexual selection, we will have to take into account the effect of what we say on other people. What good is truth if no one will act on it because it's ugly? Like intragenetic selection, the pieces of what we say have to get along with each other; that is, they will have to combine to form meaningful or comprehensible sentences. What good is truth if no one can understand it?

As with social versus geographic functions of maps, the distinction between natural and sexual selection does not always hold up. That's because the peahen's preference for the big tail is actually just another element of the peacock's environment. It's obvious to us that the peahen's sexual interest is different from the fox's predatory interest, but it's not obvious to the gene that produces the big tail. Either the gene survives and gets passed on or it doesn't. In fact, if the peacock had a choice, it would probably decide that the increased chance of having sex isn't enough compensation to make up for the risk of not being able to outrun a fox. But the animal doesn't decide; the environment does. And if there are more big-tail genes that get passed on because they arouse peahens than there are that expire because they hinder flight, then the environment has spoken. Most genes produce features that have costs (usually in the form of requiring more energy to sustain the feature) and benefits (whether making survival of the animal more likely or being a turn-on for other animals), and the environment decides whether the costs are worth the benefits. And yet it does seem helpful to distinguish the social from the geographic under some circumstances, as in explaining why peacocks have such big tails when they are an obvious hindrance.

USEFUL CLASSROOMS, THERAPIES, AND IMAGINATIONS

Imagination, therapy, theater, and classrooms all allow us to try out different approaches to situations without the costs of behavior in those situations, but the opportunity provided by these venues will only be as valuable as their essential similarities to the other situations. A useful imagination is one in which behavior works as well or as poorly as it does in life.

In a useful classroom, there is harmony between social approval of statements and their ability to inspire successful behavior outside of the classroom. In a bad classroom, the teacher approves of statements that will lead to failures out in the rest of the world. In most classrooms, the statements being taught have nothing to do with the outside world and have relevance only to other classrooms. The saying "It's academic" really means "It doesn't matter anywhere else." This sense of purely social relevance is caught in the joke about the scholar who discovered that the Iliad and the Odyssey were not written by Homer after all but by another Greek, also named Homer.

In a useful therapy, there is harmony between the therapist's agenda and what the patient needs to learn to behave successfully outside of therapy. This transposition is complicated by the fact that the harmony need not be immediate or direct—the patient shouldn't learn to corner people and talk about himself. The best way to distinguish what is only for the therapy space and what will be transcribed for later use is to manage the therapy frame carefully and explicitly. Careful, explicit framing also allows life lessons to be presented in the theater while not implying that their transcriptions should be exact.

TRUTH RARELY MATTERS

Truth is a quality of statements, discernible in the utility of conduct based on those statements. But truth rarely matters because statements rarely influence behavior any more than a sportscaster's play-by-play influences the behavior of the football players he describes. As Oscar Wilde said, "I always pass on good advice. It is the only thing to do with it. It is never of any use to oneself." People typically do whatever they are going to do and then make up statements to justify what they did. Some statements have excellent truth value—"the butter is behind the milk"—and engender useful conduct (moving the milk and getting the butter). But statements about reality, nature, or truth itself rarely engender behavior that makes a difference. That's why the medical practice of applying leeches to cure various illnesses seemed obvious and was accompanied by supportive statements until it was found to be stupid, at which time the medical practice of not applying leeches seemed obvious and was accompanied by supportive statements. Luis Alvarez (1987) summed up this problem in science in a story he told about Ernest Lawrence. A team was wondering if four subatomic particles identified in different procedures were in fact the same particle. The team reminded Lawrence that theorists had reasons why they could not be the same. Lawrence shrugged and said that if the team demonstrated that they were the same, then the theorists would show why they *had* to be. (And that's what happened—Lawrence's lab showed they were the same, and the theorists who explained why it had to be so won the Nobel Prize.)

FACTS ARE OPINIONS HELD BY THE RIGHT PEOPLE

Facts are opinions held by the right people. There's a difference between a word and what it refers to, between a statement—a fact *or* an opinion—and the underlying state of affairs. I realize that certain states of affairs exist in reality and that others are merely thought to exist. I also realize that it would be

nice to call the states of affairs that really exist *facts* and to call ideas or statements about them *opinions*, but it's not that easy. For example, my computer
is on at this moment, and it would be nice to say that this is a fact and that
anyone who thinks otherwise is simply wrong. I don't doubt that my computer is on, and I don't doubt that anyone who thinks otherwise is wrong. But
when I *say* "my computer is on," I'm making a statement—I'm not actually
turning my computer on. Everything we refer to as a fact is only a statement
about reality. It's a fact that Columbus is the capital of Ohio, but "Columbus
is the capital of Ohio" is a statement. If Columbus is the capital of Ohio, then
it's a true statement; otherwise, it's a false statement. List facts you know, and
you will find yourself listing words, phrases, and sentences about reality.
Since these are statements, they describe reality, or they guide others around
the environment, but they are not reality (well, they are a subset of reality, but
these statements do not constitute the geographical reality that concerns us for
the moment). What these statements are, then, are opinions, but they are opinions of which you can be certain.

How do we distinguish statements that are considered to be facts from
statements that are considered to be opinions? I think the answer is in the degree of certainty you have in their being true (i.e., in your being well advised
to let such statements direct and guide your behavior in the situations for
which the statements are relevant). However, no amount of certainty can be a
guarantee of truth. Indeed, if a truism is *perfectly* certain, then it is a tautology, true by its own terms, and its value is trivial. The capital of Ohio is the
capital of Ohio. For another example, if we accept that Socrates is a rat and
if we accept that all rats are rodents, then it must be perfectly true that
Socrates is a rodent. But to say that Socrates is a rodent is merely to restate
what was said before in different language; the new statement does not include any new information beyond the statements that Socrates is a rat and
that all rats are rodents. Truisms can also be perfectly certain as an article of
faith—indeed, faith's hallmark is that it does not yield to evidence. There's
nothing wrong with that, of course, until you start basing geographical behavior on it. I mean, I admire people with faith that Jesus loves and protects
them, but I don't admire them if they jump off buildings and expect to be safe.
Even Jesus did not go that far (Matthew 4:5–7).

For thousands of years, people thought the sun arose from the horizon in
the morning and sunk beyond the horizon in the evening. Then, for several
hundred years, people thought the sun went around the earth. They were
wrong, as it turns out, but in those days, everyone thought it did, and nobody
engaged in any behavior anywhere on earth that was made more difficult or
less useful as a result of that belief. (It was only when some people started
keeping careful track of stars' and planets' locations that the belief in the sta-

tionary earth made anyone's life more difficult.) It's fine to stand here in the 21st century and say that for thousands of years what everyone thought was a fact was actually an opinion. But what if you're not standing in our shoes? What if you're standing in the shoes of the ancients? From that point of view, the stationary earth is a fact. More important, we are the ancients with respect to all current facts, and we can't stand in the eventual shoes of our intellectual heirs. The only way to know which of the things we currently believe to be facts will eventually be described as wrong (as mere opinions) is to wait and see. All current factual statements are only potentially true, their potential depending on what happens in the future. In the present day, the only distinction between facts and opinions is that enough of the right people believe the facts are true and that not enough of the right people believe that the opinions are true. If everyone agreed that an opinion were true, it would be a fact. Not *everyone* has to agree, of course; if enough of the right people agree, you have a fact. Even the number of planets revolving around the sun comes down to a vote on what a planet is (Erickson, 2006).

Who the *right* people are varies with the subject and circumstances. The right people may be scientists, religious leaders, experts denoted by their credentials or experience, eyewitnesses, the general population, or the judge at a bench trial (whose written decision is preceded by a list of facts she found to be true). Unless you are a physicist, you are probably willing to accept the consensus of physicists as to whether there is such a thing as a neutrino. Regardless of how smart you are or how good you are with words, you are probably willing to accept a consensus of dictionary writers and publishers as to how to spell a word. Religious leaders used to be given a lot more deference in Western European societies than they are now, but in some parts of the world, religious leaders still get to decide what's a fact and what's not.

A system of facts is useful to the extent that, like a map and its features, it helps us get around reality without too many bumps and bruises. It used to be a fact that the earth stood still. This fact was central to a system that helped astronomers locate the current, past, and future positions of planets. Now it is a fact that the earth moves. Facts exist in the social, political sphere, even though they are *about* things in the geographical sphere. I hear you saying that it was never a fact that the earth stood still, that this was a mistake. But if we insist on calling *fact* only those things that *eventually* turn out to be true rather than those things currently believed to be true, then we have no way of knowing which of the many things we currently believe are facts. Thus, either facts are those things that turn out to be true and there are no facts until Judgment Day when God tells us what was what or facts are those things currently believed to be true by the right people.

The issue is essential to understanding the way a dispute about reality is actually almost always a dispute about framing and the way science, despite its goals, is often a party line rather than a guide to reality. That's because the empowerment of people to the status of becoming the right people to determine what's true brings with it—even when the best people are chosen—the problems of self-serving and self-preserving hegemonies. In therapy, the right person to determine what's what is usually the therapist, and it takes a system of checks and balances to keep from exploiting that position.

THE NEED TO BE YOURSELF

Discussing the difference between maps and geography helps explain how we came to be a species that talks itself out of believing in reality when it's convenient to our sense of self-importance or our sense of freedom. Because much of what we say has no bearing on our behavior, we confuse what we say with what we believe. You can tell more about what a person believes by watching what she does than by listening to what she says. She says she believes that an angel is watching over her, but she still looks both ways before crossing the street. It's the social use of communication, as opposed to the relatively nonsocial, geographic use, that sets the stage for us to develop a mythology that we can somehow escape reality.

Our beliefs about ourselves are important in determining what we do. When science challenges our beliefs about ourselves, it can be enlightening, but it can also become an oppressive party line that marginalizes our cherished beliefs. In this respect, we are all new-agers—we all have odd ideas about ourselves and our worlds that we hide from rational scrutiny. When the goal of therapy is to hunt down and clean up irrational ideas, therapy itself becomes an oppressive party line. When the goal of therapy is to show the patient how to perform the self within the constraints of her world or to change the definition of the self so that the conflict with geography is not as wearing, then science can be an ally.

One of the most powerful human motivations is the need to be yourself—to play the part I have defined as me—but it's a motivation that's largely invisible, like the human motivation to seek oxygen. You rarely see people in situations where they are oxygen deprived, so it would be hard to detect how fiercely we will struggle to get it when we don't have it just by watching us under normal conditions. But hold a person under water, and other motivations—status, sex, money, food, fame—pale in comparison to breathing. You rarely see people not being themselves because so much of our social and physical environment has been adapted by us to reflect back to us who we think we are. But drop us into a new situation, and watch how we surround ourselves with cultural and personal icons and how we generate relationships that put us in precisely the roles we find most familiar. Psychoanalysts count on this phenomenon, expecting the patient to make the newness of therapy into the familiar patterns that define her.

Being yourself is so important to us because everything good that has ever happened to us happened while we were being ourselves. If everything good that ever happened to us happened while we were hopping on one foot, stores would stop selling shoes in pairs because we would never put that other foot down. Every time my mom tousled my hair and smiled warmly at me, she strengthened not only my tendency to do what I had just been doing but also my tendency to be me. (Some unfortunate people have had so many more bad things happen to them than good things that they put a lot of energy into not being themselves: current terminology for what these persons have is *identity disorder* or *borderline personality organization*.)

Who we think we are is defined largely by reactions to the way we are treated. For example, let's say I feel discomfort at being treated as if I were important and even more discomfort at being treated as if I were unimportant and no discomfort at all at being treated as if I were important but not *that* important. I may not think consciously of my self-definition, but I can still be said to have an identity element of being "pretty important." My reactions could be assessed, and a formulation of me as a "little brother" could be developed. Then it would be accurate to say I "think of myself" as a little brother—"little brother" helps define who I am and how I act under typical conditions—even if the words "little brother" never go through my mind. The formulation could help others know how to treat me. This observation—that our identities can be usefully described in terms that we ourselves have never used—is even more obvious when the description is undesirable. If I tell you that someone I know is an arrogant prick, it can be a valid description of his identity even though he has probably never thought of himself in these terms. It's an abstraction, a reduction of his behavioral tendencies into a descriptive term that I can use to navigate him, not an engraving on his soul.

Beyond our reactions and beyond abstractions describing our reactions, there are also some statements that define us. At first glance, these statements don't seem to engender any geographical behavior, so they seem to be neither true nor false, for example, "My father was a good man" or "My mother was too self-absorbed to love me." Statements like these may seem only useful in a social context—the former can be used to get approval from one's father or from people who think that adults should honor their fathers, and the latter can get sympathy from people like therapists who respond warmly to maternal put-downs or from a romantic partner looking for an explanation as to why the speaker is so demanding. In my opinion, such statements also engender conduct of a more substantial nature: they guide the performance of the self.

In order to play a part, we have to know what part we are playing. Statements like "My father was a good man" or "Karsons say what they think" or "Americans cherish free speech" are to the performing self what *backstory* is to actors playing a part on the stage. A good actor reads a script and invents a character who will do the things the script says she does. A merely adequate actor at least invents a mood that makes sense of what she is supposed to do onstage, but a good actor will create a whole character. A good actor might even find herself wondering what the character's childhood was like to help her fully understand the part she is to play. The more the actor understands about the character, the more convincingly she will be able to do the things the character does. The same goes for performing the part of yourself. The more we know about the familial, vocational, and cultural pulls on ourselves, the better able we are to play our part. For the actor, knowing these things requires imagination and a working knowledge of human nature—for us, knowing these things is simple. We don't even have to *know* them in the sense of putting them into words; we can just do what feels right. But sometimes we put them into words, and then the statements we create can be true or false according to how conducive they are to getting us to perform the part well. "Karsons say what they think" may or may not be a valid description of how my family behaves compared to other families, but it is a true statement if it engenders behavior in me—blurting things out—that facilitates my performance of the role of me.

Our families and later our friends, culture, and work are a kind of ensemble company—actors, directors, and especially critics—that provides us with constant feedback about how well we are performing the part in which we have been cast. A girl who says a naughty word at home gets one message if she has been cast to play the virginal Doris Day and another if she has been cast to play the outspoken Madonna, and her reaction to the message she gets also depends on the definition of the role she is playing. If the little Doris Day shrugs and signals that she is indifferent to the feedback, the parents may say in shock and alarm, "Why would you say a thing like that?" This lets her know that there is no part in this particular play for the role she is trying on. (The parents, of course, don't *know* what they are doing in the sense of having reduced it to words—they're just doing what seems natural in light of their own roles and the role they envision for her.) If the little Madonna shrugs and signals that she is indifferent to the feedback, the parents may take this as a challenge: "We'll see about that," they threaten, escalating the oppositionality of the situation and daring her to be even more outspoken.

THE FANTASY OF PRECISION

The culture of scientists values precision in measurement for precision's sake. The mystique of scientific accuracy is promulgated by its subculture as persistently as the mystique of French savoir faire is promulgated by the French. Measurement is advertised as an area in which science transcends its human roots. A second is defined as the duration of 9,192,631,770 periods of something or other of the cesium-133 atom. Not 9,192,631,771 — it must be 9,192,631,770. A meter is the distance covered by a photon in a vacuum in 1/299,792,458th of a second. Such precision is an illusion, a function of scientific mythmaking. I'm not saying these tautologies are not true — I'm saying they're irrelevant. In real life, we measure things when we need to know something about them that we can't tell with the naked eye. Measurement makes things obvious.

On moving day, I want to know if the table can be carried through the door without removing the legs. It looks like it'll be close. I measure the doorway, and I measure the table. In other words, I hold a yardstick up to each and note which point on the stick each corresponds to. For this measurement, I don't even need a yardstick with markings on it — any stick would do. Once I do this, it suddenly becomes obvious that the table will fit through the door. We know when something is obvious because at that point the right people stop arguing about it. If I want to know if a polished lens will fit into a machined receptacle, then I need a yardstick that will not bend or twist and with markings on it that are much closer together than the one I used for the table. If I want to know how light is displaced by a gas to determine its elemental composition, I need not only a more precise yardstick but also a way to enhance the visual image so I can look at it. Such enhancements (provided by microscopes, computers, and digitalization) are ways to make things obvious. So even though scientific culture likes to promote itself as having transcended its humanity (as French culture likes to promote itself as having transcended its boorishness), it remains all too human. Even something as apparently pure as measurement is an exercise in social behavior.

CONCLUSION

A major source of deadliness in therapy (and elsewhere) that has attracted the focus of performance artists and theorists is the insulating effect of language. In psychology, some theorists emphasize how the misuse of language and associated logical typing errors — taking words as reality instead of taking them as about reality — are intrinsic to understanding psychopathology (Hayes,

Strosahl, & Wilson, 1999; Watzlawick, Bavelas, & Jackson, 1967). Language, once organized, becomes text, and text has a way of serving the powerful by maintaining the status quo, that is, by being deadly. Deadly text can be subverted by appealing to and celebrating that which it describes, so that reality becomes primary in importance and the way reality is defined becomes secondary, or by promulgating competing texts (although if competing texts are successful, they eventually become deadly in serving the new masters). Despite its faults, science is the human enterprise most devoted to tailoring text to reality rather than the other way around.

Science offsets its tendency to become a hegemony like any other human culture by celebrating cultural heroes who change rather than toe the party line. Science is like the United States under the Constitution. Government officials and scientists are just as likely as anyone else to exercise their power over marginalized voices and discrediting information, but at least at bottom under the Constitution and under the rubric of science, it's generally conceded that they're not supposed to. This fundamental principle gives hope and occasionally power to the marginalized. In the next chapter, we explore the possibility that the core value of science—critical thinking—can also subvert the texts that it establishes.

Chapter Nine

Critical Thinking About
Critical Thinking*

In the postmodern world, complicity and subversion are inextricably in-
tertwined.

—Carlson (1996, p. 173)

Every time anybody tells you anything, you've got to ask why. That's the
difference between us and the Nazis. We want people to ask questions.

—Frederic March, in *Tomorrow the World*

In this chapter, we examine some contexts—power and gender—in which
critical thinking occurs, articulate what we mean by critical thinking, explain
how to do it, and then explore some reasons why it's upsetting to people.

DOES CRITICAL THINKING REIFY WHAT
IT ATTEMPTS TO QUESTION?

Derrida (1978, 1982) was a critical thinker who asked questions about the implicit context of propositions, especially the context of unarticulated dualities
and dichotomies in the speaker's and listener's worldviews. Derrida himself
might not have been comfortable with being labeled a critical thinker since
it's a label often associated with an imperious attitude. He wrote that "by re-
peating what is implicit in the founding concepts . . . by using against the ed-
ifice the instruments or stones available in the house . . . one risks ceaselessly
confirming, consolidating . . . that which one allegedly deconstructs" (quoted

---

*This chapter was written with Janna Goodwin.

in Carlson, 1996, pp. 173–174). His concern was that we participate in a system by fighting it on its own terms, much as a spirited legal defense implicitly reifies our system of litigation or the way political protest via free speech and legal assembly implicitly endorses our methods of petitioning for redress. Similarly, almost every psychological symptom is both a protest and a compromise—both a problem and a solution—that challenges and facilitates relevant systems at the same time (Watzlawick, Bavelas, & Jackson, 1967).

Can deadly textual hegemonies be fought with words? Or does the use of words only reify a system of excluding the body, the individual, the marginalized, and the yin? Suspicions about the use of language to make self-serving and oppressive rules led performance theorists to explore the use of bodies and movements to challenge the status quo (Boal, 1985; Shapiro & Shapiro, 2002). And since rules are general, they can also be challenged by the specific—narrative personal stories, for example (Foss & Foss, 1991; Park-Fuller, 2000). But can rules, categories, and expectations—text—be challenged by text? In this chapter, we explore the question of whether rationality itself can challenge a definition of a situation that calls itself rational. Our view is that while critical thinking has of course been co-opted by privilege at the expense of the marginalized, as has been every change practice once its practitioners acquire power, it is still the tool par excellence for lively questioning. Critical thinking contextualizes rules, hedges expectations, and explodes categories.

CRITICAL THINKING AND POWER DYNAMICS

Is critical thinking a way of maintaining the authority of the rational? Audre Lorde (1984) wrote, "The master's tools will never dismantle the master's house" (quoted in Carlson, 1996, p. 174), but is critical thinking the master's tool, or is it only something the master claims as his tool because it's so powerful? Should the rational be trumpeted at the expense of the irrational? Our opinion is that the irrational should be celebrated not because there's something intrinsically suspicious about rationality but because it's irrational to suppose that rationality can supplant irrationality.

The party line deems the party line to be rational and deems dispute to be irrational. The marginalized voices in dispute are often voices that are upset and often express their upset right along with their critiques. Anyone who has something to say because they are upset can be dismissed as irrational. If critical thinking about such characterizations of the marginalized does not free us to listen, then the marginalized must rely on political power. And if it becomes the privileged because of political power, the marginalized will act just like the previously privileged once it gets there. Critical thinking is a way of keeping the marketplace of ideas largely unregulated. Although it can be hijacked by power motives, that does not make it intrinsically domineering.

CRITICAL THINKING AS A GENDERED COMMUNICATION

Using the terms *masculine* and *feminine* to describe gender reifies the belief that women are feminine and men are masculine, even if the terms are presented in italics or in quotation marks. This belief then stigmatizes women who don't act feminine and men who don't act masculine. Instead, we use the terms *yin* (for what is usually meant by *feminine*) and *yang* (for what is usually meant by *masculine*). We recognize that this is a little cutesy and, even worse, bound to fail because if yin becomes a true synonym for feminine, eventually women who do not manifest sufficient yin will be stigmatized. Still, the words *women* and *feminine* and *men* and *masculine* are so closely related that their use implicitly signifies that women should be feminine and men masculine.

Is critical thinking a yang enterprise such that valuing it privileges the yang by definition? Certainly, critical thinking has certain features associated with yang. It can be aggressive rather than facilitative in its approach to other people's statements since any assertion of truth is met with doubt. Indeed, critical thinking treats people's statements as assertions and contentions, and asserting and contending are yang moves that invite yang responses. But doubt isn't intrinsic to critical thinking and may only be expressed by people who are looking for absolute truths. That is, doubt is an expression of a hidden duality that includes certainty, and if one fully embraces a lack of certainty, the critical thinker may be trying to get at *when* a proposition is true and not at *whether* it is true. The assumption that the speaker has something to say of merit but is saying it without proper qualifications, is more yin than yang. Chuang-tzu (Graham, 1981) made the same point over 2,000 years ago, noting that a sorting that ranks things just ranks things, while a "sorting which evens things out" liberates us from ranking. Although critical thinking can be hijacked by yang, that does not make it intrinsically yang. Indeed, a hallmark of feminist theory has been to subject the party line to critical thinking rather than to avoid critical thinking.

WHAT IS CRITICAL THINKING?

Critical thinking is hailed as the method and the goal of education (e.g., Halpern, 2004; Meehl, 1973). Its virtues are well known: analysis, inference, interpretation, explanation, self-regulation, and evaluation (Facione, 1998). Associated personal traits include being inquisitive, systematic, judicious, analytical, truth seeking, open minded, and confident in reasoning (Facione, 1998). But how do we do it?

Critical thinking asks a series of questions that test the utility of propositions and contextualizes that utility based on the answers to those questions. A primary question we propose in this chapter will be to ask what the terms of the proposition mean, so let's explore the utility of our definition by defining its own terms. We can start by noting that the word *critical* means evaluative and has also come to mean disparaging since so much criticism is disappointing to the recipient. Critical thinking is evaluative thinking and only incidentally disparages the propositions it examines.

A *proposition* is a statement that may or may not be true. *True* means that conduct reasonably based on the statement will succeed — will comport with reality: a true statement is a good map. Some statements sound like propositions but functionally are not. "You don't love me the right way," for example, may be misinterpreted by the listener as a disputable proposition when functionally it serves as a request or a demand. If the listener attempts to employ critical thinking to demonstrate that she does love the speaker in the right way, she only proves that she does not. Other statements don't sound like propositions but functionally are. "Talk more in class," for example, sounds like a demand but may actually function as the proposition "You'll learn more if you try out your ideas on a discerning audience." Critical thinking should be employed to test propositions properly stated as such — many disputes resolve when you simply ask speakers what they're really trying to say.

Few propositions are true at all times under all circumstances. Those that are tend to be either tautologies or natural laws. A *tautology* is a statement that is true on its own terms: "All cats are cats." "People with bipolar disorder experience mood lability" is a tautology that might accidentally be used to assign the label bipolar disorder to someone who exhibits mood lability. A natural *law* is a proposition that is always true, such as those that describe the conservation of energy in a closed system or the impossibility of ascertaining both the location and the velocity of a subatomic particle. All other propositions are either false or true only in some circumstances. Critical thinking contextualizes the truth of propositions, meaning that it qualifies their truth by specifying the conditions under which they work.

Logic is the process of deriving true statements from other true statements. A *fallacy* is a way of deriving false statements from true statements.

The seven questions that we advocate as critical thinkers are the following:

1. What does the statement propose? What are you saying?
2. What is the evidence for the proposition? What is the evidence against it? How do you know that?
3. What other explanations might there be for the evidence?
4. What contexts for application of the proposition are specified or implied? (How generalizable is the evidence?)
5. Would the proposition be equally true or false if this or that were changed about the context? (Is the instant case adequately represented by the general?)
6. In what context was the proposition stated? (What motives might the speaker have besides getting at the truth?)
7. Would the meaning of the statement change if this or that about its context were changed?

What Does the Statement Propose? What Are You Saying?

"Good supervision makes therapists better." We can nail down this proposition by asking the speaker or writer to clarify what is meant on the whole. If we ask, "Are you saying that it's impossible to learn to do therapy well without good supervision?" we may learn that what is meant is "Good supervision is one way of making therapists better." We can also ask for definitions of terms—if we ask what is meant by *good* supervision and by *better* therapists, we may discover some tautologies. For example, if good supervision means exposure to discussing what is happening in the room and better therapy is described by the same terms, then we have unearthed a tautological claim such that the original proposition could be restated as "One can learn to talk about the immediate environment by talking about the immediate environment." Restating it as such lets us state a new proposition, the one really at issue: "Talking about the immediate environment in psychotherapy helps patients."

Exposing hidden tautologies is a crucial aspect of critical thinking. It's the same as identifying the fallacy of *begging the question*, where begging is a synonym for pleading (as in pleading the facts in a legal argument) and question means the proposition at stake. It is tautological to prove something by pleading it. Some premises so thoroughly contain the questions they purport to prove that only very deep critical thinking, called *deconstruction*, can reveal them. Deconstruction draws attention to the intrinsic dualities in the philosophical context in which the proposition is offered. So before evaluating the utility of the proposition about good supervision, one might first consider and question the underlying assumption that good–bad duality is a valid construct for understanding supervision and therapy. Arguments about the features of bipolar disorder not only implicitly accept the validity of the category but also implicitly accept as valid categorical diagnosis and sick–well duality.

Many disputes can be avoided if one party merely asks the other, "What are you saying?" This is especially useful when the proposition at issue involves one of the parties. "You should read Horney's *Neurosis and Human Growth*" can imply the proposition "You are not well read" or "You are a perfectionist" or "You and Horney think alike." Clarifying which definition of the relationship—friend or evaluator—was preferred by the statement can be useful before evaluating its validity. Less personally, a proposition like "Good supervision makes therapists better" might be readily translated by its proponent into "Two heads are better than one because no one can think of everything," a proposition less likely to be disputed than the original contention.

What Is the Evidence for the Proposition? What Is the Evidence against It? How do You Know That?

These questions are obviously relevant once they are asked, but all too often we forget to ask them. They also bring up two important areas of inquiry—ipse dixit and Bayes' theorem.

An *ipse dixit* is a proposition accepted on the authority of the speaker without other proof. In a way, all true propositions are ipse dixits because all evidence is only as good as its source. If we argue over the efficacy of stimulant treatment for hyperactive children, we can take Russell Barkley's (1998) word for it, or we can ask to review the evidence on which his opinion is based. We can question the method by which he identified hyperactive children, the adequacy of the control groups he used for comparison, the measure of improvement, and so on. But at some point, somewhere along the way, we will take someone's word for something, an ipse dixit. At its best, ipse dixit does not rear its head until we find an authority whose word is not disputed by anyone in the discussion. It's pragmatic to resolve a dispute over the capital of Oregon by referring to an almanac, but if a member of the discussion claims that the almanac got it wrong, then another discussion must specify which source would be considered authoritative. Articulating the ipse dixits underlying evidence for and against propositions is an important aspect of critical thinking. Even simple arithmetic is an ipse dixit. If someone insists that 2 times 2 is 5 (or that the likelihood of two SIDS deaths in one family can be determined by squaring the likelihood of its happening once in one family), they are excluded from the conversation as persons whose opinion on such matters is irrelevant. But if you had to prove to a jury that a long list of big numbers added up to a particular total, you might call a statistician to testify rather than leave the jury to its own devices. Either way, either the statistician's testimony or the calculator's display is an ipse dixit. The difference between deadly ipse dixits and necessary ipse dixits is in the believer's willingness to reconsider the speaker's authority when new evidence is adduced. But this small safeguard does not constrain ipse dixits' pervasiveness.

Bayes' theorem computes the probability of A given B from the probability of B given A. This sounds arcane, but it comes up every time anyone tries to categorize anything. To put something or someone in a category on the basis of evidence is to claim that the category exists and that the evidence is indicative of the category. For example, many people think that hypersexuality in children is indicative of a history of sexual abuse. Let's assume that hypersexuality is defined as instigating sex talk or sex activity at least once in every play episode. Suppose we find that 75% of children who have been sexually abused are hypersexual. This would at first blush appear to be strong evidence for the proposition that hypersexuality indicates sexual abuse and that a given child who exhibits hypersexuality was sexually abused. But we know only the probability of hypersexuality given a history of sexual abuse—what is the probability of a history of sexual abuse given hypersexuality?

It is easiest to follow the critical thinking required of categorizations with the 2 × 2 table. Table 9.1 provides the key concepts related to Bayes' theorem. The *cutoff score* is an algorithm by which the proponent of the proposition determines that the evidence is strong enough to warrant placement of the case at hand in the category. The gold standard is the method by which we determine, apart from the evidence under consideration, which cases are really in the category and which are not. A home pregnancy test is validated against a gold standard of actual pregnancy, where the gold standard might be

Table 9.1. The Basic 2 × 2 Table

	GOLD STANDARD	
	Actually in the category	Actually not in the category
Indicator says in the category	TP	FP
CUTOFF SCORE --------------		
Indicator says not in the category	FN	TN

Note. TP is true positive; FP is false positive; FN is false negative; TN is true negative.

ultrasound viewing of the uterus or a previously validated blood test. The cut-off score would be how blue the stick has to become to constitute a positive reading. Categorical validity is capped by the gold standard's reliability—if the same gold standard applied to the same observations doesn't produce the same categorizations, then there's a limit to how accurately a test or sign can categorize.

In order to make useful statements about the relationship between evidence and categorical propositions, we need to fill in the 2×2 table. Put differently, all propositions about categorizing something or someone should be subjected to critical thinking in the form of the questions needed to fill in the table. In our current example, we find that 75% of sexually abused children show hypersexuality. That tells us that TP is three times greater than FN. If the data were gathered by looking at 100 children with histories of sexual abuse, the 2×2 table would look like table 9.2 (so far).

What we want to know is the odds that a child who shows hypersexuality has been sexually abused. Those odds would be indicated on the 2×2 table as the ratio between TP and FP, when what we already know is the ratio between TP and FN. Given that the indicator (hypersexuality) *says* the child is in the category (of having been sexually abused), what are the odds that the child is *actually* in that category? To calculate that, we need to know the incidence of hypersexuality in children who were not sexually abused. Let's say that it's fairly rare, 5%, meaning that only 1 in 20 nonabused children show hypersexuality. Then we can generate table 9.3's interim data.

But we aren't there yet because the data in table 9.3 suggest that the number of children who have been sexually abused ($N = 100$) is the same as the number who have not. To finish filling in the table, we need to know the *base rate*—the percentage of children in the relevant population who have been sexually abused. Assume that we are inferring sexual abuse from hypersexuality in a child from the general population of the United

Table 9.2.   Hypothetical Sensitivity of Hypersexuality Among Sexual Abuse Victims

	GOLD STANDARD	
	History of sexual abuse	No history of sexual abuse
Hypersexual	TP = 75	FP
CUTOFF SCORE - - - - - - - - - - - - - -		
Not hypersexual	FN = 25	TN

Table 9.3. Hypothetical Sensitivity and Specificity of Hypersexuality by Sexual Abuse History

	GOLD STANDARD	
	History of sexual abuse |	No history of sexual abuse
Hypersexual	TP = 75	FP = 5
CUTOFF SCORE -------------		
Not hypersexual	FN = 25	TN = 95

States. The base rate is the percentage of children in America who have been sexually abused. Nobody knows what that percentage is, and on that basis alone we can float the possibility that any attempt to categorize children as sexually abused by indicators is fundamentally flawed. However, such a categorization could be offered conditionally: "Assuming the base rate of sexual abuse in children is X%, then hypersexuality as defined correctly categorized Y% of children." As an educated guess, let's say the base rate of sexual abuse is 6%. Now we can develop a table that will answer our question as to how good the evidence of hypersexuality is for indicating a sexual abuse history. Notice that the numbers on the right side of table 9.4 have been adjusted so that the 100 known sexually abused children now constitute 6% (our estimated base rate) of the entire sample but preserving the supposed 5% incidence of hypersexuality among children who have not been sexually abused.

Bayes' theorem demonstrates that under the assumptions stated previously, hypersexuality indicates a history of sexual abuse slightly less than half the time (75 true positives compared to 78 false positives).

Table 9.4. Hypothetical Sensitivity and Specificity of Hypersexuality by Sexual Abuse History, Adjusted for Base Rate

	GOLD STANDARD	
	History of sexual abuse |	No history of sexual abuse
Hypersexual	TP = 75	FP = 78
CUTOFF SCORE -------------		
Not hypersexual	FN = 25	TN = 1489

Critical thinkers ask the following questions about this 2×2 table:

a. In the original study that showed that 75% of sexually abused children were hypersexual, how was sexual abuse defined?
b. What gold standard was used to separate the children into the two groups of sexually abused and not sexually abused? If hypersexuality was used in the separation, then the whole study begs the question.
c. How was it decided which children were hypersexual and which were not? Were they observed directly or reported on by parents? How was it decided that every play session must include sexual instigation to count (i.e., what happens to the data with a different cutoff between hypersexuality and lack of it)?
d. How do we know the base rate of sexual abuse? What problems might there be with the estimate?
e. Was the finding of linkage (in this case, that 75% of sexually abused children were hypersexual) cross validated—replicated—in another sample?
f. Was the group "not actually in the category" enough like the group "actually in the category" in important ways so that it really was the categorical variable that distinguished them? (If all the children with sexual abuse histories had been from impoverished single-parent homes and all the non–sexually abused children from intact middle-class families, then hypersexuality might indicate one of the other variables and not a history of sexual abuse.)

Bayes' theorem is relevant to fairly technical propositions, such as those associated with the prediction of dangerousness and suicide, the efficacy of a medication in treating an illness, and the diagnosis of disease. It's also relevant to quotidian propositions, such as whether it's going to rain, whether plane travel is dangerous, and how you know if someone likes you. To evaluate the proposition that good supervision makes therapists better, we would need to know how therapists are rated (the gold standard for discriminating better and worse among therapists), how supervision was rated, the proportion of therapists of each quality who received good supervision, and the percentage of therapists in general who fall on each point of the goodness scale.

What Other Explanations Might There Be for the Evidence?

John Stuart Mill (1843) showed long ago that certainty about causality means that changing only one variable produces a different outcome or that changing all but one variable fails to produce a different outcome. In either case, you can say that the variable causes the outcome. However, neither case ever truly applies. You can never change all but one variable because there are always variables we don't know about or think are not important and do not change. You feel certain that you have developed an aversion to wine because you noticed that you became dyspeptic on several different days that were similar only in drinking wine (i.e., all other ingestion variables changed over the course of these dyspeptic days). But what you failed to appreciate was that when you drink wine, you drink less water because the wine quenches your thirst, and it turns out that you are averse to wine only when you also fail to drink the usual amount of water. Similarly, you can never change merely a single variable because there are always variables you don't realize are changing along with the variable you are testing as a cause. The critical thinker wonders which variables have not been considered and proposes them as alternate explanations. For example, the kinds of people who become better therapists may be the kinds of people admitted to programs where good supervision is found, so the better explanation may be that personal qualities of the therapist rather than qualities of the supervision account for eventual expertise.

What Contexts for Application of the Proposition Are Specified or Implied? (How Generalizable Is the Evidence?)

Once a proposition has been accepted as true, it's either a law of nature or else its applicability must be delimited to certain situations. A great deal of psychopathology can be productively construed as a failure to delimit the lessons of childhood to their useful contexts—people use old solutions in new situations. Critical thinking helps symptomatic individuals test the applicability of old solutions. In psychoanalytic therapy, this occurs incidentally when the dyad focuses on how those old solutions are working in the present. In cognitive therapy, the emphasis on critical thinking is direct, in what Beck (1976) calls collaborative empiricism.

Our sample proposition, "good supervision makes therapists better," from its context, implies psychotherapists as opposed to physical or occupational therapists. It might also imply individual therapy as opposed to group or family therapy. Surely it implies clinical supervision as opposed to administrative responsibility for the therapist's work. If evidence is adduced to support the proposition, that evidence might be representative of only a particular context. For example, it may delimit the proposition's applicability to supervision received in graduate school or to supervision received in a hierarchy (as opposed to that received from friends).

Would the Proposition Be Equally True or False If This or That Were Changed About the Context? (Is the Instant Case Adequately Represented by the General?)

To further delimit the applicability of a proposition to various situations, one must ask how changing something about the situation would affect the proposition's validity. Before applying the proposition to a specific situation, we must find out if there is anything about the specific situation that distinguishes it from the kinds of situations the proposition applies to. In the social sciences, there are always distinguishing features of the present case, and whether they are sufficiently important to warrant reconsideration of the proposition's validity is a matter of opinion. The opinion should be formed after argument—citing evidence and logic in support of distinguishing the current case from the typical case.

A proposition that has been widely accepted as true among forensic psychologists is that certain data in a prisoner's case record will predict recidivism. The validation of this proposition occurred in a Canadian men's prison (Quinsey, Harris, Rice, & Cormier, 1998). It is widely accepted that the algorithm does not apply to women. But can the algorithm be applied to men in a Michigan prison? An Arizona prison? An Arizona prison and a Latino prisoner? Whether such questions are asked and which answers they receive depends on the worldview of the critical thinker—one person might ask about national origin and another about skin color. Occasionally, there will be supportive or infirming evidence. For example, the algorithm may have been cross validated on Latino prisoners in Arizona, but there will always be questions about which there is no evidence—it could turn out that the Latinos in Arizona prisons on whom the algorithm was cross validated were Mexican Americans and that the Arizona prisoner of interest is Puerto Rican or from a different part of Mexico.

If a graduate student or resident wanted to become a better therapist and if our proposition were explained and accepted as valid, she would still have to ask herself if it's applicable to her particular situation. Was it validated on male therapists primarily? If she is middle aged, does that distinguish her from the validation sample enough to raise questions about whether only impressionable therapists benefit from good supervision? When examining an instant case and comparing it to the general case that produced the proposition, one relies on one's theoretical understanding of the way the world works to choose which features of the present case might be changed to make a difference.

In What Context Was the Proposition Stated? (What Motives Might the Speaker Have Besides Getting at the Truth?)

Propositions do not exist independent of speech. Speech is a behavior, an act, a communication (Searle, 1969; Skinner, 1957). The meaning of any behavior is a function of its occasioning environment. To understand the meaning of a proposition and to evaluate its validity, we need to know the context not only to which it applies but also in which it was emitted. At the simplest level, we need to know its language. If someone offers you food and says, "Gift," it makes a big difference if the context is English or German (*gift* means poison in German). At a more complex level, the question about what exactly is being proposed can be answered somewhat by the speaker, but it can also be answered independently with information about its occasioning environment.

Speakers bristle at the idea that they are not the sole determiner of what they meant by what they said. In other words, we act as if we had complete dominion over our own backstages. However, a long tradition in communication theory defines the meaning of a speech act according to how it is received, not according to what was intended. The objective theory of contracts, long embraced by British and American courts, directs a judge or jury to interpret what a contract term means by considering what it would mean to the typical, reasonable reader and not to consider what the bargainers thought they meant by it at the time. This means that once offered, a speaker loses control over any proposition. As a matter of conflict resolution, it makes sense to allow speakers to edit and amend their propositions since many conflicts will be solved as a result—but as a matter of understanding the contextual influences on a proposition, independent analysis need not be constrained by the speaker's claims of intent.

At one time, *privilege* referred to the special relationship we have with our own thoughts and feelings—we're in a position of privilege to observe ourselves, and although our declarations about what we are thinking or feeling can be disputed, it was generally thought to be necessary and polite to accede to the representations of the only person who can directly observe such things. (All that changed—or should have changed—when Skinner showed that a person's privileged self-observation can be no more valid than the ability of the verbal community to observe him because the person can learn the relevant labels and distinctions only from the verbal community.) Political privilege puts the individual in a relationship with public reality analogous to the relationship all individuals have to their own private realities. Politically unprivileged persons are expected to defer to the pronouncements of the politically privileged, just as other people are expected to defer to the pronouncements of the speaker about her interior states and motives. Performance theory is concerned with the hegemony of those pronouncements and wants to subvert them. Whoever first commented that history is written by the victors was trying to spur critical thinking about the party line by asking who created it.

A major implication of the realization that propositions are speech acts is that the speaker's motivations are relevant to an analysis of a proposition's validity. When the discovery of cold fusion was announced to the press rather

...n to the usual scientific organs, it raised serious questions in some listen-
...s' minds about the scientists' motivations and the validity of their claims.
...cientists' valid claims are usually presented to an audience of scientists who
can appreciate their validity—many commentators thought (correctly in this
case) that only invalid claims would be presented directly to the public. Just
because a speaker has idiosyncratic motivations for asserting a proposition
doesn't mean the proposition is untrue, but to ignore those motivations in
evaluating the proposition's validity is an approach that reality eventually in-
structs us to avoid. Is that a license for ad hominem arguments? No, it's a natural consequence of fully appreciating that truth seeking and truth speaking
are social acts.

"Good supervision makes therapists better," stated in a brochure for a training program, would have a different meaning from its statement by a supervisee offering credit to her supervisor for a therapeutic success. Or perhaps it
was stated in an argument as to why the state should require a year of post-
graduate supervision for licensure eligibility. Or perhaps it was the result of
an investigation of the cost-benefit analysis of requiring 3 rather than 2 years
of supervision in a training program. These contexts help us understand the
speaker's motivations and the proposition's validity. They also help us understand whether what was said was really a proposition at all or just an attempt to induce compliant behavior in others.

Would the Meaning of the Statement Change if This or That About Its Context Were Changed?

Just as we can delimit the applicability of a proposition by investigating relevant differences between the instant case and the general case, we can explore its meaning by investigating relevant differences between the environment in which it was originally asserted and the environment in which it is
currently being asserted. Even if the most scientific context imaginable produced the statement "Good supervision makes therapists better," its current
assertion may be a function of immediate characteristics of the environment.
One way to tease out the impact of immediate characteristics is to ask if the
proposition's meaning would change if those characteristics changed. For example, a patient could repeat the proposition in a conscious attempt to laud
the therapist for her pedigree while unconsciously reminding her that her
quality as a therapist depends largely on her ability to subject herself to
scrutiny. The therapist would be well served by asking herself whether it mat-
tered that he said it just after an exercise of therapeutic privilege. Perhaps the
therapist had recently framed her degree from a prestigious university and
displayed it on her office wall. The patient looks it over and says, "Good su-

pervision makes therapists better." Doesn't it affect the meaning of the proposition that it followed inspection of the diploma?

THE ROLE OF THEORY

We have listed seven questions that assist critical thinking—five about the proposition under consideration and two about the context of its utterance or writing. For questions that imagine changing "this or that" about the situation, how do we know what to change? When we ask about other explanations, where do other explanations come from? A good source of other explanations and suggestions for experimentation with the situation at hand is theory. *Theory* is a worldview or a narrative that describes reality. Goffman describes the social world as a stage, so to use Goffman to think critically about the social context of a proposition is to ask what the speaker was presenting onstage, what was left backstage, and how the proposition saved the speaker's face. Horney (1950) sees pathological functioning as a conflict between what we are and what we can imagine being. To use Horney to think critically about a proposition is to ask how its utterance helps the speaker manage imperfection. Once we learn a theorist's worldview, we can ask ourselves, "What would Goffman say?" or "What would Horney say?"

When we define the context, we're applying theory—recognition of this ensures that we won't take the frame we came up with as primary. Instead, we'll think critically about our definitions of the context and the elements of the proposition. The staunchest claim in debate is to claim that a definition is atheoretical, not socially constructed, just is. But only useless tautologies reach this height.

We can relate the discoveries of science to a specific case by letting science inform the questions we ask about the case. If a behavior is identified as problematic, we can use behaviorism or systems theory to ask what good the behavior does and what purpose it serves. These theories alert us to a behavior's consequences, while cognitive theory focuses our attention on what went through the person's mind just beforehand. Suppose a study shows that the therapists identified as most effective by their peers described their first supervisors as warm, concerned, and confronting. The study doesn't prove that good supervision makes therapists better, but it helps us frame questions about what is meant by good supervision, and it helps us constrain the proposition by asking if any concerned confrontation will do or if it has to come from someone in a supervisory role.

Specific questions to ask of psychological propositions are associated with specific theorists. For example, Horney tells us to ask about the fantasy of perfectability; Freud teaches us to inquire about sex, unconscious wishes, and parents; Adler about power and birth order; Bateson about homeostasis and logical typing; and Marx about class and money.

METATHEORY

Metatheory—theorizing about theories—produces questions about the kinds of theories a critical thinker relies upon to come to her conclusions. Identifying a critical thinker as a cognitive behaviorist, for example, can warn us that her critical thinking may overemphasize a statement's purported intent and underemphasize its effects. When we ask ourselves, "What would Derrida say?" we consider unspoken and unnecessarily entrenched dualities that haunt propositions of all theoretical bents. The proposition that hypersexuality indicates a history of sexual abuse implicitly casts a shadow over childhood sexuality and demonizes anything that resembles sexual abuse. When psychologists found that sexual abuse was not a lifelong burden and a dreadful occurrence in the lives of many abused children (Rind, Tromovitch, & Bauserman, 1998), some people (including the U.S. Senate, which took the occasion to condemn sex with children) thought they were saying that sexual abuse was okay, an inference that made sense only in the unspoken context of good and evil and an unspoken belief that all acts are one or the other.

MULTICULTURALISM

Multiculturalism can be productively thought of as a further set of questions asked of any proposition. If a proposition asserts something about people, does their race or sex matter? Does the proponent's or audience's race or sex matter? What about identified culture, ethnicity, gender, class, income, target status, stigmatized identity, or expectations of others based on one of these factors? A proposition like "Good supervision makes therapists better" seems to stand apart from factors of race or sex. Multicultural sensitivity reminds us to ask if these matter.

CRITICAL THINKING CAN BE UPSETTING

Since critical thinking lends itself to status moves and power plays, it often comes off as contemptuous. Even at its nicest, critical thinking communicates that the proponent's proposition won't be accepted at face value. To a large extent, we are all invested in face (Goffman, 1959), and critical thinking discredits any attempt to perform an oracular or authoritative face—think of doctors who won't deign to discuss evidence even when it supports their conclusions. If there is a shared understanding that pronouncements are tentative, revisable, and makeshift, critical thinking is playful and collaborative. Otherwise, it's upsetting.

For one kind of faith tradition, critical thinking attacks faith. Such faith is factual, not spiritual—faith that such and such happened or that scriptural accounts of events are literally true. Another kind of faith, faith in how we should live or faith in facts that are not subject to observation, has no problem with critical thinking. Galileo said that faith should concern itself with how to go to Heaven and not with how the heavens go. When faith addresses the latter, critical thinking undermines it.

Critical thinking involves asking what if. People sometimes link words and facts so intimately that they can't play what if. "Some philosophers seem to be angry with images for not being things, and with words for not being feelings" (Santayana, 1922, p. 131). How would you feel if you were arrested for child molesting? Some people respond, "I would never do such a thing." Critical thinking can upset people by pushing them to imagine possibilities when all they want is certainty about reality.

It's comforting to have some guiding core beliefs that reflect a coherent and consistent universe. Critical thinking subjects our beliefs to scrutiny, and very few of them emerge from the process unchanged. Critical thinking typically leads us to qualify even our accurate beliefs as probabilistic rather than lawful and as situationally true rather than universally true.

Critical thinking suggests that we probably don't know what we think we know, that facts are merely opinions, and that everything within our experience may be ultimately unknowable, or, as Gödel (1962) says, "undecidable." A socially constructed, postmodern world is an annoying world for people trying to lay foundations.

All five sources of upset—losing face, losing faith, thinking the unthinkable, challenging beliefs, and challenging believing—are analogues of the way liveliness always upsets deadliness. The powerful always want to set their definition of the world in stone, like nations trying to agree that current boundaries are the actual boundaries between countries. Marginalized groups whose sense of place is derived from community rather than imposed by drawing lines on maps will always ask just where those lines came from. Asking such questions is upsetting not only because it implies a different power structure but also because it disrupts the presentation of the lines as authoritative, God given, fixed, and dependable.

Chapter Ten

Applying Theory to the Therapy (and Not Just to the Patient's Life)

My destiny, harrying me with trials hard as yours,
led me as well, at last, to anchor in this land.
Schooled in suffering, now I learn to comfort
those who suffer too.

> —Virgil, *The Aeneid*, 1:749–52 (Robert Fagles, Trans.)

Heard melodies are sweet, but those unheard are sweeter.

> —John Keats, *Ode on a Grecian Urn*

A central tenet of performance theory is that in any system, a hegemony develops that expresses its power with self-serving rules, categories, and behavioral expectations. At first, these rules are typically promulgated for the benefit of the system, but later they are promulgated for the benefit of the hegemony. Eventually, the hegemony not only promulgates the rules, categories, and expectations but also applies them only to the masses, excepting itself from their impact. This may be done cynically, as in the case of congressmen who pursue sexual liaisons with teenagers while proclaiming their concern for children, or sincerely, as in the case of psychologists who interpret clients'—but not their own—interest in violent movies as pathological. The congressman thinks, in effect, "I can get away with it," while the psychologist thinks, in effect, "I can handle it." Well-intentioned hegemonies put themselves above the law because they believe that most people can't handle as much freedom as the members of the hegemony can (Dostoyevsky, 1950).

When those with power create rules, categories, and expectations that apply only to those with less power, they exercise what might be called colonial privilege. In Goffman's terms, they free themselves from situation consciousness

177

and avoid comparison with identity norms. In Johnstone's terms, they play a very high status. An existentialist might say they define themselves as immortal because the notion of being beyond human law is associated with the notion of being beyond natural law, a pursuit of freedom that often has roots in the denial of death. Colonial privilege needs a counterpart that is low status, restricted, categorized, and undignified.

A common example of colonial privilege is the tendency of parents to capitalize on the power differential with their children to define themselves as free to exercise will and to define their children as predictable. It's a solution to the existential dilemma—how to live with an infinite mind and a finite body—that associates the transcendence of mind with the powerful (whether they're individuals in systems or rationalities within systems) and the facticity of death with the less powerful. It's a solution that makes it toxic—not just complacent—to have less power and leads to a replication when the powerless acquire power, just as hazing in a fraternity leads pledges to mistreat the next year's pledges not so much out of revenge as a natural inclination to take advantage of the available system for hiding one's backstage and exporting one's disappointments.

In this context, psychotherapy should be a place where the person with power doesn't use power to institute a privilege of transcendence versus humiliation and instead uses it to create a subculture where it's not humiliating to have less power or lower status. The therapist can accomplish this by good-naturedly accepting her limitations, humanity, and facticity and by declining the colonial privilege of applying her rules, categories, and expectations only to the patient and not to herself.

In therapy, the privilege of rising above the rules manifests in two main ways. One way is an annoying tendency to use one set of explanatory principles for patients and another for ourselves and our friends. If a patient's husband uses pornography, he's a sexist deviant, but if we use pornography, we're free spirits who know how to enjoy ourselves. If a patient punches a wall, he's violent, but if we punch a wall, we're irritated. In social psychology, this is known as the actor-observer effect, where our own conduct is considered situational and the conduct of out-group members is considered a reflection of their character.

The privilege of rising above rules is also evident when the therapist acts as if the explanatory principles of psychology do not apply to transactions in the therapy office. This is pervasive, in my experience, and it's what this chapter is about.

GENDER AND FRAMING

It's deadly to take a concept and apply it to something in a way that turns what we are trying to understand into a slide specimen under a microscope. It's lively to take a concept and use it to surround ourselves and whatever we are trying to understand. This turns what we are trying to understand into a partner. Yang individuation dictates that I am the organizer and translator of events; yin integration feels its way in the dark. Yang jealously clings to the doctor role; yin seeks collaboration. Therapists often need yang when the frame is keyed socially (when the roles are those of professional and consumer: "You haven't paid your bill") or professionally (when the roles are those of therapist and patient: "I know you don't want to talk about your weight, but you almost died last month from starvation"). When the relationship is framed therapeutically—when the roles are those, say, of authority and impulsive child or rationalist and irrational reactor—therapists are more likely to need yin than yang, whether yin is called working in alliance, joining the system, or collaborating empirically. In a therapeutic frame, yin attitudes help us resist the therapeutic privilege that tempts us to see the patient as the object of psychological theorizing and ourselves as the godlike theorists. Even when we do apply our theory to ourselves, we can experience it as a kind of submission. Then internal privilege tempts us to see our bodies and our behaviors as the objects of psychological theorizing and to hold back a godlike part of ourselves as the part doing the theorizing. This is usually accomplished by saying, in effect, *then* I was operating according to theory, but *now* I am discussing myself from outside any theory. For example, a therapist bullies a patient into agreeing with her formulation and in the next session acknowledges that she was too aggressive, but she acknowledges her previous aggression as if the part of her acknowledging it is not an aggressive person. This is deadly because the abstraction of the self from circumstances impairs responsive interchange.

Gender and Psychoanalysis

Freud became the first modern patient in the same moment he became the first modern therapist. Freud saw himself as a conquistador (Jones, 1953), taming the wilds of the unconscious mind with his brains and daring. He was just the kind of therapist I'm talking about, excepting the part of himself doing the theorizing from his own ideas. Sometimes, the lag between theorist and subject was only a matter of seconds as he would reflect on a prior reflection as if the prior reflection were fair game for psychoanalytic interpretation but the current reflection was not. If postmodernism, deconstruction, performance theory, feminism, and psychoanalysis have taught us anything, it's that the current text is contextually meaningful, not just old texts. We should be suspicious of any text that sounds objective.

The question arises as to what I'm up to in presenting *this* current text, but you know I can't say because anything I say will be suspiciously self-serving.

The deadliest therapy of all is the therapy that demands framing the front stage as the only stage, that takes self-referential speech as the final word on the subject of what happened. Even though Freud frequently took this position with respect to his speech about himself, he taught us along the way not to believe him.

An anecdote reported by Jung (I can't remember where), although suspect in its casting of Jung in the hero role, is instructive. Jung and Freud were in the habit of telling each other their dreams, free-associating to the dream elements, and developing joint interpretations. One day, Freud balked at revealing his associations to a dream image, saying, "If I tell you that, you will lose all respect for my authority." Jung went home and wrote in his diary, "At that moment, I lost all respect for his authority." Which is more admirable: the superhuman who has no backstage or the human who laughs when it's exposed?

Gender and Radical Behaviorism

Skinner's greatest contribution to psychology is captured by the *radical* in his radical behaviorism (echoing James's radical empiricism). He inherited a behaviorism that was used by scientists to explain the publicly observable behavior of animals and that treated the private behavior of organisms as a black box (a locution borrowed from engineering), where something might be happening but is not our concern. Skinner (1953, 1957) believed that if a psychological science was to be any good at all, it must cross the threshold between scientist and subject. He used *radical* to mean thoroughgoing, not drastic or revolutionary. Skinner believed that psychological science must account not only for the behavior of rats and pigeons but also for the private behavior of people and especially the behavior of scientists and of himself. Skinner believed that the black box must be opened up and understood. Skinner's is perhaps the humblest and most yin philosophy, viewing the yang mind as an invention and the person as nothing more than a very complicated network of molecules.

Gender and Cognitive Behaviorism

Ellis writes forcefully about how he invented his therapy before anyone else, especially Beck. In his books that I've seen, he never cites Beck's earliest work, a favor Beck returns in kind. Ellis (2001) wrote that he invented his therapy not just in 1955 but in January 1955, as if the month would matter to us as much as it does to him. Both Ellis and Beck are shameless in their treatment of Horney, who anticipated much of what they have to say. They acknowledge that she came up with the idea of a "tyranny of shoulds," but they ignore her cognitive approach to helping patients, her presentation of her ideas in a format accessible to the general public, and her scheme for understanding what amount to core beliefs. More recently, Beck (Beck & Beck, 2006) seems to have discovered transference and countertransference, using those precise terms, but he still disparages psychoanalysis as "unproved," and he treats it as if it had not evolved at all since 1950 when he left it.

These yang displays of self-creation stand in contrast to their best work. Ellis (2001) has reported that he started doing therapy to get *himself* to speak in public and to approach women, and Beck (1976) is clearly interested in what goes through his patients' minds not only while they're in their problematic situations but also while they're in the therapy office. Their posturing covers a lively willingness to play a subordinate or intimate role.

Gender and Systems Theory

The systems theorists are comfortable with yin. Bateson, an anthropologist, was acutely aware of his being in rather than an observer of every system he wrote about. His conception of mind (1979) is entirely systemic—he doesn't believe that there is a way to abstract yourself from the contexts you're in. Watzlawick and his coauthors (1967) are also keenly aware that their thinking about psychology constitutes an example of what they're saying, not just text about examples. Robinson's (2006) essay on teaching a class on feminism that examines itself and its methodology and the class's teaching methods through the lens of feminist theory is another good example of including yourself in your theoretical frame.

Theoretical orientations to causality that emphasize context as opposed to internal states have an advantage when it comes to applying the theory to the theorist and the therapy because the conception of humanity and of behavior is already humble and responsive rather than willful and dignified, so being subject to a theory is not experienced as status lowering.

THE CLINICIAN IN CONTEXT

The systemic and behavioristic insistence that context is everything puts the therapist within the context that's being examined, and it's intrinsically lively. However, therapists often get carried away with themselves and forget that the therapy office is a context that includes them. Psychoanalytic and cognitive-behavioral approaches posit ego and rationality as aspects of the self that stand above the rest (ironically, since *ego* means *I*) and can therefore be deadly. However, even early psychoanalysts were fascinated by their own engagement with patients, and the past 60 years have seen a theoretical emphasis on a responsive rather than an abstracted self and a treatment emphasis on what's happening in the room. The trend toward liveliness has culminated in the communicative and intersubjective systems approaches (Buirski & Haglund, 2001; Langs, 1978; Stolorow, Brandchaft, & Atwood, 1987). Cognitive therapy also has a strong history of liveliness to counter its apparent top-down approach—Beck's (1976) main gripe with psychoanalysis in the 1950s was that it wasn't psychoanalytic *enough*. Too much emphasis was put on what was going through the patient's mind about her past and not enough on what was going through her mind *right then*. Beck's daughter, Judith Beck (1995), also a major figure in cognitive therapy, counts the working alliance as the second most important feature of cognitive treatment after the case formulation. Her book repeatedly asks the reader to examine his own automatic thoughts while reading and while doing therapy.

These four major theories vary in the centrality of context, but they all include enough contextual thinking to sustain a lively therapy, and they're all susceptible enough to the vicissitudes of their practitioners' natural privileges and gender concerns to be deadly. Psychotherapy is conflictual simply because it involves humans, who are complex bundles of conflicting goals, and because it specifically involves a conflict between therapists' hopefully salutary version of reality and patients' at least occasionally pathological version of reality. Because psychotherapy is conflictual and because therapists can get away with it, we tend to abstract ourselves from the conflict rather than enter it. Abstraction from context is a yang move, and ignoring its effects is a privileged and high-status move. The more one stays above a fray, the worse the fray gets because the part of the system abstracting itself from the fray often contains functions that could be useful in resolving conflicts, such as rationality, equanimity, and disinterest. As the fray gets worse, the motivation to stay above it increases, and pretty soon there's a systemic runaway in which ego or the rational self or the therapeutic self is tut-tutting about the fray, diagnosing it, and withdrawing into a shell of superiority. Liveliness requires an adequate feedback system and a therapist willing to submit to it.

Application of your theory to yourself and the therapy engrosses you in the therapy—the therapy includes you. Just as a good audience paying rapt attention with ready laughter occasions the best performances and just as actors who listen carefully and credulously to each other inspire each other, therapists engrossed in therapy cultivate patients at their best, solidify the therapeutic frame, and communicate that the therapy matters.

WHEN IS BEHAVIOR THERAPY BEHAVIORISTIC?

The essence of behaviorism as it applies to therapy is the conviction that the meaning of a behavior can be determined only by analyzing its function in its environment. That function will itself be a function of potentiation, reinforcement schedules, contingencies, and discriminative stimuli. *Potentiation* refers to the person's state—what will currently operate as a reinforcement or a punishment. In humans, even in rats, this is a complex question. An astonishing array of consequences can be experienced as pleasant or as aversive, with many consequences experienced as both. *Reinforcement schedules*—the relationship between behavior attempts and when reinforcement occurs—are important to consider because sometimes a behavior will be so strong that even though it no longer produces rewards, it persists. Behaviorists have long known that a variable schedule of reinforcement produces much greater response strength than a predictable schedule, even in organisms that can't do the math. The implication is that a behavior may not be paying off in the present environment but is still emitted because it developed under a variable schedule. *Contingencies* are if–then statements about what consequences follow from which behaviors in a given environment. *Discriminative stimuli* are those that define the current environment for a particular organism. For example, minor status moves can define the therapy relationship as authoritarian in one patient and as authoritative in another.

The behavioristic idea is that the environment causes behavior by selection in a perfect analogy to Darwinism's environmental causation of heredity by selection. The idea that causation lies in the environment and not in the patient's head is convenient for the therapist, who happens to be in the patient's environment and not in the patient's head. The behavioristic idea is that context is almost everything, with some schedules, deprivation histories, and learning histories thrown in the mix.

For a therapy to be behavioristic, it must treat the patient's behaviors and the therapist's behaviors as behaviors, not as exceptions because they are *about* behaviors. That means that the patient's speech, in particular, must be understood as a function of its occasioning environment, the most salient aspect of which is almost always the therapist, and that the therapist's speech must be understood as a function of the patient. However, many behaviorists discuss the patient's *reported* behaviors as if they are functionally related to the *reported* environments, and they don't consider the observed behaviors—the spoken reports—to be functionally related to the current environment. "Why did she do that when she did it?" should always prompt "And why is she telling me about it now?"

Acceptance and Commitment Therapy (ACT; Hayes, Strosahl, & Wilson, 1999) is the most systemic and psychoanalytic behavior therapy to date, but it still lags decades behind other approaches in considering what is going on in the therapeutic space. This is partly because of their insistence that everything about ACT is either new or ancient and their dedicated repudiation of the century of experience and observation that preceded them. For example, they write about "countertransference" (p. 279), but what they mean by this term is merely the therapist's own "personal issues and feared psychological content," not her idiosyncratic engagement with the patient. The therapist is admonished to accept her neurosis, modeling an important element of ACT, but the countertransference is viewed as an isolatable by-product of working together rather than a pervasive relatedness where the action is. This is psychoanalytic countertransference circa 1912. Similarly, through relational frame theory, scientifically minded behaviorists now have an accounting of language and metaphor, of communication, framing, and metacommunication, but they talk as if they invented the concepts they can now account for behavioristically. Teaching the concept of fusion—taking words and beliefs as real—is useful for helping patients get some distance on their beliefs, which is why the concept has survived for the century since Russell articulated it as the theory of logical types (Whitehead & Russell, 1910) and the half century since Bateson (1972d) adopted it as the centerpiece of his theory of psychopathology. If ACT therapists stopped claiming the invention of such concepts, they might benefit from taking a look at what other smart people working with patients have done with them (one of which is to utilize tailor-made rather than off-the-rack metaphors).

Behavior therapy is behavioristic when every behavior emitted in the therapy office is understood in functional relation to its occasioning environment—when every behavior is treated as a performance. Every time a behavior therapist takes a report of an external event as journalism rather than as literature, she is fusing with the patient's language and behaving nonbehavioristically. Every time she employs a technique or metaphor learned from a book or supervisor, she's engaging in the very kind of rule-governed behavior she's trying to teach her patients to question. Behavior therapy is behavioristic when every technique is treated as a guide and the therapist focuses on the patient's immediate reactions rather than on the guidebook.

WHEN IS COGNITIVE-BEHAVIORAL THERAPY COGNITIVE-BEHAVIORAL?

The essence of cognitive-behavioral therapy is what Beck (1976) calls collaborative empiricism. This happens when the therapist and patient put their heads together to look at what's wrong with the patient's map for negotiating problematic situations and trying to improve the map by finding things out about those situations. Cognitive therapy is to psychopathology as science is to superstition. By its nature, it's more teacherly than parental. Each patient can be viewed as an adult–child combination with adult strengths and childish fears and skill deficits. When I do psychoanalytic therapy, I ask the adult to bring the child to my office and then wait for us in the waiting room. Psychoanalytic therapy is a kind of reparenting. When I do cognitive therapy, I ask the adult to hire a babysitter and to come see me without her child. Cognitive therapy is a kind of parent coaching. (Since it's easier for parents to say good-bye to their coaches than for children to say good-bye to their parents, I prefer the cognitive approach if I think the therapy will have to end prematurely.)

For cognitive-behavioral therapy itself to be cognitive-behavioral, therapist and patient have to examine their thoughts and beliefs about the therapy relationship. This process has clear advantages. It provides examples of identifying and disputing irrational beliefs where the therapist has independent access to the activating event. In Ellis's terminology, the activating event elicits irrational beliefs that produce symptomatic consequences. In many cognitive therapies, the therapist accepts the patient's rendition of the activating event and the report of the consequences as if they are utterly objective renditions. By exploring beliefs about activating events that occurred in the therapy office, the therapist can correct the patient's inaccuracies. I have written *can* rather than *will* because all the problems of power and privilege come into play whenever the activating event sullies the doctorly image the therapist is trying to project.

Examining beliefs about the therapy allows the therapist and patient to observe the patient's *process* in applying and reporting irrational beliefs. For a semifictional example, imagine a patient who describes his problem as a tendency to get jealous of his girlfriend. He reports an activating event when his girlfriend seemed excited to attend a work-related evening meeting, and he reports the automatic thought "She must be attracted to someone attending the meeting." The therapist disputes the belief that the only reason a woman would be excited to go to an evening meeting is that she's attracted to someone else attending. But the therapist has no way of knowing that it was the aroma of the girlfriend's perfume that activated the automatic thought, not her excitement. The patient may not realize this either. The dyad is disputing the wrong belief, which should be about girlfriends smelling good and looking attractive, not about their being excited.

As soon as the girlfriend left, the patient rifled through her papers, searching for clues about the other fellow's identity. He found nothing and stewed for an hour awaiting her return. When she came home, he casually asked her about who else was there, and the cast of characters was, to him, entirely innocent. He does not tell any of this to his therapist because, while he wants to fix his jealousy, he does not want his therapist to know how childishly he handles it. The intermediate belief that actually needs disputation and behavioral intervention is not that his girlfriend only wears perfume for paramours but that he can't manage his own jealousy except by ransacking her desk.

The therapist reschedules an appointment because there is a conference she wants to attend. The patient has the automatic thought "I'm not that interesting" and continues the session in a desultory tone. Many therapists would let this tone pass, exerting the privilege of ignoring how they are using their power in the relationship. But the true cognitive-behavioral therapist recognizes that an activating event has occurred before her very eyes and asks the patient either Beck's standard question "What went through your mind when I told you I needed to reschedule?" or Ellis's (but in this case gently and curiously rather than scoffingly) "Why are you upsetting yourself about my rescheduling our appointment?" The patient's response might be "What difference does it make? You're going anyway" or "Nothing went through my mind, but I've been thinking about taking the summer off from therapy because things have gotten so busy with me and my girlfriend." These reactions show what he does with his automatic thoughts about being uninteresting, and they put the therapist in a position to dispute his beliefs about how he has to behave to manage them. The relevant intermediate belief isn't just that the therapist would only cancel a session because the patient is uninteresting— it's also relevant that feeling uninteresting can be managed only by giving up or by getting even.

Examining irrational beliefs about the therapy can help both parties fix the therapy relationship when it becomes a replica of either the patient's or the therapist's idiosyncratic expectations of what the therapy should be. Cognitive therapy assumes that the teacherly, collaboratively empirical role is being played by the therapist, but we all know that patients frequently interpret our efforts to play this role according to their personal maps of authority, and we all know that we sometimes put a personal spin on the role by playing it in a way that exaggerates our personal or professional predilections. Being cognitive-behavioral about the therapy and not just about the patient's life gets the therapy relationship back on track and uses the therapy as a learning laboratory for how to do so. In the previous example, if the patient reports that his reactions to the cancellation don't matter or that he's planning on taking the summer off, the therapist can rethink her plan to cancel the session or at least can engage in some collaborative empiricism about what the cancellation means.

WHEN IS SYSTEMIC THERAPY SYSTEMIC?

In the systemic approach, context is everything, but the specially relevant context isn't so much behaviorism's immediate environment as the system of people likely to be affected by the conduct. People behave according to the roles they acquire in their various systems. Effective interventions are directed at the way the system works, not at its components. Efforts to change a system are always met with a homeostatic response. If a system didn't have a self-correcting response, it wouldn't be a system—it would already have dissipated into something else. I am all for giving people good advice—this book is nothing but a bunch of advice. But by the time patients get to therapists, they've already heard plenty of good advice, and the reason they haven't taken it has something to do with the way advice is cast in the systemic drama and something to do with the homeostatic responses of the systems they are in.

Whether the relevant system is intrapsychic, interpersonal, marital, familial, or organizational, the therapist must either enter the system to change it or plan for the homeostatic response and judo it in the desired direction. Proponents of the judo approach have demonstrated some creative genius in its application (Erickson, as reported by Haley, 1973; Madanes, 1981; Selvini Palazzoli, Boscolo, Cecchin, & Prata, 1978). They frame the entire therapy therapeutically rather than socially and from the start use the treatment relationship to cantilever the individual or family into change. Erickson might attempt to get a patient sexually excited to facilitate her mating behavior outside of therapy. Madanes might elect to help a woman therapist married to a domineering psychiatrist by taking her into supervision and teaching her how to surpass him in skill. Selvini Palazzoli et al. might assume that a family comes in not for help but to prove that nothing will help, and they begin the therapy by recommending stasis, forcing the family into the complementary role of changing to prove that Selvini Palazzoli is wrong about *that*. Such framings are often denounced as dishonest or manipulative, but these words merely choose one frame as fundamental and real over another. Selvini Palazzoli would probably feel dreadfully dishonest letting yet another therapeutic effort founder on the frame of showing one's cards, just as a good actor playing Iago would feel more dishonest than honest by constantly winking at the audience and saying in a stage whisper, "I'm not really this devious."

To enter a system, one must choose an available role. A therapist often finds herself in the position of a fan at a football game who realizes that a screen pass would capitalize on the overly aggressive defensive line: she has a good idea, but she does not have a role that can communicate this idea to the offensive coordinator. Even one of the players would have difficulty getting an idea like this in play. She is like a bystander who has something funny to say to two famous people who are conversing near her. If one of them said her line, it would be riotously funny, but in her role (or nonrole, really), she isn't authorized to crack people up.

A few individuals, couples, and families come to therapy with the role of therapist—wise, objective, neutral, concerned—open for casting. They audition the clinician and cast her, and she comfortably proceeds to act her part. Unfortunately for us, most individuals, couples, and families who have such a role available in their dramas have already cast it. They are already receiving plenty of guidance, advice, and arbitration from themselves, their friends, and magazine writers and don't need a therapist. Indeed, much of what makes patterns of behavior problematic enough for therapy is the absence in the pattern of a therapeutic figure, and when we are consulted, we find that there is no convenient place to stand.

In my experience, systemic therapists are the most inventive change agents and also the most harmlessly ineffective. An ineffective psychoanalytic therapist can still offer some intimacy exposure, but an ineffective family therapist just pushes a little for change, and the system pushes back. Eventually, he gets aggravated by whichever part of the system has the responsibility of letting him know that there is no role for a therapist in it. He says things like, "The family has not improved because the mother is so self-absorbed," forgetting that a cornerstone of the systemic approach is to focus on the system and not its members. One of my pet peeves is therapists who blame the failure of the therapy on the presenting complaint: I can't help you with your anger problems if you don't calm down, or I can't help you with your impulsivity if you don't come to the sessions.

A systemic therapy is systemic when it views the therapy itself as a system. Setbacks or periods of poor progress have to be considered a reflection of that system, and truly systemic therapists consider how these reflect on the therapy system and what about it needs to change. Lively systemic therapists reflect on the roles available to them and how to play those roles rather than insist that they're playing a helpful role and that it's the patients who are not fitting into the therapy.

WHEN IS PSYCHOANALYTIC THERAPY PSYCHOANALYTIC?

The essence of psychoanalytic therapy is intimacy exposure. People get hurt in intimate familial relationships; they develop a fight-or-flight response to the dangers they associate with intimacy (this screws up their close relationships), and then they can be exposed to intimacy in therapy with profound honesty, skepticism about the patient's text, and certain guarantees of safety, and their aversive associations to intimacy extinguish. In this view, the framing of the relationship serves the purpose of enhancing intimacy, and interpretations are offered to demonstrate to the patient that the relationship really is all that intimate and that the social veils have fallen. The sine qua non of the psychoanalytic approach is talking about what is going on while it's going on. This process also teaches metacommunication as a form of conflict resolution.

Many therapists claim to be psychoanalytic, but they go session after session without discussing what's going on in the room at the moment. I'm not talking about elegant, mutual interpretations or pointed observations that bring the dyad closer to each other; I'm talking about simple statements like "You looked sad when I said that" or "I notice you were late" or "What was it like telling me that?" I don't endorse any of these statements for advanced therapists, but I think they are typical of the beginning psychoanalytic therapist who is learning through experimentation and exposure that she can say such mildly intimate things in therapy. When beginning therapists don't even do this much, it's usually because they think that what is psychoanalytic about the therapy they are doing is the language they use to understand the patient and an unpressured attitude toward making progress.

When trainees quote analysts who say that the relationship is primary and interpretation is secondary, I worry that they think they don't have to *do* anything to be helpful. The effective psychoanalytic therapist can indeed do very little once a restorative relationship has been established. But if the patient isn't basking in the benefits of reliable empathy, it's incumbent on the therapist to take remedial steps in the form of attunement to reactions to the therapy, frame management, privilege busting, and interpretation of what's going on.

After learning to make marginally intimate comments in sessions, good psychoanalytic therapists go on to what I call level 1 interpretations. "About your doing [or saying] [such and such], it reminds me of a type of interaction you've described with your mother [or father], where you [played such and such role] whenever they [played such and such role]. I just wonder if [that pattern applied here]." This type of interpretation takes the patient's in-session behavior as an indicator of his problematic patterns and uses the fact that the therapist has direct (rather than reported) access to the expression of the pattern to comment on its historical meaning and immediate function. In doing so, she is also enhancing intimacy exposure by saying, in effect, "I maintain my nonpunitive concern despite what you are doing, not because I have missed what you are doing." Further, she's showing the patient how to use discussion to resolve mixed impressions of an interaction rather than falling back on his outdated interpretations of how the world works and act-ing accordingly.

I call this a level 1 interpretation because it isn't truly intimate. It presents only the therapist's front stage and doesn't invite consideration even of that. The therapist uses power to disguise her backstage and uses privilege to ig-nore the way she is treating herself differently from her patient. Recognizing the power differential, as the less powerful members of interactions are al-ways sure to do, patients will tactfully treat such interventions as full-blooded intimacy, even as they experience them as a mild form of punishment that re-ally says, "You did [or said] [such and such] because you are sick."

A psychoanalytic therapy is truly psychoanalytic when it develops a tech-nology for overcoming privilege and includes the therapist's backstage (or at least enough of it so that it doesn't seem like the therapist is constantly pulling rank on the patient to define reality). One technology of considerable interest and enormous promise is Bateson, Jackson, Haley, and Weakland's (1972) idea of interpreting patient narratives as metaphorical comments on what just happened. This idea was made the centerpiece of the communicative ap-proach (Langs, 1976, 1978). Unfortunately, Langs fell victim to the tendency to memorialize innovation, and he quickly stopped using metaphor as a tech-nology for adapting to the patient's feedback and instead used it to abstract a set of rules about structuring therapy. The technology of interpreting narrative as metaphor must be used in the service of keeping the therapy lively by dis-covering what just happened rather than in the service of proving that one al-ready knows what happened. Therapists who already know what things mean are as deadly as actors waiting their turn to say their next line.

Intersubjectivity embraces a different feedback technology. If the patient provides feedback in a steady stream that varies from positive to negative and from general to specific, then the feedback can be given more weight as reli-able than if the patient's feedback is always positive, always negative, or al-ways generic. Buirski (2005) illustrates reliable feedback with examples of therapies in which the relationship, the patient's reactions within it, and the therapist's description of those reactions are ongoing topics of conversation.

Including the therapist's backstage is tricky. For one thing, it can never be done entirely intentionally, as this always creates another unrevealed backstage. It also often disturbs the power differential necessary for inti-macy exposure to be effective. The therapist's backstage must be included in the context of an assurance that it is being glimpsed or visited but not that it will become the focus of the therapy. Freud supposedly said that at every self-disclosure, the patient undertakes the analysis of the analyst, an apt ob-servation of what happens when superiors act like subordinates. In families, parents who act like children parentify the actual children. But there is no breach of structural clarity when parents are occasionally joyous, sad, self-indulgent, or foolish because the child frames these behaviors not as primary representations of the parent but as plays within the play of security. Similarly, therapists can frame comments that acknowledge their own backstages as plays within a play, where the larger play is framed by a secure and reliable relationship.

The intersubjective approach (Buirski, 2005; Buirski & Haglund, 2001; Stolorow et al., 1987) is acutely concerned with addressing dramaturgical problems associated with revealing and using the therapist's backstage and equally concerned with status and privilege problems arising from the power differential. It has addressed these concerns by framing the relationship as cocreated within a larger frame of helping, just as a skilled and famous actor doing a scene with a less accomplished partner could productively frame their work together as mutual. My own efforts in this direction have led me to frame my interpretations as those of a couple's therapist, where the patient and I constitute the couple. The change in role from me-interacting to me-interpreting allows me to comment directly on my backstage and to do so in a way that does not presume that either of us, the patient or me, is at fault for whatever just happened. Me-interpreting is the role that constitutes the therapy frame and me-interacting is the role that constitutes the play within the play. Me-interpreting, of course, does not or cannot reveal *his* backstage, but neither does he pretend not to have one.

Good psychoanalytic therapy often looks like you're doing nothing, but that doesn't mean that doing nothing is good psychoanalytic therapy. The therapist has to connect the therapy relationship to the treatment goals ("You can't sleep at night because you don't know what it's like to feel supported and secure while things are tough at work; let's find out what keeps you from feeling supported and secure"). The therapist has to establish a solid framing of the relationship to set it off from but make it relevant to the rest of life. The therapist has to cultivate free association by helping the patient experience its advantages. The therapist has to demonstrate reliable empathy and a willingness to be seen as all too human. The therapist must exemplify sympathetic honesty, especially about the relationship. Only then, for long periods, can the therapist appear to be doing nothing.

THEORY AS A PAVILION

These four major theoretical approaches to clinical problems all lend themselves to liveliness and to deadliness depending on how they are used. A major component of their lively use, as we would expect from the privilege and gender issues that arise in a power differential, is the application of the approach not just to the patient's life but also to the therapy and the therapist. A theoretical orientation should be not a template but a pavilion. Like a pavilion at Epcot Center, the players using—embraced by—a theoretical orientation must take it seriously in terms of costume, staging, language, and narrative, but they must also understand that it is only a mock-up and that there are other pavilions.

Chapter Eleven

Deadly Supervision

Preachers say, Do as I say, not as I do. But if a physician has the same disease upon him that I have, and he should bid me do one thing, and he do quite another, could I believe him?

—John Selden, *Table Talk*, 1689

Some, valuing those of their own side or mind,
Still make themselves the measure of mankind:
Fondly we think we honour merit then,
When we but praise ourselves in other men.

—Alexander Pope, *An Essay on Criticism*, 1711

SUPERVISORY FRAMES

An actress at the conservatory carefully prepares for the first scene she will perform for the class. She has seen other students run off the stage in fear, bark with anger, or collapse in tears when the gruff but good-natured teacher has interrupted their scenes with such hearty comments as "You're screeching like a fishwife," "Is the character supposed to be sleepwalking?," and the pervasive "What are you doing up there?" She enters the scene confident that she has made deliberate choices and can defend her approach to the material. But before she even gets to her spot onstage, the teacher bellows, "You're walking like a cow!" The actress calls out, "Can I do it again?" And the teacher shouts back, "Yes!"

Acting training is different from clinical supervision in that acting itself is public, while psychotherapy is fairly private. Unlike a therapy trainee, an

193

actor cannot nod and act compliant with the acting teacher only to go off and ignore his input because the teacher and anyone else can go see what she's doing onstage. Other actors, critics, and even old acting teachers will tell her what they really think of her performance. Those over whom she has some power will only find things to compliment, but an actress can't fully confine her performance to those over whom she has power. (There have been some notable exceptions, as when Nero insisted on performing as a singer in public and received only praise for his efforts.)

Acting's public nature has produced a culture among theater professionals in which criticism, or *notes*, are offered and accepted in a friendly spirit because there's no use in just pretending to accept them. Also, criticism is especially valuable to the recipient because she will eventually have to show her work, so she needs to get better at what she does and not just pretend to improve. The bombastic acting teacher didn't say that the actress had the voice of a fishwife but that she was using her voice as a fishwife does. The performance, not the person, is fair game. The conservatory teacher in the story was acculturating the students to the world of theater by making criticism playful and instructive. He was defining a relationship in which students had to recognize that their cherished ownership of what they thought they were doing is always subordinate to the audience's response.

I'm holding this actress's behavior up as a model of being a good supervisee, but I'm not holding this teacher's behavior up as a model of good supervision. It's too sudden, too yang, and too privileged to be optimally effective for the dual goals of teaching acting and weeding out trainees who'll never make it. By "too sudden," I mean that the students were not put on notice for what class would be like. The teacher didn't help them frame the activity as playful except by his tone of voice and general demeanor, and he didn't show them how to transition to useful supervision from the natural and predictable desire to show off what they already knew. Metacommunication about the framing of rehearsals could have brought out the best in everyone, not just the actress who framed the situation as educational and comedic. I try to help trainees frame supervision as educational and comedic by telling them this story about acting. The actress's definition of comedy is instructive: comedy acknowledges that a backstage—its contents as well as our self-consciousness about having one—is universal.

By "too yang," I mean that the teacher's emphasis on verbal jousting and his own joyous self-expression stemmed from the power differential in the relationship. When the gender roles are cast in a group, those in power take the fun, yang things to do and then label the fun stuff in a way that justifies their taking those roles. In a patriarchy, the fun stuff is labeled boyish or masculine, while the subordinate, facilitative, compliant stuff is labeled girlish or feminine. If women hold power over men, say by reason of seniority, then the fun stuff is labeled the reward of lasting group membership. In therapy, the justification for being the one who gets to tell instructive stories, hold forth, and be right is mental health, and in supervision, it's clinical experience.

By "too privileged," I mean that the teacher in the story exploited his power to define the situation by construing the crying, barking, stifled students as bad acting prospects rather than as victims of his approach. He also exploited his power to ignore the students' construction of the situation by not attending to their implicit feedback.

Many of the same performance issues that inform psychotherapy also apply to supervision. The similarities are in the power differentials in the relationships and the fiduciary responsibilities of the person in power for the subordinate. A lively supervision makes use of this analogy to enhance supervision, just as lively therapy uses rather than ignores the performance, privilege, and gender issues in therapy. Lively supervision becomes a laboratory for exploring performance, power, and gender for the purpose of helping the therapist become more adept when she is on her own, just as lively therapy becomes a laboratory for the patient's management of power differentials when he is on his own.

SUPERVISION AS REHEARSAL

Brook's (1968) view is that the stage director sits in for the audience. At an obvious level, she makes sure that the actors are speaking loudly enough to be heard throughout the house and that the staging allows the audience to follow the narrative. More subtly, she monitors the performance for audience satisfaction. Is the presentation entertaining and coherent? Even more subtly, she checks to see if she is engrossed, using her own involvement as a gauge of the audience's engrossment. These more subtle aspects of directing are particularly difficult because of her familiarity with the material and her identification with what the actors are doing. It's hard to tell if a joke is funny or a speech is moving the hundredth time, but the accomplished director is able to imagine hearing it for the first time. It's hard to become engrossed in something that has no novelty, so her own reactions must be translated into what the audience will feel. It's also hard to eliminate performance ideas as ineffective when they were her ideas in the first place. These technical problems aside, Brook's point is that the director is the audience's viceroy, and it's her job to ensure that the performance is successful by voicing boredom or confusion and by offering suggestions for improvement. Gibson (1950) places the editor of a magazine in an analogous role, representing the magazine's readers.

The ability to hear and see things as if for the first time and as if they were not one's own products is essential to good art and good therapy. The good artist observes each brushstroke, each line of text, and each dramaturgical choice as if she were evaluating it afresh and as if she were not attached to it—she is her own director. "You have to kill your little darlings," said Hemingway, in his yang way, describing the detachment necessary to improve your own writing. A good artist is both a writer and an editor, a painter and a critic, whose feedback loop between the two aspects of the self is friendly and collaborative. A good therapist must let go of her comments and evaluate their effectiveness with similar detachment. Too often, therapists preface their comments with behavior meant to deflect criticism ("I was wondering if maybe there was some chance that perhaps you are angry with me") and follow them similarly ("I mean, if that makes sense to you, sort of, and maybe not really 'angry,' maybe more like, you know"). Lively supervision teaches trainees that the feedback loop can be friendly but objective by exposing them to a supervisor who is both blunt and warm.

Just as the director sits in for the audience, the clinical supervisor sits in for the patient, who needs representation not because the performance must be reasonably set before the patient's input is available but because the patient's input is subject to the distorting influences of the power differential in the relationship and to the patient's ambivalence about making the therapy as effective as possible. The patient, as audience to the therapist's performance, is more like Nero's listeners than like moviegoers. The power differential drives the patient toward appreciating the therapist's efforts or at least saying he does. To the extent that the patient is also caught up in cognitive dissonance ("if I'm paying all this money, the therapy must be good"), he's like the theatergoer who has coughed up so much money for the seats that he dare not find the performance disappointing. To the extent that the patient has developed affection for the therapist, he's like parents attending a high school play, and his critical reactions are suspended. To the extent that the patient is ambivalent about relinquishing his symptoms (and all the major schools of therapy suggest that he would have relinquished them long before meeting the therapist if they were not doing him or others *some* good), he is also ambivalent about providing the therapist with useful feedback about what's working and what's not. Deadly therapy, like deadly theater, puts up the performance without tailoring it to the patient, without engrossing the patient, and without changing the patient. Deadly supervision assists deadly therapy by not highlighting the patient's reactions of involvement, engrossment, and change, instead highlighting the extent to which the therapy performance conforms with the supervisor's prior expectation, which could be called the supervisory party line.

SUPERVISION AS RULES

Supervision raises the Zen Buddhist problem of the master pointing at the moon and the student looking at the master's finger rather than at the moon. The supervisor tries to teach contingency-shaped behavior to the trainee and to bring the trainee's behavior under the influence of the patient's reactions but does so by telling the trainee the rules about how to do it. The trainee attends to the supervisor's rules rather than to the patient's reactions. The baseball coach tells the infielder to look at the ball, not at me, and this works fine because catching the ball is rewarding to the infielder. The supervisor tells the trainee to listen to the patient, not to me, but this doesn't work so well because the trainee needs the supervisor to tell him whether he caught the ball. The infielder knows if he caught the ball. The trainee doesn't know if the patient has reacted well to an intervention because the patient's reaction is overlain with the patient's efforts to please the therapist, to avoid criticizing the therapist, to maintain a sense that the therapist is helping, and to resist change. The patient, like all subordinates, may not even know whether he has benefited from an intervention because the role of compliant and appreciative subordinate is easier to play effectively if the performer convinces himself that it is not just a role. People who laugh at their boss's jokes aren't manipulative—they truly think their boss is funny. But the boss who wants to be truly funny rather than merely obtain laughter should pay closer attention to the reactions of her employees who have tenure than to those who are on probation.

IDENTIFYING USEFUL FEEDBACK

The problem for the supervisor is to teach the trainee how to tell when he has scored, independent of the communicative distortions brought on by the power, gender, and affection issues in the therapy relationship. Analogously, parents need a way of finding out which of their techniques are beneficial to their children, and it's clear that just asking the children doesn't produce useful information. Children, like patients, are likely to undervalue frustration, for example, and are likely to offer unmerited compliments for a variety of reasons. Needless to say, the supervisor has little chance of accomplishing this central task of supervision if she has never herself considered the problem of identifying useful feedback and has never articulated a basis for tailoring her therapy techniques to patients other than to avoid frustrating them and to pursue their compliments.

The next great obstacle for lively supervision is to help trainees attend to the patient's reactions rather than to the supervisor's own. The old saw "If you meet the Buddha on the road, kill him" addresses the student's need to attend to business and not to the word of the master. Supervisors are mapmakers, not safari guides, because the therapist journeys on her own. Even a really good map should only be seen as a general idea when the landscape it depicts shifts as quickly as therapy does. Supervisory advice should be perennially framed as what the supervisor would say to the patient she imagines, and the trainee will have to tailor that advice to the actual patient, the actual moment, and the trainee's personal style. That said, though, I think a good way to learn therapy is first to do it as an expert might and then to do it as I might. I am in a better position to consider what *I* might say having first learned to say what Beck, Horney, Madanes, and Kohut might say.

The third great obstacle to lively supervision is the tendency for the supervisory conversation to become a party line. This tendency increases when the supervisor is especially intelligent and thoughtful because the trainee's admiration can fixate the supervisor's articulations into truths that seem to transcend the situations that occasion them. This party-line tendency is also exacerbated by the power differential in the relationship, as all human text from the powerful tends to become a party line. It's also exacerbated by trainee anxiety.

TRAINEE ANXIETY

Anxiety is the feeling that accompanies not knowing what to do (Skinner, 1953). Anxiety is our friend, as in the old joke that if you can keep your head when all about you are losing theirs, maybe you don't realize what is going on. Anxiety tells us that our map may not be suitable for the terrain. Anxiety is not the problem. The problem is the avoidance of anxiety, the management of the aversive experience in some way other than revising the map. Anxiety's aversiveness is compounded when the individual not only doesn't know what to do but also doesn't know how to look at a map with a critical eye, doesn't know how to revise a map, and doesn't know how to explore the terrain for enough information to create a better map. Part of the supervisor's job is to assuage this second-order anxiety, to make the trainee feel that even though she is anxious about not knowing how to do the therapy, she need not be anxious about her ability to solve the problem eventually. This is what is meant by the holding function of the supervisory relationship. The supervisor's warm confidence turns the surrounding abysses into potholes and allows the therapist to use her anxiety productively rather than be paralyzed with fear or cling to her supervisor's map.

Another way to look at this second-order anxiety is to see it as anxiety about the role of therapist. If I'm confident that I'm a good therapist—confident that I can play this role—then anxiety about a particular clinical situation doesn't get out of hand. This is especially true if my definition of the role of therapist doesn't include always knowing what to do. To the extent that I view myself as some kind of mastermind or oracle, my performance will be too easily discredited, and like all oracles, I will start speaking in vague generalizations to avoid that fate. To the extent that I view myself as an explorer and a mutual partner in understanding what happens, my role is not so easily discredited, and devising defensive maneuvers is unnecessary. The supervisor's job is partly to help the trainee define a role of therapist that is personally sustainable and good for patients. Her job is also to critique the trainee's performance of that role in the same way a theater director gives notes to an actor. "Juliet must be clever for the story to make sense, and she must be delighted by her own cleverness. When you smile like that, Juliet seems more immature than clever." This is precisely analogous to saying, "Jack's therapist must communicate that his fantasy life will not upset her. When you repeatedly reassure him that it's okay to think such things, his therapist seems like she's protesting too much."

THE ROLE OF THERAPIST

The therapist role must exude integrity, bigheartedness, confidence, warmth, intelligence, and hope. As some Hollywood wag once said, "The hardest thing to show on screen is integrity, but once you learn to fake integrity, you've got it made." What's wrong with teaching trainees how to act confident, warm, and bighearted? The prospect raises the issue of authenticity. We want the trainee to *be* bighearted, not just to *act* bighearted, the difference apparently being that to act is conniving, a false face put on a miserly and blaming backstage. But how do humans become bighearted if not by acting that way, experiencing its rewards, and then identifying with the behavior that produces them? Nietzsche (1996) made the same point about becoming a benevolent person, and it has been made many times since about other traits: identity doesn't produce behavior—behavior produces identity. There's nothing wrong with training therapists to take control of their presentations of self. I have already mentioned the student I told to stop bobbing her head in order to project her actual competence. Another student had a Jimmy Carter smile, natural, glowing, and warm, but like Carter's it read as insincere to many people. Reportedly, Carter had to learn not to smile during his run for the White

House in order to project himself as a potential leader. I told the trainee that her smile was lovely with children, but adults might need to see a more serious and reflective face on a therapist. Afterward, I felt terrible when I saw her impassive visage in the clinic, until I realized that I had not depressed her— she was merely not smiling.

I also like to talk with trainees about such performance topics as what to say when you don't know what to say (you have the right to remain silent), what to do with your narcissistic glee when you see a therapist in therapy for the first time, how to describe what you do and how to explain it to your family, and how to express affection for patients. These discussions are geared toward helping the trainee learn how to play the role by helping her master her backstory, just as an actress learns a role by articulating the character's backstory. A friend asked me what I'm doing backstage while I'm performing the role of therapist. Listening, I replied. What, I asked her back, are you doing backstage when you're performing the role of Madame Jourdain? Listening, she said.

SUPERVISORY POWER DIFFERENTIALS

Supervisions founder on many of the same shoals as therapies do. Power, privilege, and gender can combine to make the supervisor brilliant, expressive, and cheerful and mold the trainee into the complementary audience. Supervisors shine and trainees polish. This is impossible to avoid at least sometimes (especially for a show-off like me), but a feedback loop can be established to even things out. Supervisory ideas can become a party line, the worst implication of which is that the supervisor's ideas become the box outside of which the trainee can't think, just as adherence to a theory, rather than playful envelopment in it, can be deadly. Supervisors and trainees must give each other a backstage pass to see the qualms and questions of the other, or else their teamwork fails. But their team formation must be on the patient's behalf, not at the patient's expense, just as the teamwork between director and actor must be in the service of reaching the audience, not in the service of demeaning the audience. The power distribution presses supervisor and trainee to blame the patient for any inadequacies in the therapy's progress. Some supervisors protect the patient and blame the therapist, which can be a good learning experience if the therapist is heroic enough to use it, but then the therapist's vision of the therapist role tends to become equally heroic, and heroic therapists have patients who become damsels in distress. Some supervisors go so far as to blame themselves, which is fine as long as blame is only a metaphor for inward looking and self-improvement. The liveliest supervisions are those in which therapist and supervisor collaborate on the patient's behalf and set-backs, like boredom in the theater, are greeted with creative thinking rather than as a sign that someone needs to be blamed.

A major difference between supervision and therapy is the evaluative function of supervision. Many therapies and many rehearsals are also evaluative, but they don't need to be after the initial decision about whether to continue working with the people in question. Trainees, in contrast, work to please their supervisors not only because of the immediate power differential but also because of potentially lifelong ramifications for their careers, including grades, letters of recommendation, clinical appointments, and so on. This is a tricky problem for supervisors, who are often accomplished in nonjudgmental relationships but have little experience as administrators. Like all people, they tend to split between unreflective evaluation and none at all, either un-self-consciously making judgments about their trainees' abilities or refusing to make judgments of any kind. Both of these paths are deadly because both exacerbate the power differential. Supervisors who comfortably rate one trainee as excellent and another as very good isolate the evaluative function from discussion. These yardsticks become the party line that deconstructionists and critical thinkers are trying to question. At the other end of the evaluative spectrum, the supervisor who loves all the trainees equally merely makes them wonder what the real yardstick looks like, where it is kept, and how it will be used.

The lively way to teach trainees how to make the unspeakable speakable is to encourage discussion of the power differential in supervision. I tell my trainees that as a member of the human race, I am bound to exercise my privilege and to ignore the power differential between us. As a member of the clinical community, I am bound to treat their voiced hints and complaints as signs of their inexperience and ignorance—I'm pretty good about not pathologizing them, but that too is a risk. My commitment is to take a swing at the third strike, to be responsive at last when they voice concern over my ignoring their complaints about the power differential. Sometimes I find the grace to respond immediately, but this three-strike convention encourages the trainee to stick with it a few times to give me a chance to respond.

As for the evaluation itself, I use the same model I use as a therapist. I start off unsure whether a patient and I can work together, but once I make an offer, I revisit the question only if something alarming emerges. In law, there is a convention that a contract can be voided if an event occurs "the nonoccurrence of which was a basic assumption of the contract." In therapy contracts, there is usually a basic assumption that a psychotic transference will not develop, that frequent phone calls or extra sessions will not be needed, and that self-harm or substance abuse will not interfere with the relationship. If these occur, I feel entitled to raise the question of whether continuing to work together makes sense. In supervision, there is a third alternative between working together and not working together, a work plan such as those imposed on probationary employees. After an initial period of mutual assessment, I either end the supervision (unless it is part of an organizational duty), explain my judgment that the trainee has passed muster and why (usually because they have exhibited intelligence, diligence, an absence of character pathology, and a sense of humor), or spell out what they need to do to continue in the supervision. This work plan then becomes the central feature of the supervision, and although it's painful for both of us, it at least avoids the deadliness of not talking about the main thing between us. An analogous work plan can address the evaluative function of supervision even when the relationship is institutionally mandated, as in a training program. This requires the supervisor to specify what the trainee needs to change to stay in school or keep his job rather than just evaluating him.

Chapter Twelve

Fourteen Things We Can Do to Make Our Therapies Livelier

Man is
the symbol-using (symbol-making, symbol-misusing) animal
inventor of the negative (or moralized by the negative)
separated from his natural condition by instruments of his own making
goaded by the spirit of hierarchy (or moved by the sense of order)
and rotten with perfection.

—Burke (1966, p. 16)

Turn in the direction of the skid.

—Anonymous driving tip

THINGS WE CAN DO TO SUBVERT THE PARTY LINE

Humans are the rule-making animal, but "the Tao that can be told is not the eternal Tao" (Lao-Tzu, 1988, No. 1). Rules and categories are made to describe situations so we can negotiate them better, but then the rules come to define situations, the definitions suit those with the authority to concoct them, and then the authorities defend the rules by turning them into a party line. Many therapy problems arise because of the effect of words. The voiceless aspects of the self or the family are restless because they cannot be heard. The rules derived for one situation are revered, but they are unsuitable for a new situation. Treatment requires hearing the marginalized or challenging the rules. In either case, the party line must be subverted.

One reason people behave symptomatically is that they find that they can't advocate for themselves effectively from an inferior position. The unprivileged voice in advocacy sounds litigious, angry, pathological, or, worst of all, confirming of the reason for the inferiority. If a person is stigmatized because she is a woman, advocacy sounds shrill. If as a man, it sounds threatening. If as a black, it sounds accusatory. If as a mental patient, it sounds symptomatic. Every party line has a way of accounting for efforts to question it. If you disagree with this, you're passive-aggressive or just plain stupid.

As therapists, we must welcome subversion of the party line, even when it's our own, without rushing to pathologize attempts to subvert it.

1. Respond to Data, Not to Rules

Trainees frequently ask us what to do if a patient comes late, whether they are qualified to treat rape victims, how much notice we demand for missed sessions, and what the rules are for self-disclosure. Which patient? Which rape victim? Which session? Which self-disclosure? Policies are instances generalized into rules and applied to novel situations. They are the exact equivalent of most psychopathology, using an old map on new terrain. Why not base our behavior on an understanding of the instant situation and what we want to accomplish? Codifying rules is deadly because it constrains response alternatives and turns the therapy into an example of a hypothetical, typical therapy. My policy is to have no policy.

Will a lack of policies generate unethical or unprofessional conduct? No, there should be an absence of policies only for decisions not covered by law or ethics. If there is a general rule of law or ethics, just obey it. But that doesn't mean that one must inject these rules into conversations that might otherwise develop into meaningful dialogues. The pronouncement that one will not write a letter to a judge (in light of a rule of professional conduct that forbids mixing therapy and custody evaluations) kills the discussion, where an open curiosity can unpack different definitions of the relationship. Consider the young boy who tells his mother he wants to marry her some day—the deadly mother informs him that it is impossible, while the lively mother asks him what that would be like. The deadly therapist forestalls exploration by imposing rules at the outset of the treatment with a flurry of consent forms and mandatory disclosures. The deadly therapist forestalls exploration of content by imposing theoretical constructs on the patient's story. If theories are like languages, there is no need to pick one for deciphering the patient's story until, at the very least, one has heard the story. What is wanted, in religious terms, is a pastoral rather than a doctrinal response to therapy problems.

Whether rules are legal, professional, or theory based, there is no need to start with them. We have trained a generation of therapists who think that therapy starts with a list of mandatory disclosures, informed consent forms, fee policies, and brief assessment instruments rather than an inquiry about what is troubling the patient, the context of the presenting problem, a demonstration of therapeutic intervention, an explanation of how therapy can help, and an offer to work together. Only after there is a tentative agreement on doing therapy can informed consent and mandatory disclosure become relevant. Trainees ask me what I do if the patient reveals child abuse before I have warned the patient about the legal limits of confidentiality. I tell them that I have no obligation to disclose the legal limits of confidentiality until we're talking about how confidential the relationship will be. It's true that a therapist incurs a responsibility to keep things confidential from the outset, but patients are not entitled to assume that this responsibility embraces the commission of a crime until the matter is discussed explicitly. Mandatory disclosure of the limits of confidentiality makes sense only in the context of saying that, other than those exceptions, everything said here will stay here. Until I have promised confidentiality, I don't need to circumscribe its limits. If some day I practice in a jurisdiction that requires disclosure before beginning, I will say then what I say now after offering to help—that the help I offer is regulated by the state I work in and that one of those regulations requires the following disclosures. I will act like I'm obeying the relevant law in the societal frame, not like I'm a legal robot that starts a helping relationship with a set of rules.

2. Learn Multiple Theoretical Orientations

Theory drives our understanding of what constitutes relevant data, and it shapes our perception of events into patterns that resemble what the theory predicts. Theory is a Procrustean bed that can lop off or stretch important data that don't fit. Since there is no such thing as an atheoretical approach (no perception without expectations derived from history and rules), the best guard against subservience to a theoretical party line is to learn many theories. A therapist should at least be conversational in behaviorism, cognitive theory, systems theory, and psychoanalysis, plus a few assorted personally meaningful dialects, such as self psychology or existentialism. A therapist should be fluent in at least a few of these approaches. One theoretical orientation that every clinician should learn is the patient's.

Theories usually come with prescriptions about how to do therapy, and multilingualism will present alternatives to the clinician. Options are what liveliness is all about. Learning multiple theories can help therapists understand that no frames are primary and that their own perspectives are just perspectives. The English speaker who learns that *casa* is Spanish for *house* may also learn that *house* itself is an arbitrary way to denote a house.

3. Don't Categorize

Therapy is about unpacking the verbal boxes people use to define themselves and their situations, which demonstrates that moribund ways and old definitions may not apply to new situations. In that context, there are few good reasons to put people in boxes, however politically correct or multiculturally sensitive the boxes may seem to be. There are good reasons to find out which categories the patient uses to define herself (Ossorio, 1983), but that's usually to demonstrate how constricting those categories are. There are not three or four sexual orientations—there are 6 billion. There are not 8 or 12 races— there are as many races and ethnicities as there are ways of grouping people. Lively multiculturalism analyzes types of situations, not types of people.

4. Think Critically About Ourselves and Our Therapies

Critical thinking is the greatest verbal tool ever devised to mend the harms done by verbal tools that turn words into party lines that ignore or disqualify invalidating information. It's an antidote to confirmation bias (the tendency to see what one expects to see) and cognitive dissonance (the tendency to resolve conflicting ideas by trashing one of them). Critical thinking requires the complacent, self-assured therapist to ask, "Am I doing a good job?" "Could I have handled that better?" "Am I selling a bill of goods?" "Is the patient getting better or just telling me she's getting better to cope with the power differential between us?"

When you're in a position of power, it's human nature to find disconsonant or questioning voices irritating. Reminders of this tendency are easily undermined when the person in power says to herself, "Generally, yes, that is a problem, but this particular complaint really is too much." A therapist who installs critical thinking as the primary value in her professional life loses her complacency and a good deal of satisfaction, but she gains a source of liveliness. Pontification is a deadly practice, whether it's a blanket statement of self-assurance, a holding forth that your theoretical orientation is the only one supported by research, or a statement of infallibility in interpretation or intervention. It's deadly because it excludes argument, disconfirming information, and uncertainty. Liveliness is uncertainty, whether it's a question of how a dog's reaction to being kicked is harder to predict than a billiard ball's (Bateson, 1972b) or a question of what I will do with my life. Uncertainty is scary, and we all occasionally take a vacation from it by pontificating. Perhaps the greatest challenge of any clinical training program is to teach therapists productive ways to manage anxiety and uncertainty when the alluring alternative of ossifying and idealizing a point of view continually presents itself. We all want a place to stand in an uncertain world, and critical thinking gives us a place to stand while we are deconstructing places to stand.

THINGS WE CAN DO TO MANAGE
THE POWER DIFFERENTIAL

Humans are a status-conscious animal. Possibly, this is because the advantages of a prolonged childhood—minimal hardwiring and maximal learning on the fly—require prolonged exposure to a power differential with our parents. Whatever the reason, we are exquisitely aware of pecking orders above us and blithely unconcerned with pecking orders below us. The therapy relationship has a power differential that offers the opportunity to remediate misuses of power in the patient's history. Our power should not be dispersed, but it must be continually recognized and appreciated, or we will engage in the natural human tendency to exploit it.

5. Find Ways to Evaluate What We Did That
Don't Depend on the Patient's Report

The patient's report is suspect because it's offered in the context of a power differential. The information in the report probably isn't nearly as salient as the function of the report in the relationship. Those afraid of power, invested in pleasing power, or trying to cope with their own uncertainties and anxieties by adhering to the therapist's party line tend to exaggerate the therapist's beneficence and effectiveness. Those antagonistic to, jealous of, or suspicious of power tend to exaggerate the therapist's malevolence or ineffectiveness. As therapists, we like to rely on patients' reports because they tend to be positive (those inclined to criticize usually leave treatment). We justify this reliance with thoughts about empowering "clients," as if it's in the patient's best interests to become our supervisor. Imagine a parent asking a child if a fixed bedtime is a good idea.

I use three main alterative sources of information to evaluate myself. One, the metaphorical content of ensuing speech may be treated as a sort of commentary on an intervention (Bateson, Jackson, Haley, & Weakland, 1972; Langs, 1978). Two, collateral behaviors in the office can be monitored for independent verification of improvement, as when the depressed patient is more spirited or the narcissistic patient is less conceited. Three, a communicative dyad can be established where the patient's running commentary on her experience of me is so textured, variable, and situation specific that I can assume that I'm receiving some good information about her experience of me

among the inevitable concern that my power in the relationship is overly influencing its presentation.

6. Be Curious About What Embarrasses or Discredits Us

It's human nature to present a picture of yourself that defines the situation and
the relationship advantageously or familiarly. Only in early childhood are
such presentations transparent; so it's in early childhood, typically, that a person can learn a comfortable relationship with her own backstage. Intimacy
exposure and remediation of presentation problems require a comfortable relationship between front stage and backstage. We can facilitate this restorative factor in therapy by being curious about our own discrediting moments.
Curiosity helps to establish a miniculture in which exposure is experienced as
comfortable and useful rather than as humiliating.

In order to foster intimacy and comfort with being discredited, we should
avoid using the disattend channel in therapy. This means that we should avoid
communicating on the channel that is normally used to carry offstage messages
since its presence in therapy undermines the effort to establish a culture where
everything is welcome and openly acknowledged (to facilitate the extinguish-
ing effects of exposure). No mm-hmms, no nods, no excuse me's, no muttering, and no sighs of relief. But there is a danger here that disuse of the disattend
channel will become a rule, a party line that will hound the therapist into hiding rather than celebrating openness, as when the therapist remains in an uncomfortable posture rather than risk self-expression or when the therapist feels
bad rather than curious about having sneezed or yawned. The supervisor should
reinforce silence and front-stage speech, punishing asides only mildly, and
should demonstrate comfort with her own openness. The goal is for the patient's use of the disattend channel to become a subject of conversation, and this
can happen without embarrassment only if the therapist's relationship to his
own disattended and discrediting communications is welcoming.

7. Don't Diagnose

This is the psychotherapy-specific version of "don't categorize." There are
few situations where diagnosis is helpful. Labels like *hyperactivity*, *psychosis*, *obsessive-compulsive disorder*, and *bipolar disorder*, if used properly,
help direct treatment. Labels like *personality disorder* remind us to anticipate
that the therapeutic encounter will be subsumed into an idiosyncratic pattern
for making sense of the world rather than a respite from the pattern. But most
of the time, diagnosis just puts people in boxes that reify expectations and
limit options.

Diagnosis is also the clinical community's method of disqualifying those who subvert the party line. When colleagues don't yield to our superior insight or clerical staff don't do as we ask, we label them passive-aggressive. When students pass notes in class, we suspect authority problems. The analysts are narcissistic, the behaviorists obsessive-compulsive, the humanists passive-dependent. In a group of clinicians, it's almost impossible to disagree with the consensus without getting diagnosed. Every group has a vocabulary for maintaining the party line by disqualifying protest. The Church has *bedevilment*, minorities have terms like *sellout* and *Oreo cookie* and *banana*, and we have *diagnoses*. When diagnostic thoughts occur to us in therapy, we should remember that they're probably occurring to us to affirm our line and to refute the patient's.

THINGS WE CAN DO TO DEFINE THE RELATIONSHIP

Humans are the situation-defining animal. The power of definitions and their effect on which roles can be played in them drives us to define situations. Treatment involves the resolution of discrepancies between the patient's definition of situations and ours. When the situation at stake is the therapy, we are both likely, at least on occasion, to push for an idiosyncratic and ineffective definition, and we're both there to witness firsthand the evidence supporting or refuting one definition or another. Discussion of the therapy relationship is a fertile field for change. While all definitions run the risk of becoming party lines, some articulation of the desirable features of therapy helps both parties stay on track when idiosyncrasies, defensive maneuvers, and power plays predominate.

8. Be on a Team with the Patient

Establish an alliance around presenting a performance to others. When discussing events that occurred outside the office, make it clear that we're on the patient's side. Even if the patient is dead wrong and the other person was absolutely in the right, we should still be organized around what it was like for the patient. Our point can be to wonder why the patient would act is such a manner, not whether she should have. When discussing events that happened in the therapy, we should be teammates around understanding them rather than adversaries, oracles, or dictators. People need a base where they can roll their eyes and lick their wounds, loosen their belts, and kick off their shoes. Without a base, the demands of performance are too great. Provide one for our patients.

9. Make the Patient Our Audience and Be the Patient's Audience

How is it possible to be teammates—allies before an audience—and at the same time be each other's audience? Construe therapy as rehearsal, not as the real thing. We perform for each other as if we were planning a performance for others. Like a good rehearsal, therapy should be confidential so that new ideas can be played without fear of embarrassment. Treating therapy as a rehearsal also helps the patient learn what it's like to experience a transaction as real and not real at once, a familiarity that is supposed to be learned as a child at play but for which, at least concerning some topics, the patient may not have had sufficient playful opportunities (Bateson, 1972d).

Talk for the patient, not for a supervisor or an imagined audience of peers. Treat the patient's speech, no matter how artificial or barriered, as speech for us. Be engrossed, and the patient's engrossment will follow.

10. Be a Teacher or a Foster Parent or a Gadfly and Stay in Character

Define the relationship according to the approach you're using and the approach that best serves the patient. A family therapist may play the gadfly in a stultified family or the fool in a family where someone else is impulsively distracting the family from sadness. Most cognitive therapies cast the therapist in the role of teacher/senior colleague in a joint enterprise of collaborative empiricism. Most psychoanalytic therapies require a role that I have defined as foster parent, where we reparent a child for money. Whatever the role—whatever the definition of the relationship—it's important to stay in character. The reason to stay in character is not to avoid being discredited—the character must be defined richly enough that a wide range of behaviors can be supported within it, making it a hard role to discredit. Rather, one must stay in character to support the definition of the relationship so that it can compete successfully with the patient's definitions. The patients are committed to theirs, and we must be committed to ours.

THINGS WE CAN DO TO ACT THE PART

Humans are the dramaturgical animal. We are experts at playing roles and hiding the fact that we are keeping something in reserve, only pretending. We generally believe that we personally are the only ones who are this aware of our dramaturgy, so we feel guilty about it, convinced that most people are more sincere than we are. The parts we play as therapists are too important to constrain with concerns about sincerity, so let's prepare for the performance by studying the lessons of the stage about how to do it convincingly and engagingly.

11. Cast Ourselves and Design the Set

Look in the mirror. Can you play the wise old psychoanalytic sage? Can you pull off the rational-emotive curmudgeon? Are you a Meryl Streep or Paul Muni, able to play any part, or are you a *type*, constrained by your body, voice, hair, and posture to play a more limited array? What can you change to broaden your repertoire? What can you not change that you have to take into account?

Design your office and wear clothing to reduce the patient's situation consciousness. Find an outfit and a set that fits the role you anticipate playing and find props and makeup that probably suit the patient's expectations. Ask people you trust what you look like and listen for commentary on your office. It's there—we just don't want to hear it.

12. Play Gender and Status Flexibly and Deliberately

Two crucial features of any interpersonal exchange are gender and status. Some of us are constrained by our bodies to play only certain roles, but we can all learn how to play any role flexibly with respect to gender and status. Many patients are struggling with difficulties defining relationships on these dimensions, and they need us to teach them that neither is a fundamental frame, neither is a fact about themselves, and each is a constructed definition of a situation or relationship. To accomplish this and to remediate patients' deadly categorization of themselves in gender roles and status roles, we have to be able to show them how flexibly these factors can be played. Further, to play the array of roles patients need us to play, we have to be able to play different genders and different statuses. The ideal therapist is sometimes high status, occasionally low, sometimes equal, sometimes yin, and sometimes yang, depending on the situation. Those who cannot play all these are constrained in their freedom to interact as needed and are therefore deadly on many occasions.

13. Know Our Characters' Backstories

Amateur actors look at the text and think about how to say it. Professionals look at the text and think about what the character is up to, what the situation is, what the character is trying to hide and what to reveal, what the character is feeling and trying not to feel, how the character will stand, and where she will look. Good actors make even a first reading come alive.

When a good actor takes a serious part, she invents or infers a backstory for her character. The backstory may be a biography that helps the actor know what person she is pretending to be, or it may be a personality description that fleshes out the character's motives for behaving as she does at any moment. The backstory serves the same function for the actress on stage as it does for any individual in life: our self-knowledge tells us how to behave, which reduces anxiety and enhances our ability to plan for ourselves.

Such is the nature of performance that no matter how adept a presentation is, something can always happen to discredit it. A polished comic knows how to manage hecklers, and a skillful actor knows how to handle missed cues, flubbed lines, and uncooperative props. Actors must know their characters' backstories so that they can manage chance occurrences without discrediting their performances. A therapist must know the backstory of the character she construes a therapist to be and also the backstories of characters the patient casts her as so that she will understand the lines she has, so that she will know what to do when the patients flub *their* lines, and so that she will not discredit her definition of her role as a therapist.

The best way to learn useful and convincing backstories is to read literature, history, philosophy, and science. These are stories about how the world works, and the more stories one has read, the more schemas one can apply to new information for the purpose of creating new stories that fit. A lifelong commitment to reading (and theatergoing, film watching, and curiosity about others) ensures that we will be positioned as lifelong learners. There is nothing more deadly in therapy than "I already know." The lifelong learner is committed to managing her ignorance, uncertainty, and anxiety more productively.

14. Pay Attention to the Man Behind the Curtain

Therapists and patients often imbue the role of therapist with lofty expectations. Trainees have a natural tendency to try to skip over the part where they learn how to do therapy and get to the part where they already know. What they come to discover, I hope, is that "I already know" is just a clumsy form of not knowing, while adept not knowing implies curiosity, a welcoming attitude, a policy of not having policies, a search for feedback not tainted by privilege, and flexibility when it comes to theoretical orientation.

Therapists often manage their ignorance and anxiety by other means, including analogues of the usual defense mechanisms. Therapists may deny evidence of their ordinariness or inadequacy, forget that they are not always successful, put their own feelings of inadequacy into their patients by attributing bumps in the road to the patient's psychology, and so on. The key element of psychotherapy training is teaching students how to manage their ignorance, uncertainty, and anxiety productively. This is summed up in the single word "oops," which I first heard in this context at a Keith Johnstone workshop and which I've already mentioned as essential to a scientific attitude. It captures the nonnarcissistic commitment to doing it well in a playful manner with a readiness to improve. If "I already know" is deadly subtext and if "I will never know" is deadly subtext, then "I didn't know that" is lively.

Trying to fulfill their lofty expectations of the role, therapists often pretend either to have no backstage or to have fully exposed it. "I am not hiding anything from you" or "I have nothing to hide from you" produces a personal coalition between therapist and patient against whatever is professional. This is as deadly a stance as a professional coalition against the personal (as in "I am the doctor and you are the patient, and we have no personal relationship") still seen pervasively in mental hospitals and offender treatment. Pretending to have no backstage or to have fully exposed it is so easily discredited by information readily available in any human interaction that the patient will either learn to be as blind in therapy as she was taught to be at home or become disheartened about her therapist's ability to help her when his line is discredited. A better stance is the one a good parent takes—affectionately but unwaveringly maintaining her emotional connection to her child while affectionately but unwaveringly communicating that her backstage is off limits. We want our children to know that we are having sex with our coparent, but we don't want them to know what positions we use. We never want them to know that sometimes we glance at their college friends in their bathing suits and think wild thoughts.

Having a backstage doesn't mean that the performance is inauthentic—it allows the performance to be *more* authentic. Parents can be more genuinely engaged, attentive, and patient if they know they get to stop at bedtime. Police officers can be more tolerant and more helpful if they know there is an off-duty self who gets to make fun of people. If a cast putting up *Hamlet* had to always stay in character, their personal selves would seep into their performances and ruin the play. Having an offstage enables them to keep the performance more real, not less real.

One strategy for comfortable backstage management is to make the backstage presentable. If the audience catches a glimpse of an actor's backstage in a theater, its discrediting effect depends on what is glimpsed. An actor's offstage anti-Semitic rant or marriage to his own stepdaughter can discredit any future performance, while merely catching the character breathing heavily from exertion or adjusting his costume might not. As a therapist and as a parent, I want my backstage to be off limits only because I don't think its exposure is conducive to growth, not because I'm embarrassed about what's back there. In this way, practicing psychotherapy and raising children has made me a better person because they've given me strong incentives for behaving in ways that I endorse.

CODA

Bateson (1972a) was at first alarmed that Balinese mothers tease their infants with the breast. But he soon realized that the custom prepared children for later life in a world of abundance. In Bali, the cost-benefit analysis of fighting over property heavily dictated avoidance of conflict since food was plentiful and shelter was virtually unnecessary. Maternal teasing taught children not to covet or expect ownership.

In America, we prepare our children for an adult economy that punishes deviance and public indolence by educating them in punitive, regimented institutions. Our schools prepare our children for their cubicles, where workers must blend in and look busy.

Our patients may justly wonder what psychotherapy with us prepares them for. Perhaps my patients will meet people who want lifelong teammates, intimacy and authenticity, joint and mutual solitude, and relationships based on how things actually go between the partners and not on rules and categorical expectations. I would be happy to think that their time with me has helped prepare them to participate in such a relationship. Likewise, I'd like to think that therapy with me prepared my patients for work that integrates the personal and professional and for privilege-busting, gender-bending, humanity-celebrating acts of social justice.

*   *   *

I'm not conflicted about saying that practicing psychotherapy has made me a better person, but it is a short path from better to superior. I'm always tempted to claim that I've resolved my conflicts and that my backstage is in such good order that I need no curtain to stand behind.

In his introduction to *Listening with the Third Ear*, Reik (1964) recounts the story of a famous actor who declined the part of Prospero in *The Tempest*. Prospero is the ultimate puppeteer: having learned by scholarship to pull strings so skillfully that he becomes the master of both the spiritual and the earthly, he schemes the restoration of his crown, his daughter's romance, and the comeuppance of his enemies. The actor declined the part, saying that to play Prospero, one must be not only a great actor but also a great man. And what great man would become an actor?

Reik draws the analogy to therapy, saying that to do the job, one must be not only a great therapist but also a great person. But what great person would become a therapist? Obviously, Reik rejected the point of the story, as he not only remained a therapist but also encouraged others to do therapy as well. Even Prospero decides to "abjure," at the end of the play, the "rough magic"—the verbal mastery of nature—that led to all his troubles. But before that, Prospero lords it over those he helps: "Thou best know'st what torment I did find thee in. . . . It was mine art, when I arrived and heard thee, that made gape the pine and let thee out" (I.ii.288–295). And he shows off: "I must bestow upon the eyes of this young couple some vanity of mine art. It is my promise and they expect it from me" (IV.i.39–42).

Reik poses a conundrum that every therapist wrestles with: How can I undertake the enormous responsibility and complexity of psychotherapy without either feeling secretly inadequate or talking myself into thinking that I am brilliant, wise, and transcendently healthy? This book is my answer to that question, the short version of which is that Prospero—the powerful figure exerting control over his world and the people in it by virtue of his intellectual dominion over the sublime and the magical—is an enticing but deadly model for a therapist.

References

Adler, A. (1937). *What life should mean to you* (Alan Porter, Ed.). Boston: Little, Brown. (Original work published 1931)

Alvarez, L. (1987). *Alvarez: Adventures of a physicist.* New York: Basic Books.

American Psychiatric Association. (1994). *Diagnostic and statistical manual of mental disorders* (4th ed.). Washington, DC: Author.

American Psychological Association. (2001). Study relates desire for death in the terminally ill to depression, hopelessness. *Monitor on Psychology, 32*(3). Washington, DC: Author.

American Psychological Association. (2002). *Ethical principles of psychologists and code of conduct.* Washington, DC: Author.

Andersen, H. C. (1993). The emperor's new clothes. In L. Owens (Ed.), *The complete Hans Christian Andersen fairy tales.* New York: Gramercy. (Original work published 1837)

Aristotle. (1997). *Poetics.* (Malcolm Heath, Trans.). London: Penguin Books. (Original work published 350 B.C.E.)

Arnheim, R. (1966). *Toward a psychology of art.* Berkeley: University of California Press.

Asch, S. E. (1956). Studies of independence and conformity: A minority of one against a unanimous majority. *Psychological Monographs, 70* (Whole No. 416).

Ashcroft, J. (2001, December 6). Statement to the Senate Judiciary Committee. Retrieved December 6, 2006, from http://archives.cnn.com/2001/US/12/06/ inv .ashcroft.hearing

Asimov, I. (1969). *Asimov's guide to the Bible: Volume 2. The New Testament.* New York: Random House.

Asimov, I. (1970). *Asimov's guide to Shakespeare.* New York: Doubleday.

Barkley, R. (1998). *Attention-deficit hyperactivity disorder: A handbook for diagnosis and treatment.* New York: Guilford Press.

Bateson, G. (1972a). Bali: The value system of a steady state. In *Steps to an ecology of the mind.* Chicago: University of Chicago Press. (Original work published 1949)

217

Bateson, G. (1972b). The group dynamics of schizophrenia. In *Steps to an ecology of the mind*. Chicago: University of Chicago Press. (Original work published 1960)

Bateson, G. (1972c). *Steps to an ecology of mind*. Chicago: University of Chicago Press.

Bateson, G. (1972d). A theory of play and fantasy. In *Steps to an ecology of the mind*. Chicago: University of Chicago Press. (Original work published 1954)

Bateson, G. (1979). *Mind and nature*. New York: Dutton.

Bateson, G., Jackson, D., Haley, J., & Weakland, J. (1972). Toward a theory of schizophrenia. In G. Bateson, *Steps to an ecology of mind*. Chicago: University of Chicago Press. (Original work published 1956)

Beck, A. (1976). *Cognitive therapy and the emotional disorders*. New York: International Universities Press.

Beck, A., & Beck, J. (2006, August). *Advances in cognitive therapy*. Invited address presented at the annual convention of the American Psychological Association, New Orleans, LA.

Beck, J. (1995). *Cognitive therapy: Basics and beyond*. New York: Guilford Press.

Bion, W. R. (1967). Notes on memory and desire. *Psycho-analytic Forum, 2*(3), 271–280.

Blake, W. (1794). *Europe, a prophecy*. London: Author.

Boal, A. (1985). *Theatre of the oppressed*. (C. & M. Leal McBride, Trans.). New York: Theatre Communications Group. (Original work published 1974)

Bosnak, R. (1984). The dirty needle: Images of the inferior analyst. *Spring, 44*, 105–115.

Brackett, C. (Producer), & Lang, W. (Director). (1956). *The King and I* [Motion picture]. United States: 20th Century Fox.

Brockett, O. G. (1982). *History of the theatre* (4th ed.). Boston: Allyn and Bacon.

Brook, P. (1968). *The empty space*. New York: Atheneum.

Brook, P. (1993). *The open door: Thoughts on acting and theatre*. New York: Random House.

Broyard, A. (1950). Portrait of the inauthentic Negro. *Commentary, 10*(1), 56–64.

Buirski, P. (2005). *Practicing intersubjectively*. Lanham, MD: Jason Aronson.

Buirski, P. (2006, October 27). *Discussion of case presentation by Amy Eldridge: Evolving perspectives on the selfobject transference*. Paper presented at the 29th annual Self Psychology Conference, Chicago, IL.

Buirski, P., & Haglund, P. (2001). *Making sense together: The intersubjective approach to psychotherapy*. New York: Jason Aronson.

Bullough, E. (1912–1913). Psychical distance as a factor in art and an aesthetic principle. *British Journal of Psychology, 5*, 87–118.

Burke, K. (1945). *A grammar of motives*. New York: Prentice Hall.

Burke, K. (1966). *Language as symbolic action*. Berkeley: University of California Press.

Butler, J. (1990). *Gender trouble: Feminism and the subversion of identity*. New York: Routledge.

Butler, J. (1993). *Bodies that matter: On the discursive limits of sex*. New York: Routledge.

Butler, J. (1999). Introduction. In *Gender trouble*. New York: Routledge.

Butler, J. (2004). Performative acts and gender constitution: An essay in phenomenology and feminist theory. In H. Bial (Ed.), *The performance studies reader* (pp. 270–282). New York: Routledge. (Original work published 1988)

Carlson, M. (1996). *Performance: A critical introduction.* New York: Routledge.

Coleridge, S. T. (1985). *Biographia literaria.* Princeton, NJ: Princeton University Press. (Original work published 1817)

Dale, P. S., Loftus, E. F., & Rathburn, L. (1978). The influence of the form of the question on the eyewitness memory of preschool children. *Journal of Psycholinguistic Research, 7,* 269–277.

Dawkins, R. (1986). *The blind watchmaker.* London: Penguin Books.

Derrida, J. (1978). *Writing and difference* (A. Bass, Trans.). Chicago: University of Chicago Press.

Derrida, J. (1982). *Margins of philosophy* (A. Bass, Trans.). Chicago: University of Chicago Press.

Dewey, J. (1934). *Art as experience.* New York: Perigee Books.

Diamond, J. (1997). *Guns, germs, and steel: The fates of human societies.* New York: Norton.

Dostoyevsky, F. (1950). The grand inquisitor. In *The Brothers Karamazov* (C. Garnett, Trans.). New York: Modern Library. (Original work published 1880)

Dvoskin, J. (1978). *Contextual determinants of attitude change in a field setting: Time as a limiting factor.* Unpublished master's thesis, University of Arizona, Tucson.

Eliot, G. (1995). *Daniel Deronda.* London: Penguin Books. (Original work published 1876)

Ellis, A. (2001). *Overcoming destructive beliefs, feelings, and behaviors: New directions for Rational Emotive Behavior Therapy.* Amherst, NY: Prometheus Books.

Ellis, A., & Harper, R. (1975). *A guide to rational living* (3rd rev. ed.). Chatsworth, CA: Wilshire Book Co.

Erickson, J. (2006, August 25). Pluto booted off roster of planets. *Rocky Mountain News.* Retrieved August 25, 2006, from http://www.msnbc.msn.com/id/14510837

Erikson, E. H. (1954). The dream specimen of psychoanalysis. *Journal of the American Psychoanalytic Association, 2,* 5–56.

Facione, P. (1998). *Critical thinking: What it is and why it counts.* Millbrae, CA: California Academic Press. [Online]

Foreman, J. (Producer), & Hill, G. R. (Director). (1969). *Butch Cassidy and the Sundance Kid* [Motion picture]. United States: 20th Century Fox.

Foss, S., & Foss, K. (1991). *Women speak: The eloquence of women's lives.* Skokie, IL: Waveland Press.

Freud, S. (1953). *The interpretation of dreams.* In J. Strachey (Ed. and Trans.), *The standard edition of the complete psychological works of Sigmund Freud* (Vol. 5, pp. 339–630). London: Hogarth Press. (Original work published 1900)

Freud, S. (1961). *Civilization and its discontents.* In J. Strachey (Ed. and Trans.), *The standard edition of the complete psychological works of Sigmund Freud* (Vol. 21, pp. 57–145). London: Hogarth Press. (Original work published 1930)

Friedan, B. (1963). *The feminine mystique.* New York: Norton.

Fry, R. (1920). *Vision and design*. London: Penguin Books.

Geisinger, M. (1971). *Plays, players, and playwrights: An illustrated history of the theatre*. New York: Hart.

Gibson, W. (1950). Authors, speakers, readers, and mock readers. *College English, 11*, 265–269.

Gilbert, L. (Producer & Director). (1966). *Alfie* [Motion picture]. United Kingdom: Lewis Gilbert.

Gilligan, C. (1982). *In a different voice*. Cambridge, MA: Harvard University Press.

Gödel, K. (1962). *On formally undecidable propositions of Principia mathematica and related systems* (B. Meltzer, Trans.). New York: Basic Books. (Original work published 1931)

Goffman, E. (1959). *The presentation of self in everyday life*. New York: Doubleday.

Goffman, E. (1961). *Asylums: Essays on the social situation of mental patients and other inmates*. Garden City, NY: Anchor Books.

Goffman, E. (1963). *Stigma: Notes on the management of spoiled identity*. New York: Simon and Schuster.

Goffman, E. (1967). *Interaction ritual*. New York: Doubleday.

Goffman, E. (1974). *Frame analysis: An essay on the organization of experience*. Boston: Northeastern University Press.

Goodwin, J. (2001, March 31). *Challenging and transforming deadly spaces of authority: Steps towards a responsible and responsive educational body*. Paper presented at Borderlands: Remapping Zones of Cultural Practice and Representation, University of Massachusetts, Amherst.

Gould, S. J. (1981). *The mismeasure of man*. New York: Norton.

Graham, A. C. (Ed. and Trans.). (1981). *Chuang-tzu: The inner chapters*. London: George Allen & Unwin.

Greenhut, R. (Producer), & Gordon, S. (Director). (1981). *Arthur* [Motion picture]. United States: Orion Pictures.

Griffin, S. (1981). *Pornography and silence: Culture's revenge against nature*. New York: Harper & Row.

Grotstein, A. (1980). Irma's injection. In *Sigmund Freud's dreams* (pp. 21–46). New York: International Universities Press.

Haley, J. (1965). The art of being schizophrenic. *Voices, 1*, 133–142.

Haley, J. (1973). *Uncommon therapy: The psychiatric techniques of Milton H. Erickson*. New York: Norton.

Halpern, D. (2004). I dare you to try this at home (or at work) (President's column). *Monitor on Psychology, 35*(2), 5.

Harford, T. (2005). *The undercover economist*. New York: Random House.

Hayes, S. C., Strosahl, K. D., & Wilson, K. G. (1999). *Acceptance and commitment therapy: An experiential approach to behavior change*. New York: Guilford Press.

Helms, J., Jernigan, M., & Mascher, J. (2005). The meaning of race in psychology and how to change it: A methodological perspective. *American Psychologist, 60*(1), 27–36.

Herskovits, M. (1959). Art and value. In R. Redfield, M. Herskovits, & G. Ekholm, *Aspects of primitive art*. New York: University Publishers.

Holmes, O. (1881). *The common law*. Boston: Little, Brown.

Horney, K. (1950). *Neurosis and human growth*. New York: Norton.

Hughes, J. (Producer & Director). (1986). *Ferris Bueller's day off* [Motion picture]. United States: Paramount.

Hymes, D. (1973). *Toward linguistic competence*. Unpublished manuscript.

Irigaray, L. (1985). *The sex which is not one*. (C. Porter with C. Burke, Trans.). Ithaca, NY: Cornell University Press.

Janoff-Bulman, R. (1982). Esteem and control bases of blame: Adaptive strategies for victims versus observers. *Journal of Personality, 50*, 180–191.

Johnstone, K. (1981). *Impro: Improvisation and the Theatre*. New York: Routledge.

Jones, E. (1953). *Sigmund Freud: Life and work* (Vol. 1). London: Hogarth Press.

Joyce, R. (2000). *Gender and power in prehispanic Mesoamerica*. Austin: University of Texas Press.

Kaplan, A. G. (Ed.). (1976). *Beyond sex-role stereotypes: Readings toward a psychology of androgyny*. Glenview, IL: Scott Foresman.

Karson, M. (2001). *Patterns of child abuse: How dysfunctional transactions are replicated in individuals, families, and the child welfare system*. New York: Haworth Press.

Karson, M. (2005). Over-interpretation of the Rorschach and the MMPI-2 when standard error is ignored. *Scientific Review of Mental Health Practice, 3*(2), 25–29.

Karson, M. (2006). *Using early memories in psychotherapy: Roadmaps to presenting problems and treatment impasses*. Lanham, MD: Jason Aronson.

Knoblauch, S. (2001). High risk, high gain: Commentary on paper by Philip A. Ringstrom. *Psychoanalytic Dialogues, 11*(5), 785–795.

Kohlberg, L. (1958). *The development of modes of moral thinking in the years ten to sixteen*. Unpublished doctoral dissertation, University of Chicago.

Kohut, H. (1971). *The analysis of the self*. New York: International Universities Press.

Kohut, H. (1977). *The restoration of the self*. New York: International Universities Press.

Kubie, L. (1958). *Neurotic distortion of the creative process*. Lawrence: University Press of Kansas.

Kuhn, T. (1962). *The structure of scientific revolutions*. Chicago: University of Chicago Press.

Langs, R. J. (1976). *The bipersonal field*. New York: Jason Aronson.

Langs, R. J. (1978). *The listening process*. New York: Jason Aronson.

Lao-Tzu. (1988). *Tao te ching*. (S. Mitchell, Trans.). New York: Harper & Row. (Original work published ca. 300 B.C.E.)

Lao-Tzu. (1993). *Tao te ching*. (S. Addiss & S. Lombardo, Trans.). Indianapolis: Hackett. (Original work published ca. 300 B.C.E.)

Lerner, G. (1986). *The creation of patriarchy*. New York: Oxford University Press.

LeRoy, M. (Producer), & Fleming, V. (Director). (1939). *The Wizard of Oz* [Motion picture]. United States: MGM.

Loftus, E., & Ketcham, K. (1991). *Witness for the defense: The accused, the eyewitness, and the expert who puts memory on trial*. New York: St. Martin's Press.

Longino, H. (1990). *Science as social knowledge: Values and objectivity in scientific inquiry*. Princeton, NJ: Princeton University Press.

Lorde, A. (1984). *Sister/outsider: Essays and speeches*. Freedom, CA: Cross Press.

Madanes, C. (1981). *Strategic family therapy*. San Francisco: Jossey-Bass.

Madison, J. (1945). The particular structure of the new government and the distribution of power among its parts. In A. Hamilton, J. Madison, & J. Jay, *The Federalist or The new constitution* (No. 47, pp. 321–329). New York: Heritage Press. (Original work published 1788)

McCullough, D. (2005). *1776*. New York: Simon & Schuster.

Meares, R. (2001). What happens next? A developmental model of therapeutic spontaneity: Commentary on paper by Philip A. Ringstrom. *Psychoanalytic Dialogues, 11*(5), 755–770.

Meehl, P. (1973). Why I do not attend case conferences. In *Psychodiagnosis: Selected papers* (pp. 225–302). Minneapolis: University of Minnesota Press.

Mehlman, J. (1987). Trimethylamin: Notes on Freud's specimen dream. In H. Bloom (Ed.), *Modern critical interpretations: Sigmund Freud's* The Interpretation of Dreams. New York: Chelsea House.

Meltsner, M., & Schrag, P. (1974). Negotiating tactics for legal services lawyers. In *Public interest advocacy: Materials for clinical legal education* (pp. 18–23). Boston: Little, Brown.

Melville, H. (2004). *Bartleby, the scrivener: A tale of Wall Street*. Hoboken, NJ: Melville House. (Original work published 1853)

Milgram, S. (1963). Behavioral study of obedience. *Journal of Abnormal and Social Psychology, 67*, 371–378.

Mill, J. S. (1843). *A system of logic*. London: Longmans.

Miller, G. (2000). *The mating mind: How sexual choice shaped the evolution of human nature*. New York: Doubleday.

Nietzsche, F. (1966a). *Beyond good and evil* (W. Kaufmann, Trans.). New York: Vintage Books. (Original work published 1886)

Nietzsche, F. (1966b). *The birth of tragedy*. In W. Kaufmann (Ed. and Trans.), *Basic writings of Nietzsche*. New York: Modern Library. (Original work published 1872)

Nietzsche, F. (1967). *On the genealogy of morals*. (W. Kaufmann and R. J. Hollingdale, Trans.). New York: Vintage Books. (Original work published 1887)

Nietzsche, F. (1977). *Thus spake Zarathustra*. In W. Kaufmann (Ed. and Trans.), *The portable Nietzsche*. New York: Penguin Books. (Original work published 1891)

Nietzsche, F. (1996). *Human, all too human: A book for free spirits*. (R. J. Hollingdale, Trans.). Cambridge: Cambridge University Press. (Original work published 1878)

Ossorio, P. G. (1983). A multicultural psychology. In K. E. Davis & R. M. Bergner (Eds.), *Advances in descriptive psychology* (pp. 13–44). Ann Arbor, MI: Descriptive Psychology Press.

Park-Fuller, L. (2000). Performing absence: The staged personal narrative as testimony. *Text and Performance Quarterly, 20*(1), 20–42.

Parker, D. (1978). The standard of living. In D. Parker, *The Penguin Dorothy Parker*. London: Penguin Books. (Original work published 1941)

Pope, A. (1970). An essay on criticism. In J. Butt (Ed.), *The poems of Alexander Pope*. New Haven, CT: Yale University Press. (Original work published 1711)

Quinsey, V. L., Harris, G. T., Rice, M. E., & Cormier, C. A. (1998). *Violent offenders: Appraising and managing risk*. Washington, DC: American Psychological Association.

Rank, O. (1936). *Will therapy* and *Truth and reality*. New York: Knopf. (Original work published 1931)

Rank, O. (1989). *Art and artist*. New York: Norton. (Original work published 1932)

Reik, T. (1964). *Listening with the third ear: The inner experience of a psychoanalyst*. New York: Arena. (Original work published 1948)

Rind, B., Tromovitch, P., & Bauserman, R. (1998). A meta-analytic examination of assumed properties of child sexual abuse using college samples. *Psychological Bulletin, 124*(1), 22–53.

Ringstrom, P. (2001a) Cultivating the improvisational in psychoanalytic treatment. *Psychoanalytic Dialogues, 11*(5), 727–754.

Ringstrom, P. (2001b). "Yes, and . . ."—How improvisation *is* the essence of good psychoanalytic dialogue. *Psychoanalytic Dialogues, 11*(5), 797–806.

Robinson, T. (2006). *Teaching activist intelligence: Feminism, the educational experience and the Applied Women's Studies Department at CGU*. Unpublished master's thesis, Claremont Graduate University, Claremont, CA.

Santayana, G. (1922). *Soliloquies in England and later soliloquies*. New York: Scribner's.

Schechner, R. (1973). Performance and the social sciences. *The Drama Review, 17*, 5–36.

Schechner, R. (1988). *Performance theory*. New York: Routledge.

Schur, M. (1966). Some additional "day residues" of "The specimen dream of psychoanalysis." In R. Loewenstein, L. Newman, M. Schur, & A. Solnit (Eds.), *Psychoanalysis—A general psychology: Essays in honor of Heinz Hartmann*. New York: International Universities Press.

Schwary, R. L. (Producer), & Redford, R. (Director). (1980). *Ordinary people* [Motion picture]. United States: Paramount Pictures.

Searle, J. (1969). *Speech acts: An essay in the philosophy of language*. Cambridge: Cambridge University Press.

Selvini Palazzoli, M., Boscolo, L., Cecchin, G., & Prata, G. (1978). *Paradox and counterparadox*. New York: Jason Aronson.

Selvini Palazzoli, M., Boscolo, L., Cecchin, G., & Prata, G. (1980). Hypothesizing–circularity–neutrality: Three guidelines for the conductor of the session. *Family Process, 19*, 3–13.

Shapiro, S., & Shapiro, S. (2002). *Body movements: Pedagogy, politics and social change*. Cresskill, NJ: Hampton Press.

Skinner, B. F. (1953). *Science and human behavior*. New York: Free Press.

Skinner, B. F. (1957). *Verbal behavior*. New York: Appleton-Century-Crofts.

Smith, S. T. (2003). *Surviving aggressive people: Practical violence prevention skills for the workplace and the street*. Boulder, CO: Sentient Publications.

Stolorow, R. D., Brandchaft, B., & Atwood, G. E. (1987). *Psychoanalytic treatment: An intersubjective approach*. Hillsdale, NJ: Analytic Press.

Trivers, R. L. (1985). *Social evolution*. Menlo Park, CA: Benjamin/Cummings.

Turner, V. (1969). *The ritual process: Structure and anti-structure*. Chicago: Aldine.

Twain, M. (1946). *Huckleberry Finn*. In B. DeVoto (Ed.), *The portable Mark Twain*. New York: Viking. (Original work published 1885)

Twain, M. (1968). *Letters from the earth*. New York: Fawcett. (Original work published 1962)

Wallis, H. (Producer), & Rapper, I. (Director). (1942). *Now, voyager* [Motion picture]. United States: Warner Bros. Pictures.

Watzlawick, P., Bavelas, J. B., & Jackson, D. (1967). *Pragmatics of human communication*. New York: Norton.

Whitehead, A. N., & Russell, B. (1910). *Principia mathematica*. Cambridge: Cambridge University Press.

Winer, G. A., Cottrell, J. E., Gregg, V., Fournier, J. S., & Bica, L. A. (2002). Fundamentally misunderstanding visual perception: Adults' beliefs in visual emissions. *American Psychologist, 57*, 417–424.

Winnicott, D. W. (1965). The capacity to be alone. In *The maturational processes and the facilitating environment* (pp. 29–36). New York: International Universities Press. (Original work published 1958)

Wood, M. (2003). *Shakespeare*. New York: Basic Books.

Zahavi, A., & Zahavi, A. (1997). *The handicap principle*. Oxford: Oxford University Press.

Index

Acceptance and Commitment Therapy (ACT), 184
actor-observer effect, 178
Adler, A., 10, 119, 174
advice, 187
aesthetic engrossment, 51–55, 125, 136, 182
aggression, 69–70
Allen, Woody, 42
Alvarez, Luis, 151
Andersen, Hans Christian, 139
Aristotle, 4
Arnheim, R., 16
Arthur, 75
Asch, S., 130
Ashcroft, John, 127
Asimov, I., 2, 5
audience, 46, 51, 210
authenticity, 43–55, 154–56, 199–200

backstages, xii, 5, 25, 43–44, 46, 49–50, 67, 90, 99, 131, 171, 212–14
Barkley, Russell, 164
Bateson, G., 21, 32–38, 44, 55, 104, 119, 135, 174, 181, 184, 190, 206–7, 210, 214
Bayes' Theorem, 165–68
Beck, A., 99, 103, 169, 180–81, 182, 184–86

Beck, J., 182
begging the question, 163
behaviorism, 4, 39, 47, 180, 183–84
binds. *See* paradoxical communication
Bion, W., 23
Blake, William, 94
Boal, A., 160
Bono, Sonny, 75
Bosnak, R., 60, 63
Brockett, O., 5
Broderick, Matthew, 54
Brook, P., 3, 9, 11, 14–18, 20–22, 24–26, 30, 31, 90, 118, 120, 136, 195
Broyard, A., 113
Buddha, 15, 198
Buirski, P., 9, 14, 24, 66, 182, 190, 191
Bullough, E., 18, 52
Burke, K., 31
Bush, George W., 78–79
Butch Cassidy and the Sundance Kid, 52
Butler, J., 87–88, 90

Caine, Michael, 42, 54
Carlson, M., 30
Carter, Jimmy, 199
categories, ix–x, 87, 89–90, 105–7, 109–10, 115–16, 160, 165–67, 177, 206

celebration, 5, 51
channels, 44–46
Chuang-Tzu, 96, 102, 161
Churchill, Winston, 70
circular questions, 38
clinically relevant behaviors, 47
cognitive therapy, 4, 21, 24, 40, 45, 53,
    54, 103, 112, 169, 180–81, 182,
    184–86
Coleridge, S., 53, 125
colonial privilege, 177
comedy, 194
competence, 6–9
confidentiality, 15, 50–51, 55, 64, 205
confirmation bias, x, 206
Confucius, 102
countertransference, 2, 184
couple's therapy, 17, 191
critical thinking, 103, 108–9, 147,
    159–75, 206–7
cultural competence, 10, 106–7, 109–10

Dale, P., 130
Dante, 145
Darwin, C., 103, 138, 147
Dawkins, R. 34
deadliness, 3–4
deconstruction, 30, 163, 179
definition of the situation, xi, 17, 32,
    35–41, 45, 49, 117–19, 126–32,
    209–10
Derrida, J., 96, 159–60, 174
Dewey, J., 5, 48, 51
diagnosis, x, 2, 24, 164, 208–9
Diamond, J., 70
Dickinson, Emily, 38
doorknob disclosures, 128
Dostoyevsky, Fyodor, 177
Dvoskin, J., 130

Ecclesiastes, 138
Eliot, George, 35
Ellis, A., 91, 103, 180–81, 185–86
empathy, 66
The Emperor's New Clothes, 139

Erickson, J., 153
Erickson, Milton, 20, 67
Erikson, E., 60, 62
exposure, 13, 18, 52, 60, 85. *See also*
    intimacy exposure

Facione, P., 161
fact versus opinion, 151–54
faith, 175
Fisher, R. A., 140
Foss, S., 160
frames, 26, 32, 38–41, 49, 53, 57,
    93–94, 125, 137, 151, 178–79, 191
free association, 47–48, 56–57
Freud, S., 10, 41, 47, 59–67, 70, 99,
    174, 179–80, 190
Friedan, Betty, 100
Fry, R., 52
fusion, 37, 40–41, 184

game theory, 32, 33–35, 56–57
Galileo, 143–44, 175
Gandhi, M., 1
Garner, James, 49–50
Geisinger, M., 5
gender, 31, 87–104, 111–12, 178–81,
    194–95, 211; and critical thinking,
    161; and existentialism, 97–101;
    labels, 89; as performance, 87–89;
    and the pornographic mind, 97–101;
    and reproduction, 96–97; in the
    therapy relationship, 91–96, 125–26;
    as a therapy topic, 90–91
Gibson, W., 195
Gilligan, C., 102, 103
Giotto, 52
Gödel, K., 175
Goffman, E., xii, 1, 6–8, 21, 25, 26, 30,
    31, 38, 42–57, 75, 88, 90, 99,
    110–15, 125, 173, 175
goodness, 71–72
Goodwin, J., 3, 110
Gould, S., 138
grand rounds, 101
gratification, 20–21, 54

gratitude, 13–14
Griffin, S., 97
Grotstein, A., 60, 62–63

Haley, J., 20, 37, 122
Halpern, D., 161
Harford, T., 140
Hayes, S., 157, 184
health, 9–11, 122–23
hegemony, xi, xii, 1–2, 30, 87, 90, 110,
    118, 126–28, 138, 154, 160, 177, 198
Helms, J., 107
Henley, William, 101
Herskovitz, M., 53
hierarchy, 70–71
Hirsch, Judd, 14, 85
Holmes, O., 103
homeostasis, 85, 187
Homer, 100, 150
honesty, 84, 187
Horney, K., 72, 99, 173, 180–81
Hymes, D., 33

identity: and multiculturalism, 108;
    norms, xii, 110–16; as performance,
    xii, 88, 155–56, 199
imagination, 150–51
improvisation, 24–26
insight versus change, 18–20
intellectualization, 18
intersubjectivity. *See* psychoanalysis
intimacy exposure, 47–48, 56, 104, 123,
    188–91, 208
ipse dixit, 164–65
Irigaray, L., 98

James, W., 38, 180
Janoff-Bulman, R., 96
Jesus, 2, 152
Johnstone, K., 25, 73, 82–84, 121, 178,
    213
joining, 85
Jones, E., 179
Julius Caesar, 21
Jung, Carl, 180

Kaplan, A., 90
Karson, M., 13, 19, 45, 64, 79, 103
The King and I, 145
King Lear, 18, 92
King, Martin Luther, Jr., 113
Knoblauch, S., 25
Kohlberg, L., 102, 103
Kohut, H., 21, 92
Kubie, L., 4
Kuhn, T., 140

lamination, 7, 21, 52–53
Langs, R., 25, 103–4, 135, 182, 190,
    207
Lao-Tzu, 80, 91, 123, 203
Lawrence, Ernest, 151
Lecter, Hannibal, 98
Lerner, G., 96
Lewis, Carl, 140
lobotomy, 122
logical types, 32, 35, 157, 184
Longino, H., xi, 126, 140
Lorde, A., 160

Madanes, C., 67, 98, 187
Madison, James, 128
Madonna, 98, 156
Malleus Maleficarum, 99
Mao Zedong, 140
maps, 64, 103, 144–47, 185, 198
marginalized voices, 30–31, 105–7,
    160–61, 203
Marx, Karl, 174
McCullough, D., 44
Meares, R., 25
Measure for Measure, 100
Meehl, P., 161
Mehlman, J., 60, 63–64
Meltsner, M., 81
Melville, Herman, 100
Mendel, Gregor, 140
metacommunication, 21, 32, 35–38, 44,
    49, 53, 189
metaconflict, 81
Midsummer Night's Dream, 16, 39

Milgram, S., 130
Mill, John Stuart, 104, 168
Miller, G., 6
Minnesota Multiphasic Personality
Inventory (MMPI), 79–80
Minuchin, S., 19, 91
money, 11–13
multiculturalism, 105–16, 174, 206

Nero, 194, 196
Nietzsche, F., 4, 5, 48, 70, 71–72, 98,
100, 110, 199
Now, Voyager, 85

obedience, x–xi, 40, 129
office decor, 21–23
"oops," 142, 213
Ordinary People, 85
Ossorio, P., 110, 206
out of line, 1–3, 30
Owens, Jesse, 126

paradoxical communication, 23, 35–38
Parker, Dorothy, 100, 141
Park-Fuller, L., 160
party line. *See* hegemony
patient: deadly motives of, 16–21;
feedback from, 133–36, 190, 196–98,
207–8; role of, 23–24, 30–31, 43,
54–55; suicidal, 54
pecking order. *See* hierarchy
perfectionism, 72–73
performance, 33, 46
performance art, 29–31, 160
performance theory, xii, 29, 31, 59, 118,
177
personality disorder, 53, 111
Pope, Alexander, 39
postmodernism, 30, 175, 179
power, 74–76, 86, 92, 101, 117–23,
160–61, 207–9
PowerPoint, 16
privilege, 1, 14, 117–36, 171
projective testing, 47, 55

psychoanalysis, 4, 9, 21, 45–47, 54,
66–67, 112, 155, 169, 179–80, 182,
188–91
psychopathology, xi, 3–4, 17, 36, 43,
55, 95, 111–12, 119, 127–28, 155,
157

Quinsey, V., 170

Rank, O., 30, 55, 122
Read, Herbert, 118
Reik, T., 214–15
relational frame theory, 184
Renoir, Jean, 2
reputation, 6–9, 14–15, 31
resistance, 57
revelry. *See* celebration
Rind, B., 174
Ringstrom, P., 25
ritual, 5
Robinson, T., 110, 181
Roemer, Ole, 143–44
Romeo and Juliet, 24, 54
rules, 42–43, 74–76, 203–7
rule-governed behavior, ix–xii, 22, 40,
101–4, 184, 197
runaway, 2, 182
Russell, B., 32, 35, 184

Sacajawea, 65
Santayana, G., 175
Schechner, R., 1
Schur, M., 60
science, 137–58; and gender, 140–41;
geographic versus social, 144–47;
nomothetic, 103, 141; and
objectivity, 140, 141, 151–54, 157;
and status, 77; as subculture, xi, 126,
137–44
Searle, J., 170
Selvini, M., 38, 187
sex and therapy, 49, 53, 93, 99, 101, 121
sexual orientation, 44, 100, 109–13,
116, 127, 149, 206

sexual selection, 6, 148, 150
Shakespeare, William, 85, 100, 145
Shapiro, S., 160
Shedler, J., 4
signs and signals, 33–35, 47, 71, 134
situation consciousness, 52, 124–25, 129
Skinner, B. F., xi, 34, 88, 108, 109, 144, 170, 171, 180, 198
Smith, S., 80
status, 73–86, 124, 211; behaviors, 73–74, 81–84; and the body, 78; conflicts over, 80–81; and death, 78, 101, 178; and gender, 85, 92; and interpretations, 78–79; in psychotherapy, 84–86; and social capital, 76–77
stigma, 88, 90, 110–16
Stolorow, R., 9, 182, 191
supervision: case by case, 204; framing of, 193–95; power in, 200–202; as rehearsal, 195–96; as rules, 197–98. *See also* trainee anxiety
symptoms: as metaphors, 60, 135; as protests, 2, 55, 160
systems theory, 4, 32–33, 96, 117, 181, 182, 187–88

teams, 45, 46, 50–51, 209
The Tempest, 214–15
theater: as culture, 16; defined, 30; history, 4–6; as protest, xii, 2, 30, 118
theory choice, 27, 40–41, 142, 173–74, 191–92, 205
therapist: as actor, 210–14; anonymity of, 55; as artist, 8; as blamer, 188; deadly motives of, 6–17; as

hegemony, 2; as hero, 200; as human, 67, 95, 178; as inspiration, 40, 57; mistakes by, 50; as parent, 54, 91, 119–23, 185, 210, 213; pregnant, 42; race of, 7, 42, 124, 132; role of, 13, 23, 26, 42–43, 54–55, 92, 199–200, 208; as teacher, 185, 210; values of, 9–10, 27, 122–23, 206
Thoreau, Henry, 72
Tolkien, J. R. R., 146
Tolstoy, Leo, 100
tragedy, 5
trainee anxiety, 198–99, 206–7
transference, 47, 53
trauma, 52
trial-and-error learning, x, 21, 43, 102–3
Trivers, R., 31
truth, 144–54, 161–62, 172
Turner, V., 99
Twain, Mark, 7, 99

underdistancer, 18, 20–21, 52–53

Washington, George, 44–45
Watzlawick, P., 44, 60, 158, 160, 181
Welles, Orson, 52
Wilde, Oscar, 151
Winer, G., 143
Winnicott, D., 51
The Wizard of Oz, 131
Wood, M., 2

Yeats, W. B., 140
yin and yang. *See* gender

Zahavi, A., 31

About the Author

Michael Karson teaches in the Graduate School of Professional Psychology at the University of Denver. Prior to that, he practiced psychotherapy and consulted in the child welfare system for 25 years in Massachusetts. He is the author of *Patterns of Child Abuse: How Dysfunctional Transactions Are Replicated in Individuals, Families, and the Child Welfare System*, and *Using Early Memories in Psychotherapy: Roadmaps to Presenting Problems and Treatment Impasses*. He is senior author of *16PF Interpretation in Clinical Practice: A Guide to the Fifth Edition*. He is also an attorney.